THE AWAKENING OF CHINA

LECTOR HOUSE PUBLIC DOMAIN WORKS

THE AWAKENING OF CHINA

WILLIAM ALEXANDER PARSONS MARTIN

ISBN: 978-93-90215-12-6

Published: 1907

LECTOR HOUSE LLP
E-MAIL: lectorpublishing@gmail.com

The Emperor of China.

THE AWAKENING OF CHINA

BY

WILLIAM ALEXANDER PARSONS MARTIN, D.D., LL.D

Formerly President of the Chinese Imperial University

Author of "A Cycle of Cathay," "The Siege in Peking," "The Lore of Cathay," etc.

1907

PREFACE

China is the theatre of the greatest movement now taking place on the face of the globe. In comparison with it, the agitation in Russia shrinks to insignificance; for it is not political, but social. Its object is not a changed dynasty, nor a revolution in the form of government; but, with higher aim and deeper motive, it promises nothing short of the complete renovation of the oldest, most populous, and most conservative of empires. Is there a people in either hemisphere that can afford to look on with indifference?

When, some thirty years ago, Japan adopted the outward forms of Western civilisation, her action was regarded by many as a stage trick—a sort of travesty employed for a temporary purpose. But what do they think now, when they see cabinets and chambers of commerce compelled to reckon with the British of the North Pacific? The awakening of Japan's huge neighbour promises to yield results equally startling and on a vastly extended scale.

Political agitation, whether periodic like the tides or unforeseen like the hurricane, is in general superficial and temporary; but the social movement in China has its origin in subterranean forces such as raise continents from the bosom of the deep. To explain those forces is the object of the present work.

It is the fascination of this grand spectacle that has brought me back to China, after a short visit to my native land—and to this capital, after a sojourn of some years in the central provinces. Had the people continued to be as inert and immobile as they appeared to be half a century ago, I might have been tempted to despair of their future. But when I see them, as they are to-day, united in a firm resolve to break with the past, and to seek new life by adopting the essentials of Western civilisation, I feel that my hopes as to their future are more than half realised; and I rejoice to help their cause with voice and pen.

Their patriotism may indeed be tinged with hostility to foreigners; but will it not gain in breadth with growing intelligence, and will they not come to perceive that their interests are inseparable from those of the great family into which they are seeking admission?

Every day adds its testimony to the depth and genuineness of the movement in the direction of reform. Yesterday the autumn manœuvres of the grand army came to a close. They have shown that by the aid of her railways China is able to assemble a body of trained troops numbering 100,000 men. Not content with this formidable land force, the Government has ordered the construction of the nucleus of a navy, to consist of eight armoured cruisers and two battleships. Five of these and three naval stations are to be equipped with the wireless telegraph.

Not less significant than this rehabilitation of army and navy is the fact that a few days ago a number of students, who had completed their studies at foreign universities, were admitted to the third degree (or D. C. L.) in the scale of literary honours, which means appointment to some important post in the active mandarinate. If the booming of cannon at the grand review proclaimed that the age of bows and arrows is past, does not this other fact announce that, in the field of education, rhyming and caligraphy have given place to science and languages? Henceforth thousands of ambitious youth will flock to the universities of Japan, and growing multitudes will seek knowledge at its fountain-head beyond the seas.

Still more surprising are the steps taken toward the intellectual emancipation of woman in China. One of the leading ministers of education assured me the other day that he was pushing the establishment of schools for girls. The shaded hemisphere of Chinese life will thus be brought into the sunshine, and in years to come the education of Chinese youth will begin at the mother's knee.

The daily deliberations of the Council of State prove that the reform proposals of the High Commission are not to be consigned to the limbo of abortions. Tuan Fang, one of the leaders, has just been appointed to the viceroyalty of Nanking, with *carte blanche* to carry out his progressive ideas; and the metropolitan viceroy, Yuan, on taking leave of the Empress Dowager before proceeding to the manœuvres, besought her not to listen to reactionary counsels such as those which had produced the disasters of 1900.

In view of these facts, what wonder that Chinese newspapers are discussing the question of a national religion? The fires of the old altars are well-nigh extinct; and, among those who have come forward to advocate the adoption of Christianity as the only faith that meets the wants of an enlightened people, one of the most prominent is a priest of Buddha.

May we not look forward with confidence to a time when China shall be found in the brotherhood of Christian nations?

W. A. P. M.

Peking, October 30, 1906.

CONTENTS

PART I
THE EMPIRE IN OUTLINE

PART II
HISTORY IN OUTLINE FROM THE EARLIEST TIMES TO
THE EIGHTEENTH CENTURY

PART III
CHINA IN TRANSFORMATION

APPENDIX

LIST OF ILLUSTRATIONS

INTRODUCTION

How varied are the geological formations of different countries, and what countless ages do they represent! Scarcely less diversified are the human beings that occupy the surface of the globe, and not much shorter the period of their evolution. To trace the stages of their growth and decay, to explain the vicissitudes through which they have passed, is the office of a philosophic historian.

If the life history of a silkworm, whose threefold existence is rounded off in a few months, is replete with interest, how much more interesting is that of societies of men emerging from barbarism and expanding through thousands of years. Next in interest to the history of our own branch of the human family is that of the yellow race confronting us on the opposite shore of the Pacific; even more fascinating, it may be, owing to the strangeness of manners and environment, as well as from the contrast or coincidence of experience and sentiment. So different from ours (the author writes as an American) are many phases of their social life that one is tempted to suspect that the same law, which placed their feet opposite to ours, of necessity turned their heads the other way.

To pursue this study is not to delve in a necropolis like Nineveh or Babylon; for China is not, like western Asia, the grave of dead empires, but the home of a people endowed with inexhaustible vitality. Her present greatness and her future prospects alike challenge admiration.

If the inhabitants of other worlds could look down on us, as we look up at the moon, there are only five empires on the globe of sufficient extent to make a figure on their map: one of these is China. With more than three times the population of Russia, and an almost equal area, in natural advantages she is without a rival, if one excepts the United States. Imagination revels in picturing her future, when she shall have adopted Christian civilisation, and when steam and electricity shall have knit together all the members of her gigantic frame.

It was by the absorption of small states that the Chinese people grew to greatness. The present work will trace their history as they emerge, like a rivulet, from the highlands of central Asia and, increasing in volume, flow, like a stately river, toward the eastern ocean. Revolutions many and startling are to be recorded: some, like that in the epoch of the Great Wall, which stamped the impress of unity upon the entire people; others, like the Manchu conquest of 1644, by which, in whole or in part, they were brought under the sway of a foreign dynasty. Finally, contemporary history will be treated at some length, as its importance demands; and the transformation now going on in the Empire will be faithfully depicted in its relations to Western influences in the fields of religion, commerce and arms.

As no people can be understood or properly studied apart from their environment, a bird's-eye view of the country is given.

PART I
THE EMPIRE IN OUTLINE

THE AWAKENING OF CHINA

CHAPTER I

CHINA PROPER

Five Grand Divisions—Climate—Area and Population—The Eighteen Provinces

The empire consists of five grand divisions: China Proper, Manchuria, Mongolia, Turkestan, and Tibet. In treating of this huge conglomerate it will be most convenient to begin with the portion that gives name and character to the whole.

Of China Proper it may be affirmed that the sun shines nowhere on an equal area which combines so many of the conditions requisite for the support of an opulent and prosperous people. Lying between 18° and 49° north latitude, her climate is alike exempt from the fierce heat of the torrid zone and the killing cold of the frigid regions. There is not one of her provinces in which wheat, rice, and cotton, the three staples of food and clothing, may not be cultivated with more or less success; but in the southern half wheat gives place to rice, while in the north cotton yields to silk and hemp. In the south cotton is king and rice is queen of the fields.

Traversed in every direction by mountain ranges of moderate elevation whose sides are cultivated in terraces to such a height as to present the appearance of hanging gardens, China possesses fertile valleys in fair proportion, together with vast plains that compare in extent with those of our American prairie states. Furrowed by great rivers whose innumerable affluents supply means of irrigation and transport, her barren tracts are few and small.

A coast-line of three thousand miles indented with gulfs, bays, and inlets affords countless harbours for shipping, so that few countries can compare with her in facilities for ocean commerce.

As to her boundaries, on the east six of her eighteen provinces bathe their feet in the waters of the Pacific; on the south she clasps hands with Indo-China and with British Burma; and on the west the foothills of the Himalayas form a bulwark more secure than the wall that marks her boundary on the north. Greatest of the works of man, the Great Wall serves at present no other purpose than that of a mere geographical expression. Built to protect the fertile fields of the "Flowery Land" from the incursions of northern nomads, it may have been useful for some generations; but it can hardly be pronounced an unqualified success, since China in whole or in part has passed more than half of the twenty-two subsequent centuries under the domination of Tartars.

With an area of about 1,500,000 square miles, or one-half that of Europe, China has a busy population of about four hundred millions; yet, so far from being exhausted, there can be no doubt that with improved methods in agriculture, manufactures, mining, and transportation, she might very easily sustain double the present number of her thrifty children.

Within this favoured domain the products of nature and of human industry vie with each other in extent and variety. A bare enumeration would read like a page of a gazetteer and possibly make no more impression than a column of figures. To form an estimate of the marvellous fecundity of the country and to realise its picturesqueness, one ought to visit the provinces in succession and spend a year in the exploration of each. If one is precluded from such leisurely observation, undoubtedly the next best thing is to see them through the eyes of those who have travelled in and have made a special study of those regions.

To more than half of the provinces I can offer myself as a guide. I spent ten years at Ningpo, and one year at Shanghai, both on the southern seacoast. At the northern capital I spent forty years; and I have recently passed three years at Wuchang on the banks of the Yang-tse Kiang, a special coign of vantage for the study of central China. While residing in the above-mentioned foci it was my privilege to visit six other provinces (some of them more than once), thus gaining a personal acquaintance with ten out of the eighteen and being enabled to gather valuable information at first hand.

A glance at the subjoined table (from the report of the China Inland Mission for 1905) will exhibit the magnitude of the field of investigation before us. The average province corresponds in extent to the average state of the American Union; and the whole exceeds that portion of the United States which lies east of the Mississippi.

CHINA PROPER

PROVINCES	AREA SQ. MILES	POPULATION
Kwangtung (Canton)	99,970	31,865,000
Kwangsi	77,200	5,142,000
Fukien	46,320	22,876,000
Chéhkiang	36,670	11,580,000
Kiangsu	38,600	13,980,000
Shantung	55,970	38,248,000
Chihli	115,800	20,937,000
Shansi	81,830	12,200,000
Shensi	75,270	8,450,000
Kansuh	125,450	10,385,000

Honan	67,940	35,316,000
Hupeh	71,410	35,280,000
Hunan	83,380	22,170,000
Nganhwei(Anhwei)	54,810	23,670,000
Yünnan	146,680	12,325,000
Szechuen	218,480	68,725,000
Kiangsi	69,480	26,532,000
Kweichau	67,160	7,650,000
Totals	1,532,420	407,331,000

Parade Ground, Hong Kong

CHAPTER II

A JOURNEY THROUGH THE PROVINCES— KWANGTUNG AND KWANGSI

Hong Kong—A Trip to Canton—Macao—Scenes on Pearl River—Canton Christian College—Passion for Gambling—A Typical City—A Chief Source of Emigration

Let us take an imaginary journey through the provinces and begin at Hong Kong, where, in 1850, I began my actual experience of life in China.

From the deck of the good ship *Lantao*, which had brought me from Boston around the Cape in one hundred and thirty-four days, I gazed with admiration on the Gibraltar of the Orient. Before me was a land-locked harbour in which all the navies of the world might ride in safety. Around me rose a noble chain of hills, their slopes adorned with fine residences, their valleys a chessboard of busy streets, with here and there a British battery perched on a commanding rock.

Under Chinese rule Hong Kong had been an insignificant fishing village, in fact a nest of pirates. In 1841 the island was ceded by China to Great Britain, and the cession was confirmed by the treaty of Nanking in August, 1842. The transformation effected in less than a decade had been magical; yet that was only the bloom of babyhood, compared with the rich maturity of the, present day.

A daily steamer then sufficed for its trade with Canton; a weekly packet connected it with Shanghai; and the bulk of its merchandise was still carried in sailing ships or Chinese junks. How astounding the progress that has marked the last half-century! The streets that meandered, as it were, among the valleys, or fringed the water's edge, now girdle the hills like rows of seats in a huge amphitheatre; a railway lifts the passenger to the mountain top; and other railways whirl him from hill to hill along the dizzy height. I Trade, too, has multiplied twenty fold. In a commercial report for the year ending June, 1905, it is stated that in amount of tonnage Hong Kong has become the banner port of the world.

Though politically Hong Kong is not China, more than 212,000 of its busy population (about 221,000) are Chinese; and it is preëminently the gate of China. By a wise and liberal policy the British Government has made it the chief emporium of the Eastern seas.

We now take a trip to Canton and cross a bay studded with islands. These are clothed with copious verdure, but, like all others on the China coast, lack the crowning beauty of trees. In passing we get a glimpse of Macao, a pretty town under the flag of the Portuguese, the pioneers of Eastern trade. The oldest foreign settlement in China, it dates from 1544—not quite a half-century after the discovery of the route to India, an achievement whose fourth centenary was celebrated in 1898. If it could be ascertained on what day some adventurous argonaut pushed the quest of the Golden Fleece to Farther India, as China was then designated, that exploit might with equal appropriateness be commemorated also.

The city of Macao stands a monument of Lusitanian enterprise. Beautifully situated on a projecting spur of an island, it is a favourite summer resort of foreign residents in the metropolis. It has a population of about 70,000, mostly Chinese, and contains two tombs that make it sacred in my eyes; namely, that of Camöens, author of "The Lusiad" and poet of Gama's voyage, and that of Robert Morrison, the pioneer of Protestant missions, the centennial of whose arrival had in 1907 a brilliant celebration.

Entering the Pearl River, a fine stream 500 miles in length, whose affluents spread like a fan over two provinces, we come to the viceregal capital, as Canton deserves to be called, though the viceroy actually resides in another city. The river is alive with steamboats, large and small, mostly under the British flag; but native craft of the old style have not yet been put to flight. Propelled by sail or oar, the latter creep along the shore; and at Pagoda Anchorage near the city they form a floating town in which families are born and die without ever having a home on *terra firma*.

Big-footed women are seen earning an honest living by plying the oar, or swinging on the scull-beam with babies strapped on their backs. One may notice also the so-called "flower-boats," embellished like the palaces of water fairies. Moored in one locality, they are a well-known resort of the vicious. In the fields are the tillers of the soil wading barefoot and bareheaded in mud and water, holding plough or harrow drawn by an amphibious creature called a carabao or water-buffalo, burying by hand in the mire the roots of young rice plants, or applying as a fertiliser the ordure and garbage of the city. Such unpoetic toils never could have inspired the georgic muse of Vergil or Thomson.

The most picturesque structure that strikes the eye as one approaches the city is a Christian college—showing how times have changed. In 1850 the foreign quarter was in a suburb near one of the gates. There I dined with Sir John Bowring at the British Consulate, having a letter of introduction from his American cousin, Miss Maylin, a gifted lady of Philadelphia. There, too, I lodged with Dr. Happer, who by the tireless exertions of many years succeeded in laying the foundations of that same Christian college. For him it is a monument more lasting than brass; for China it is only one of many lighthouses now rising at commanding points on the seacoast and in the interior.

Amoy, Province of Fukien

In passing the Fati, a recreation-ground near the city, a view is obtained of the amusements of the rich and the profligate. We see a multitude seated around a cockpit intent on a cock-fight; but the cocks are quails, not barnyard fowls. Here, too, is a smaller and more exclusive circle stooping over a pair of crickets engaged in deadly combat. Insects of other sorts or pugnacious birds are sometimes substituted; and it might be supposed that the people must be warlike in their disposition, to enjoy such spectacles. The fact is, they are fond of fighting by proxy. What attracts them most, however, is the chance of winning or losing a wager.

A more intellectual entertainment to be seen in many places is the solving of historical enigmas. Some ancient celebrity is represented by an animal in a rhyming couplet; and the man who detects the hero under this disguise wins a considerable sum. Such is the native passion for gambling that bets are even made on the result of the metropolitan examinations, particularly on the province to which will fall the honour of the first prize, that of the scholar-laureateship.

Officials in all parts and benevolent societies take advantage of this passion for gambling in opening lotteries to raise funds for worthy objects—a policy which is unwise if not immoral. It should not be forgotten, however, that our own forefathers sometimes had recourse to lotteries to build churches.

The foreign settlement now stands on Shamien, a pretty islet in the river, in splendid contrast with the squalor of the native streets. The city wall is not conspicuous, if indeed it is visible beyond the houses of a crowded suburb. Yet one may be sure that it is there; for every large town must have a wall for protection, and the whole empire counts no fewer than 1,553 walled cities. What an index to the insecurity resulting from an ill-regulated police! The Chinese are surprised to hear that in all the United States there is nothing which they would call a city, because the American cities are destitute of walls.

Canton with its suburbs contains over two million people; it is therefore the most populous city in the empire. In general the houses are low, dark, and dirty, and the streets are for the most part too narrow for anything broader than a sedan or a "rickshaw" (jinriksha). Yet in city and suburbs the eye is dazzled by the richness of the shops, especially of those dealing in silks and embroideries. In strong contrast with this luxurious profusion may be seen crowds of beggars displaying their loathsome sores at the doors of the rich in order to extort thereby a penny from those who might not be disposed to give from motives of charity. The narrow streets are thronged with coolies in quality of beasts of burden, having their loads suspended from each end of an elastic pole balanced on the shoulder, or carrying their betters in sedan chairs, two bearers for a commoner, four for a "swell," and six or eight for a magnate. High officials borne in these luxurious vehicles are accompanied by lictors on horse or foot. Bridegrooms and brides are allowed to pose for the nonce as grandees; and the bridal chair, whose drapery blends the rainbow and the butterfly, is heralded by a band of music, the blowing of horns, and the clashing of cymbals. The block and jam thus occasioned are such as no people except the patient Chinese would tolerate. They bow to custom and smile at inconvenience. Of horse-cars or carriages there are none except in new streets. Rickshaws and wheelbarrows push their way in the narrowest alleys, and compete with sedans for a share of the passenger traffic.

In those blue hills that hang like clouds on the verge of the horizon and bear the poetical name of White Cloud, there are gardens that combine in rich variety the fruits of both the torrid and the temperate zones. Tea and silk are grown in many other parts of China; but here they are produced of a superior quality.

Enterprising and intelligent, the people of this province have overflowed into the islands of the Pacific from Singapore to Honolulu. Touching at Java in 1850, I found refreshments at the shop of a Canton man who showed a manifest superiority to the natives of the island. Is it not to be regretted that the Chinese are excluded from the Philippines? Would not the future of that archipelago be brighter if the shiftless native were replaced by the thrifty Chinaman?

It was in Canton that American trade suffered most from the boycott of 1905, because there the ill-treatment of Chinese in America was most deeply felt, the Chinese in California being almost exclusively from the province of Canton.

The viceroy of Canton has also the province of Kwangsi under his jurisdiction. Mountainous and thinly peopled, it is regarded by its associate as a burden, being in an almost chronic state of rebellion and requiring large armies to keep its turbulent inhabitants in order.

CHAPTER III

PROVINCE OF FUKIEN

Amoy—Bold Navigators—Foochow—Mountain of Kushan—The Bridge of Ten Thousand Years

Following the coast to the north some three hundred miles we come to Amoy, the first important seaport in the adjacent province of Fukien. The aspect of the country has undergone a change. Hills attain the altitude of mountains, and the alluvial plains, so conspicuous about Canton, become contracted to narrow valleys.

The people, too, are changed in speech and feature. Taller, coarser in physiognomy, with high cheek-bones and harsh voices, their dialect is totally unintelligible to people of the neighbouring province. As an example of the diversity of dialects in China, may be cited the Chinese word for man. In some parts of Fukien it is long; in Canton, yan or yin; at Ningpo, ning; and at Peking, jin.

One is left in doubt whether the people or the mountains which they inhabit were the most prominent factors in determining the dividing line that separates them from their neighbours on the south and west. In enterprise and energy they rival the Cantonese. They are bold navigators; the grand island of Formosa, now ceded to Japan, was colonised by them; and by them also the savage aborigines were driven over to the east coast. A peculiar sort of black tea is grown on these mountains, and, along with grass cloth, forms a staple in the trade of Amoy. The harbour is not wanting in beauty; and a view from one of the hill-tops, from which hundreds of villages are visible, is highly picturesque. Of the town of Amoy with its 200,000 people there is not much to be said except that several missions, British and American, which opened stations there soon after the first war with Great Britain, have met with encouraging success. At Swatow, a district in Canton Province beyond the boundary, the American Baptists have a flourishing mission.

Entering the Formosan Channel we proceed to the mouth of the Min, a fine river which leads up to Foochow (Fuchau), some thirty miles inland. We do not stop to explore the Island of Formosa because, having been ceded to Japan, it no longer forms a part of the Chinese Empire. From the river the whole province is sometimes described as "the country of Min"; but its official name is Fukien. This name does not signify "happily established," as stated in most books, but is compounded of the names of its two chief cities by taking the first syllable of each, somewhat as the pioneer settlers of Arkansas formed the name of the boundary town of Texarkana. The names of some other provinces of China are formed in the same way; e.g. Kiangsu, Kansuh, and that of the viceregal district of Yünkwei.

Kushan, a mountain on the bank of the river, is famed for its scenery; and, as with mountains everywhere else in China, it has been made the seat of a Buddhist monastery, with some scores of monks passing their time not in contemplation, but in idleness.

The city of Foochow is imposing with its fine wall of stone, and a long stone bridge called Wansuik'iao "the bridge of ten thousand years." It has a population of about 650,000. To add to its importance it has a garrison or colony of Manchus who from the date of the conquest in 1644 have lived apart from the Chinese and have not diminished in numbers.

The American Board and the Methodist Episcopal Board have large and prosperous missions at this great centre, and from this base they have ramified through the surrounding mountains, mostly following the tributaries of the Min up to their sources. In 1850 I was entertained at Foochow by the Rev. Dr. C. C. Baldwin, who, I am glad to say, still lives after the lapse of fifty-five years; but he is no longer in the mission field.

View of Amoy, Looking toward River

CHAPTER IV

PROVINCE OF CHÉHKIANG

Chusan Archipelago—Putu and Pirates—Queer Fishers and Queer Boats—Ningpo—A Literary Triumph—Search for a Soul—Chinese Psychology—Hangchow—The Great Bore

Chéhkiang, the next province to the north, and the smallest of the eighteen, is a portion of the highlands mentioned in the last chapter. It is about as large as Indiana, while some of the provinces have four or five times that area. There is no apparent reason why it should have a distinct provincial government save that its waters flow to the north, or perhaps because the principality of Yuih (1100 B.C.) had such a boundary, or, again, perhaps because the language of the people is akin to that of the Great Plain in which its chief river finds an outlet. How often does a conqueror sever regions which form a natural unit, merely to provide a principality for some favourite!

Lying off its coast is the Chusan archipelago, in which two islands are worthy of notice. The largest, which gives the archipelago its name, is about half the length of Long Island, N. Y., and is so called from a fancied resemblance to a junk, it having a high promontory at either end. It contains eighteen valleys—a division not connected with the eighteen provinces, but perpetuated in a popular rhyme which reflects severely on the morals of its inhabitants. Shielded by the sea, and near enough to the land to strike with ease at any point of the neighbouring coast, the British forces found here a secure camping-ground in their first war.

To the eastward lies the sacred Isle of Putu, the Iona of the China coast. With a noble landscape, and so little land as to offer no temptation to the worldly, it was inevitable that the Buddhists should fix on it as a natural cloister. For many centuries it has been famous for its monasteries, some of which are built of timbers taken from imperial palaces. Formerly the missionaries from neighbouring seaports found at Putu refuge from the summer heat, but it is now abandoned, since it afforded no shelter from the petty piracy at all times so rife in these waters.

In 1855 Mr. (afterward Bishop) Russell and myself were captured by pirates while on our way to Putu. The most gentlemanly freebooters I ever heard of, they invited us to share their breakfast on the deck of our own junk; but they took possession of all our provisions and our junk too, sending us to our destination in a small boat, and promising to pay us a friendly visit on the island. One of them, who had taken my friend's watch, came to the owner to ask him how to wind it. The Rev. Walter Lowrie, founder of the Presbyterian Mission at Ningpo, was not so fortunate. Attacked by pirates nearly on the same spot, he was thrown into the sea and drowned.

Passing these islands we come to the Ningpo River, with Chinhai, a small city, at its mouth, and Ningpo, a great emporium, some twelve miles inland. This curious arrangement, so different from what one would expect, confronts one in China with the regularity of a natural law: Canton, Shanghai, Foochow, and Tientsin, all conform to it. The small city stands at the anchorage for heavy shipping; but the great city, renouncing this advantage, is located some distance inland, to be safe from sea-robbers and foreign foes.

The Sacred Island of Putu

As we ascend the river we are struck with more than one peculiar mode of taking fish. We see a number of cormorants perched on the sides of a boat. Now and then a bird dives into the water and comes up with a fish in its beak. If the fish be a small one, the bird swallows it as a reward for its services; but a fish of considerable size is hindered in its descent by a ring around the bird's neck and becomes the booty of the fisherman. The birds appear to be well-trained; and their sharp eyes penetrate the depths of the water. Another novelty in fishing is a contrivance by which fish are made to catch themselves—not by running into a net or by swallowing a hook, but by leaping over a white board and falling into a boat. More strange than all are men who, like the cormorants, dive into the water and emerge with fish—sometimes with one in either hand. These fishermen when in the water always have their feet on the ground and grope along the shore. The first time I saw this method in practice I ran to the brink of the river to save, as I thought, the life of a poor man. He no sooner raised his head out of the water, however, than down it went again; and I was laughed at for my want of discernment by a crowd of people who shouted *Ko-ng, Ko-ng,* "he's catching fish."

The natives have a peculiar mode of propelling a boat. Sitting in the stern the boatman holds the helm with one hand, while with the other he grasps a long pipe which he smokes at leisure. Without mast or sail, he makes speed against wind or current by making use of his feet to drive the oar. He thus gains the advantage of weight and of his strong sartorial muscles. These little craft are the swiftest boats on the river.

At the forks of the river, in a broad plain dotted with villages, rise the stone walls of Ningpo, six miles in circuit, enclosing a network of streets better built than those of the majority of Chinese cities. The foreign settlement is on the north bank of the main stream; but a few missionaries live within the walls, and there I passed the first years of my life in China.

Above the walls, conspicuous at a distance, appears the pinnacle of a lofty pagoda, a structure like most of those bearing the name, with eight corners and nine stories. Originally designed for the mere purposes of look-outs, these airy edifices have degenerated into appliances of superstition to attract good influences and to ward off evil.

Not only has this section of the province a dialect of its own, of the mandarin type, but its people possess a finer physique than those of the south. Taller, with eyes less angular and faces of faultless symmetry, they are a handsome people, famed alike for literary talent and for commercial enterprise. During my residence there the whole city was once thrown into excitement by the news that one of her sons had won the first prize in prose and verse in competition, before the emperor, with the assembled scholars of the empire—an an honour comparable to that of poet laureate or of a victor in the Olympic games. When that distinction falls to a city, it is believed that, in order to equalise matters, the event is sure to be followed by three years of dearth. In this instance, the highest mandarins escorted the wife of the literary athlete to the top of the wall, where she scattered a few handfuls of rice to avert the impending famine.

My house was attached to a new church which was surmounted by a bell-tower. In a place where nothing of the sort had previously existed, that accessory attracted many visitors even before the bell was in position to invite them. One day a weeping mother, attended by an anxious retinue, presented herself and asked permission to climb the tower, which request of course was not refused.

Scene in the Island of Putu

Uncovering a bundle, she said: "This is my boy's clothing. Yesterday he was up in the tower and, taking fright at the height of the building, his little soul forsook his body and he had to go home without it. He is now delirious with fever. We think the soul is hovering about in this huge edifice and that it will recognise these clothes and, taking possession of them, will return home with us."

When a bird escapes from its cage the Chinese sometimes hang the cage on the branch of a tree and the bird returns to its house again. They believe they can capture a fugitive soul in the same way. Sometimes, too, a man may be seen standing on a housetop at night waving a lantern and chanting in dismal tones an invitation to some wandering spirit to return to its abode. Whether in the case just mentioned the poor woman's hopes were fulfilled and whether the *animula vagula blandula* returned from its wanderings I never learned, but I mention the incident as exhibiting another picturesque superstition.

Chinese psychology recognises three souls, viz., the animal, the spiritual, and the intellectual. The absence of one of the three does not, therefore, involve immediate death, as does the departure of the soul in our dual system.

But I tarry too long at my old home. We have practically an empire still before us, and will, therefore, steer west for Hangchow.

In the thirteenth century this was the residence of an imperial court; and the provincial capital still retains many signs of imperial magnificence. The West Lake with its pavilions and its lilies, a pleasance fit for an emperor; the vast circuit of the city's walls enclosing hill and vale; and its commanding site on the bank of a great river at the head of a broad bay—all combine to invest it with dignity. Well do I recall the day in 1855 when white men first trod its streets. They were the Rev. Henry Rankin and myself. Though not permitted by treaty to penetrate even the rind of the "melon," as the Chinese call their empire, to a distance farther than admitted of our returning to sleep at home, we nevertheless broke bounds and set out for the old capital of the Sungs. On the way we made a halt at the city of Shaohing; and as we were preaching to a numerous and respectful audience in the public square, a well-dressed man pressed through the crowd and invited us to do him the honour of taking tea at his house. His mansion exhibited every evidence of affluence; and he, a scholar by profession, aspiring to the honours of the mandarinate, explained, as he ordered for us an ample repast, that he would have felt ashamed if scholars from the West had been allowed to pass through his city without anyone offering them hospitality. What courtesy! Could Hebrew or Arab hospitality surpass it?

Priests of the Island of Putu

Two things for which the city of Shaohing is widely celebrated are (1) a sort of rice wine used throughout the Empire as being indispensable at mandarin feasts, and (2) clever lawyers who are deemed indispensable as legal advisers to mandarins. They are the "Philadelphia lawyers" of China.

As we entered Hangchow the boys shouted *Wo tsei lai liao*, "the Japanese are coming "—never having seen a European, and having heard their fathers speak of the Japanese as sea-robbers, a terror to the Chinese coast. Up to this date, Japan had no treaty with China, and it had never carried on any sort of regular commerce with or acknowledged the superiority of China. Before many years had passed, these youths became accustomed to Western garb and features; and I never heard that any foreigner suffered insult or injury at their hands.

In 1860 the Rev. J. L. Nevius, one of my colleagues, took possession of the place in the name of Christ. He was soon followed by Bishop Burden, of the English Church Mission, whose apostolic successor, Bishop Moule, now makes it the seat of his immense diocese.

Another claim to distinction not to be overlooked is that its river is a trap for whales. Seven or eight years ago a cetaceous monster was stranded near the river's mouth. The Rev. Dr. Judson, president of the Hangchow Mission College, went to see it and sent me an account of his observations. He estimated the length of the whale at 100 feet; the tail had been removed by the natives. To explain the incident it is necessary to say that, the bay being funnel-shaped, the tides rise to an extraordinary height. Twice a month, at the full and the change of the moon, the attractions of sun and moon combine, and the water rushes in with a roar like that of a tidal wave. The bore of Hangchow is not surpassed by that of the Hooghly or of the Bay of Fundy. Vessels are wrecked by it; and even the monsters of the deep are unable to contend with the fury of its irresistible advance.

CHAPTER V

PROVINCE OF KIANGSU

Nanking—Shanghai—The Yang-tse Kiang—The Yellow River

Bordering on the sea, traversed by the Grand Canal and the Yang-tse Kiang, the chief river of the Empire, rich in agriculture, fisheries, and commerce, Kiang-su is the undisputed queen of the eighteen provinces. In 1905 it was represented to the throne as too heavy a burden for one set of officers. The northern section was therefore detached and erected into a separate province; but before the new government was organised the Empress Dowager yielded to remonstrances and rescinded her hasty decree—showing how reluctant she is to contravene the wishes of her people. What China requires above all things is the ballot box, by which the people may make their wishes known.

The name of the province is derived from its two chief cities, Suchow and Nanking. Suchow, the Paris of the Far East, is coupled with Hangchow in a popular rhyme, which represents the two as paragon cities:

"Shang yu t'ien t'ang hia yu Su-Hang."

"Su and Hang, so rich and fair,
May well with Paradise compare."

The local dialect is so soft and musical that strolling players from Suchow are much sought for in the adjacent provinces. A well-known couplet says:

"I'd rather hear men wrangle in Suchow's dulcet tones
Than hear that mountain jargon, composed of sighs and groans."

Farther inland, near the banks of the "Great River," stands Nanking, the old capital of the Ming dynasty. The Manchus, unwilling to call it a *king, i.e.* seat of empire, changed its name to Kiangning; but the old title survives in spite of official jealousy. As it will figure prominently in our history we shall not pause there at present, but proceed to Shanghai, a place which more than any other controls the destinies of the State.

Formerly an insignificant town of the third order (provincial capitals and prefectural towns ranking respectively first and second), some sapient Englishman with an eye to commerce perceived the advantage of the site; and in the dictation of the terms of peace in 1842 it was made one of the five ports. It has come to over-shadow Canton; and more than all the other ports it displays to the Chinese the marvels of Western skill, knowledge, and enterprise.

On a broad estuary near the mouth of the main artery that penetrates the heart of China, it has become a leading emporium of the world's commerce. The native city still hides its squalor behind low walls of brick, but outside the North Gate lies a tract of land known as the "Foreign Concessions." There a beautiful city styled the "model settlement" has sprung up like a gorgeous pond-lily from the muddy, paddy-fields. Having spent a year there, I regard it with a sort of affection as one of my Oriental homes.

Suchow: One of the Water Gates

In Suchow City

Shanghai presents a spectacle rare amongst the seaports of the world. Its broad streets, well kept and soon to be provided with electric trolleys, extend for miles along the banks of two rivers, lined with opulent business houses and luxurious mansions, most of the latter being surrounded by gardens and embowered in groves of flowering trees. Nor do these magazines and dwelling-houses stand merely for taste and opulence. Within the bounds of the Concessions is the reign of law—not, as elsewhere in China, the arbitrary will of a magistrate, but the offspring of freedom and justice. Foreigners live everywhere under the protection of their own national flags: and within the Concessions. Chinese accused of crimes are tried by a mixed court which serves as an object-lesson in justice and humanity. Had one time to peep into a native *yamên*, one might see bundles of bamboos, large and small, prepared for the bastinado; one might see, also, thumb-screws, wooden boots, wooden collars, and other instruments of torture, some of them intended to make mince-meat of the human body. The use of these has now been forbidden.[1]

In Shanghai there are schools of all grades, some under the foreign municipal government, others under missionary societies. St. John's College (U. S. Episcopal) and the Anglo-Chinese College (American M. E.) bear the palm in the line of education so long borne by the Roman Catholics of Siccawei. Added to these, newspapers foreign and native—the latter exercising a freedom of opinion impossible beyond the limits of this city of refuge—the Society for the Diffusion of Christian Knowledge and other translation bureaux, foreign and native, turning out books by the thousand with the aid of steam presses, form a combination of forces to which China is no longer insensible.

Resuming our imaginary voyage we proceed northward, and in the space of an hour find ourselves at the mouth of the Yang-tse Kiang, or Ta Kiang, the "Great River," as the Chinese call it. The width of its embouchure suggests an Asiatic rival of the Amazon and La Plata. We now see why this part of the ocean is sometimes described as the Yellow Sea. A river whose volume, it is said, equals that of two hundred and forty-four such rivulets as Father Thames, pours into it its muddy waters, making new islands and advancing the shore far into the domain of Neptune.

Notice on the left those long rows of trees that appear to spring from the bosom of the river. They are the life-belt of the Island of Tsungming which six centuries ago rose like the fabled Delos from the surface of the turbid waters. Accepted as the river's tribute to the Dragon Throne, it now forms a district of the province with a population of over half a million. About the same time, a large tract of land was carried into the sea by the Hwang Ho, the "Yellow River," which gave rise to the popular proverb, "If we lose in Tungking we gain in Tsungming."

---

[1] In another city a farmer having extorted a sum of money from a tailor living within the Concession, the latter appealed to the British consul for Justice. The consul, an inexperienced young man, observing that the case concerned only the Chinese, referred it to the city magistrate, who instantly ordered the tailor to receive a hundred blows for having applied to a foreign court.

Suchow: A Waterway within the Walls

The former river comes with its mouth full of pearls; the latter yawns to engulf the adjacent land. At present, however, the Yellow River is dry and thirsty, the unruly stream, the opposite of Horace's *uxorius amnis*, having about forty years ago forsaken its old bed and rushed away to the Gulf of Pechili (Peh-chihli). This produced as much consternation as the Mississippi would occasion if it should plough its way across the state that bears its name and enter the Gulf of Mexico at Mobile Bay. The same phenomenon has occurred at long intervals in times past. The wilful stream has oscillated with something like periodical regularity from side to side of the Shantung promontory, and sometimes it has flowed with a divided current, converting that territory into an island. Now, however, the river seems to have settled itself in its new channel, entering the gulf at Yang Chia Kow—a place which foreign sailors describe as "Yankee cow"—and making a portentous alteration in the geography of the globe.

CHAPTER VI

PROVINCE OF SHANTUNG

Kiao-Chao — Visit to Confucius's Tomb — Expedition to the Jews of K'ai-fung-fu — The Grand Canal — Chefoo

In Shantung the people appear to be much more robust than their neighbours to the south. Wheat and millet rather than rice are their staple food. In their orchards apples, pears and peaches take the place of oranges.

At Kiao-chao (Kiau-Chau) the Germans, who occupied that port in 1897, have built a beautiful town opposite the Island of Tsingtao, presenting a fine model for imitation, which, however, the Chinese are not in haste to copy. They have constructed also a railway from the sea to Tsinan-fu, very nearly bisecting the province. Weihien is destined to become a railroad centre; and several missionary societies are erecting colleges there to teach the people truths that Confucius never knew. More than half a century ago, when a missionary distributed Christian books in that region, the people brought them back saying, "We have the works of our Sage, and they are sufficient for us." Will not the new arts and sciences of the West convince them that their Sage was not omniscient?

In 1866 I earned the honours of a *hadji* by visiting the tomb of Confucius — a magnificent mausoleum surrounded by his descendants of the seventieth generation, one of whom in quality of high priest to China's greatest teacher enjoys the rank of a hereditary duke.

One of the Gates of Nanking .

On that occasion, I had come up from a visit to the Jews in Honan. Having profited by a winter vacation to make an expedition to K'ai-fung-fu, I had the intention of pushing on athwart the province to Hankow. The interior, however, as I learned to my intense disappointment, was convulsed with rebellion. No cart driver was willing to venture his neck, his steed, and his vehicle by going in that direction. I accordingly steered for the Mecca of Shantung, and, having paid my respects to the memory of China's greatest sage, struck the Grand Canal and proceeded to Shanghai. From K'ai-fung-fu I had come by land slowly, painfully, and not without danger. From Tsi-ning I drifted down with luxurious ease in a well-appointed house-boat, meditating poetic terms in which to describe the contrast.

The canal deserves the name of "grand" as the wall on the north deserves the name of "great." Memorials of ancient times, they both still stand unrivalled by anything the Western world has to show, if one except the Siberian Railway. The Great Wan is an effete relic no longer of use; and it appears to be satire on human foresight that the Grand Canal should have been built by the very people whom the Great Wall was intended to exclude from China. The canal is as useful to-day as it was six centuries ago, and remains the chief glory of the Mongol dynasty.

Kublai having set up his throne in the north, and completed the conquest of the eighteen provinces, ordered the construction of this magnificent waterway, which extends 800 miles from Peking to Hangchow and connects with other waterways which put the northern capital in roundabout communication with provinces of the extreme south. His object was to tap the rice-fields of Central China and obtain a food supply which could not be interfered with by those daring sea-robbers, the redoubtable Japanese, who had destroyed his fleets and rendered abortive his attempt at conquest. Of the Great Wall, it may be said that the oppression inseparable from its construction hastened the overthrow of the house of its builder. The same is probably true of the Grand Canal. The myriads of unpaid labourers who were drafted by *corvée* from among the Chinese people subsequently enlisted, they or their children, under the revolutionary banner which expelled the oppressive Mongols.

Another port in this province which we cannot pass without an admiring glance, is Chefoo (Chifu). On a fine hill rising from the sea wave the flags of several nations; in the harbour is a cluster of islands; and above the settlement another noble hill rears its head crowned with a temple and groves of trees. On its sides and near the seashore are the residences of missionaries. There I have more than once found a refuge from the summer heat, under the hospitable roof of Mrs. Nevius, the widow of my friend Dr. J. L. Nevius, who, after opening a mission in Hangchow, became one of the pioneers of Shantung. In Chefoo he planted not only a church, but a fruit garden. To the Chinese eye this garden was a striking symbol of what his gospel proposed to effect for the people.

Shanghai: Mouth of Suchow Creek

Shanghai: River View Up-stream

CHAPTER VII

PROVINCE OF CHIHLI

Taku — Tientsin — Peking — The Summer Palace — Patachu — Temples of Heaven, Earth, and Agriculture — Foreign Quarter — The Forbidden City — King-Han Railway — Paoting-fu

Crossing the gulf we reach Taku, at the mouth of the Peiho, and, passing the dismantled forts, ascend the river to Tientsin.

In 1858 I spent two months at Taku and Tientsin in connection with the tedious negotiations of that year. At the latter place I became familiar with the dusty road to the treaty temple; and at the former witnessed the capture of the forts by the combined squadrons of Great Britain and France. The next year on the same ground I saw the allied forces repulsed with heavy loss — a defeat avenged by the capture of Peking in 1860.

In the Boxer War the relief force met with formidable opposition at Tientsin. The place has, however, risen with new splendour from its half-ruined condition, and now poses as the principal residence of the most powerful of the viceroys. Connected by the river with the seaboard, by the Grand Canal with several provinces to the south, and by rail with Peking, Hankow and Manchuria, Tientsin commands the chief lines of communication in northern China. In point of trade it ranks as the third in importance of the treaty ports.

Three hours by rail bring us to the gates of Peking, the northern capital. Formerly it took another hour to get within the city. Superstition or suspicion kept the railway station at a distance; now, however, it is at the Great Central Gate. Unlike Nanking, Peking has nothing picturesque or commanding in its location. On the west and north, at a distance of ten to twenty miles, ranges of blue hills form a feature in the landscape. Within these limits the eye rests on nothing but flat fields, interspersed with clumps of trees overshadowing some family cemetery or the grave of some grandee.

Between the city and the hills are the Yuen Ming Yuen, the Emperor's summer palace, burnt in 1860 and still an unsightly ruin, and the Eho Yuen, the summer residence of the Empress Dowager. Enclosing two or three pretty hills and near to a lofty range, the latter occupies a site of rare beauty. It also possesses mountain water in rich abundance. No fewer than twenty-four springs gush from the base of one of its hills, feeding a pretty lake and numberless canals. Partly destroyed in 1860, this palace was for many years as silent as the halls of Palmyra. I have often wandered through its neglected grounds. Now, every prominent rock is crowned with pagoda or pavilion. There are, however, some things which the slave of the lamp is unable to produce even at the command of an empress—there are no venerable oaks or tall pines to lend their majesty to the scene.

Patachu, in the adjacent hills, used to be a favourite summer resort for the legations and other foreigners before the seaside became accessible by rail. Its name, signifying the "eight great places," denotes that number of Buddhist temples, built one above another in a winding gorge on the hillside. In the highest, called Pearl Grotto, 1,200 feet above the sea, I have found repose for many a summer. I am there now (June, 1906), and there I expect to write the closing chapters of this work. These temples are at my feet; the great city is in full view. To that shrine the emperors sometimes made excursions to obtain a distant prospect of the world. One of them, Kien Lung, somewhat noted as a poet, has left, inscribed on a rock, a few lines commemorative of his visit:

Memorial of the German Occupation of Kiautschou (Kiao-Chao)

German Government Building

"Why have I scaled this dizzy height?
Why sought this mountain den?
I tread as on enchanted ground,
Unlike the abode of men.

"Beneath my feet my realm I see
As in a map unrolled,
Above my head a canopy
Adorned with clouds of gold."

The capital consists of two parts: the Tartar city, a square of four miles; and the Chinese city, measuring five miles by three. They are separated by imposing walls with lofty towers, the outer wall being twenty-one miles in circuit. At present the subject people are permitted to mingle freely with their conquerors; but most of the business is done in the Chinese city. Resembling other Chinese towns in its unsavoury condition, this section contains two imperial temples of great sanctity. One of these, the Temple of Heaven, has a circular altar of fine white marble with an azure dome in its centre in imitation of the celestial vault. Here the Emperor announces his accession, prays for rain, and offers an ox as a burnt sacrifice at the winter solstice—addressing himself to Shang-ti, the supreme ruler, "by whom kings reign and princes decree justice."

The Temple of Agriculture, which stands at a short distance from that just mentioned, was erected in honour of the first man who cultivated the earth. In Chinese, he has no name, his title, Shin-nung signifying the "divine husbandman"—a masculine Ceres. Might we not call the place the Temple of Cain? There the Emperor does honour to husbandry by ploughing a few furrows at the vernal equinox. His example no doubt tends to encourage and comfort his toiling subjects.

Another temple associated with these is that of Mother Earth, the personified consort of Heaven; but it is not in this locality. The eternal fitness of things requires that it should be outside of the walls and on the north. It has a square altar, because the earth is supposed to have "four corners." "Heaven is round and Earth square," is the first line of a school reader for boys. The Tartar city is laid out with perfect regularity, and its streets and alleys are all of convenient width.

Passing from the Chinese city through the Great Central Gate we enter Legation Street, so called because most of the legations are situated on or near it. Architecturally they make no show, being of one story, or at most two stories, in height and hidden behind high walls. So high and strong are the walls of the British Legation that in the Boxer War of 1900 it served the whole community for a fortress, wherein we sustained a siege of eight weeks. A marble obelisk near the Legation gate commemorates the siege, and a marble gateway on a neighbouring street marks the spot where Baron Ketteler was shot. Since that war a foreign quarter has been marked out, the approaches to which have been partially fortified. The streets are now greatly improved; ruined buildings have been repaired; and the general appearance of the old city has been altered for the better.

Tomb of Dr. Ernest Faber in Tsing-Tau

Two more walled enclosures have to be passed before we arrive at the palace. One of them forms a protected barrack or camping-ground for the palace guards and other officials attendant on the court. The other is a sacred precinct shielded from vulgar eyes and intrusive feet, and bears the name "Forbidden City." In the year following the flight of the court these palaces were guarded by foreign troops, and were thrown open to foreign visitors.

Marble bridges, balustrades, and stairways bewilder a stranger. Dragons, phœnixes and other imaginary monsters carved on doorways and pillars warn him that he is treading on sacred ground. The ground, though paved with granite, is far from clean; and the costly carvings within remind one of the saying of an Oriental monarch, "The spider taketh hold with her hands and is in kings' houses." None of the buildings has more than one story, but the throne-rooms and great halls are so lofty as to suggest the dome of a cathedral. The roofs are all covered with tiles of a yellow hue, a colour which even princes are not permitted to use.

Separated from the palace by a moat and a wall is Prospect Hill, a charming elevation which serves as an imperial garden. On the fall of the city in 1643 the last of the Mings hanged himself there—after having stabbed his daughter, like another Virginius, as a last proof of paternal affection.

From the gate of the Forbidden City to the palace officials high and low must go on foot, unless His Majesty by special favour confers the privilege of riding on horseback, a distinction which is always announced in the *Gazette* by the statement that His Majesty has "given a horse" to So-and-So. No trolleys are to be seen in the streets, and four-wheeled carriages are rare and recent. Carts, camels, wheel-barrows, and the ubiquitous rickshaw are the means of transport and locomotion. The canals are open sewers never used for boats.

Not lacking in barbaric splendour, as regards the convenience of living this famous capital will not compare with a country village of the Western world. On the same parallel as Philadelphia, but dryer, hotter, and colder, the climate is so superb that the city, though lacking a system of sanitation, has a remarkably low death-rate. In 1859 I first entered its gates. In 1863 I came here to reside. More than any other place on earth it has been to me a home; and here I am not unlikely to close my pilgrimage.

On my first visit, I made use of Byron's lines on Lisbon to express my impressions of Peking. Though there are now some signs of improvement in the city the quotation can hardly be considered as inapplicable at the present time. Here it is for the convenience of the next traveller:

Lake at Tsinan

"...Whoso entereth within this town,
That, sheening far, celestial seems to be,
Disconsolate will wander up and down,
'Mid many things unsightly to strange ee:
For hut and palace show like filthily:

The dingy denizens are rear'd in dirt;
Ne personage of high or mean degree
Doth care for cleanness of surtout or shirt..."

(Childe Harold's Pilgrimage, Canto the First, st. xvii.)

Returning to the station we face about for the south and take tickets for Paoting-fu. We are on the first grand trunk railway of this empire. It might indeed be described as a vertebral column from which iron roads will ere long be extended laterally on either side, like ribs, to support and bind together the huge frame. Undertaken about twelve years ago it has only recently been completed as far as Hankow, about six hundred miles. The last spike in the bridge across the Yellow River was driven in August, 1905, and since that time through trains have been running from the capital to the banks of the Yang-tse Kiang.

This portion has been constructed by a Belgian syndicate, and their task has been admirably performed. I wish I could say as much of the other half (from Hankow to Canton), the contract for which was given to an American company. After a preliminary survey this company did no work, but, under pretext of waiting for tranquil times, watched the fluctuations of the share market. The whole enterprise was eventually taken over by a native company opposed to foreign ownership— at an advance of 300 per cent. It was a clever deal; but the Americans sacrificed the credit and the influence of their country, and a grand opportunity was lost through cupidity and want of patriotism.

This iron highway is destined in the near future to exert a mighty influence on people and government. It will bring the provinces together and make them feel their unity. It will also insure that communication between the north and the south shall not be interrupted as it might be were it dependent on sea or canal. These advantages must have been so patent as to overcome an inbred hostility to development. Instead of being a danger, these railways are bound to become a source of incalculable strength.

Paoting-fu was the scene of a sad tragedy in 1900, and when avenging troops appeared on the scene, and saw the charred bones of missionaries among the ashes of their dwellings, they were bent on destroying the whole city, but a missionary who served as guide begged them to spare the place. So grateful were the inhabitants for his kindly intervention that they bestowed on the mission a large plot of ground—showing that, however easily wrought up, they were not altogether destitute of the better feelings of humanity.

Continuing our journey through half a dozen considerable cities, at one of which, Shunteh-fu, an American mission has recently been opened, we reach the borders of the province of Honan.

CHAPTER VIII

PROVINCE OF HONAN

A Great Bridge—K'ai-fung-fu—Yellow Jews

Passing the border city of Weihwei-fu, we find ourselves arrested by the Hwang Ho—not that we experience any difficulty in reaching the other bank; but we wish to indulge our curiosity in inspecting the means of transit. It is a bridge, and such a bridge as has no parallel on earth. Five miles in length, it is longer than any other bridge built for the passage of a river. It is not, however, as has been said, the longest bridge in the world; the elevated railway of New York is a bridge of much greater length. So are some of the bridges that carry railways across swamplands on the Pacific Coast. Bridges of that sort, however, are of comparatively easy construction. They have no rebellious stream or treacherous quicksands to contend with. Cæsar's bridge over the Rhine was an achievement worthy to be recorded among the victories of his Gallic wars; but it was a child's plaything in comparison with the bridge over the Yellow River. Cæsar's bridge rested on sesquipedalian beams of solid timber. The Belgian bridge is supported on tubular piles of steel of sesquipedalian diameter driven by steam or screwed down into the sand to a depth of fifty feet.

There have been other bridges near this very spot with which it might be compared. One of them was called Ta-liang, the "Great Bridge," and gave name to a city. Another was Pien-liang, "The Bridge of Pien," one of the names of the present city of K'ai-fung-fu. That bridge has long since disappeared; but the name adheres to the city.

What an unstable foundation on which to erect a seat of empire! Yet the capital has been located in this vicinity more than once or twice within the last twenty-five centuries. The first occasion was during the dynasty of Chou (1100 B. c.), when the king, to be more central, or perhaps dreading the incursions of the Tartars, forsook his capital in Shensi and followed the stream down almost to the sea, braving the quicksands and the floods rather than face those terrible foes. Again, in the Sung period, it was the seat of government for a century and a half.

The safest refuge for a fugitive court which, once established there, has no reason to fear attack by sea or river, it is somewhat strange that in 1900 the Empress Dowager did not direct her steps toward K'ai-fung-fu, instead of escaping to Si-ngan. Being, however, herself a Tartar, she might have been expected to act in a way contrary to precedents set by Chinese dynasties. Obviously, she chose the latter as a place of refuge because it lay near the borders of Tartary. It is noteworthy that a loyal governor of Honan at that very time prepared a palace for her accommodation in K'ai-fung-fu, and when the court was invited to return to Peking, he implored her not to risk herself in the northern capital.

Honan is a province rich in agricultural, and probably in mineral, resources, but it has no outlet in the way of trade. What a boon this railway is destined to be, as a channel of communication with neighbouring provinces!

Tomb of Confucius at Kewfow

I crossed the Yellow River in 1866, but there was then no bridge of any kind. Two-thirds of a mile in width, with a furious current, the management of the ferry-boat was no easy task. On that occasion an object which presented stronger attractions than this wonderful bridge had drawn me to K'ai-fung-fu—a colony of Jews, a fragment of the Lost Tribes of Israel. As mentioned in a previous chapter, I had come by land over the very track now followed by the railroad, but under conditions in strong contrast with the luxuries of a railway carriage—"Alone, un-friended, solitary, slow," I had made my way painfully, shifting from horse to cart, and sometimes compelled by the narrowness of a path to descend to a wheelbar-row. How I longed for the advent of the iron horse. Now I have with me a jovial company; and we may enjoy the mental stimulus of an uninterrupted session of the Oriental Society, while making more distance in an hour than I then made in a day.

Of the condition of the Jews of K'ai-fung-fu, as I found them, I have given a detailed account elsewhere.[2] Suffice it to say here that the so-called colony con-sisted of about four hundred persons, belonging to seven families or clans. Under-mined by a flood of the Yellow River, their synagogue had become ruinous, and, being unable to repair it, they had disposed of its timbers to relieve the pressure of their dire poverty. Nothing remained but the vacant space, marked by a single stone recording the varying fortunes of these forlorn Israelites. It avers that their remoter ancestors arrived in China by way of India in the Han dynasty, before the Christian era, and that the founders of this particular colony found their way to K'ai-fung-fu in the T'ang dynasty about 800 A. D. It also gives an outline of their Holy Faith, showing that, in all their wanderings, they had not forsaken the God of their fathers. They still possessed some rolls of the Law, written in Hebrew, on sheepskins, but they no longer had a rabbi to expound them. They had forgotten the sacred tongue, and some of them had wandered into the fold of Mohammed, whose creed resembled their own. Some too had embraced the religion of Buddha.

My report was listened to with much interest by the rich Jews of Shanghai, but not one of them put his hand in his pocket to rebuild the ruined synagogue; and without that for a rallying-place the colony must ere long fade away, and be absorbed in the surrounding heathenism, or be led to embrace Christianity.

I now learn that the Jews of Shanghai have manifested enough interest to bring a few of their youth to that port for instruction in the Hebrew language. Also that some of these K'ai-fung-fu Jews are frequent attendants in Christian chapels, which have now been opened in that city. To my view, the resuscitation of that ancient colony would be as much of a miracle as the return from captivity in the days of Cyrus.

---

[2] See "Cycle of Cathay." Revell & Co., New York.

Temple of Confucius

CHAPTER IX

THE RIVER PROVINCES

Hupeh—Hankow—Hanyang Iron Works—A Centre of Missionary Activity—Hunan—Kiangsi—Anhwei—Native Province of Li Hung Chang

By the term "river provinces" are to be understood those provinces of central and western China which are made accessible to intercourse and trade by means of the Yang-tse Kiang.

Pursuing our journey, in twelve hours by rail we reach the frontier of Hupeh. At that point we see above us a fortification perched on the side of a lofty hill which stands beyond the line. At a height more than double that of this crenelated wall is a summer resort of foreigners from Hankow and other parts of the interior. I visited this place in 1905. In Chinese, the plateau on which it stands is called, from a projecting rock, the "Rooster's Crest"; shortened into the more expressive name, the "Roost," it is suggestive of the repose of summer. It presents a magnificent prospect, extending over a broad belt of both provinces.

Six hours more and we arrive in Hankow, which is one of three cities built at the junction of the Han and the Yang-tse, the Tripolis of China, a tripod of empire, the hub of the universe, as the Chinese fondly regard it. The other two cities are Wuchang, the capital of the viceroyalty, and Hanyang, on the opposite bank of the river.

In Hankow one beholds a Shanghai on a smaller scale, and in the other two cities the eye is struck by indications of the change which is coming over the externals of Chinese life.

At Hanyang, which is reached by a bridge, may be seen an extensive and well-appointed system of iron-works, daily turning out large quantities of steel rails for the continuation of the railway. It also produces large quantities of iron ordnance for the contingencies of war. This is the pet enterprise of the enlightened Viceroy Chang Chi-tung; but on the other side of the Yang-tse we have cheering evidence that he has not confined his reforms to transportation and the army. There, on the south bank, you may see the long walls and tall chimneys of numerous manufacturing establishments—cotton-mills, silk filatures, rope-walks, glass-works, tile-works, powder-works—all designed to introduce the arts of the West, and to wage an industrial war with the powers of Christendom. There, too, in a pretty house overlooking the Great River, I spent three years as aid to the viceroy in educational work. In the heart of China, it was a watch-tower from which I could look up and down the river and study the condition of these inland provinces.

This great centre was early preëmpted by the pioneers of missionary enterprise. Here Griffith John set up the banner of the cross forty years ago and by indefatigable and not unfruitful labours earned for himself the name of "the Apostle of Central China." In addition he has founded a college for the training of native preachers. The year 1905 was the jubilee of his arrival in the empire. Here, too, came David Hill, a saintly man combining the characters of St. Paul and of John Howard, as one of the pioneers of the churches of Great Britain. These leaders have been followed by a host who, if less distinguished, have perhaps accomplished more for the advancement of the Kingdom of Christ. Without the coöperation of such agencies all reformatory movements like those initiated by the viceroy must fall short of elevating the people to the level of Christian civilisation.

Chefoo: City and Harbour

Chefoo Hill

The London Mission, the English Wesleyans, and the American Episcopalians, all have flourishing stations at Wuchang. The Boone school, under the auspices of the last-named society, is an admirable institution, and takes rank with the best colleges in China.

At Hankow the China Inland Mission is represented by a superintendent and a home for missionaries in transit. At that home the Rev. J. Hudson Taylor, the founder of that great society, whom I call the Loyola of Protestant missions, spent a few days in 1906; and there Dr. John and I sat with him for a group of the "Three Senior Missionaries" in China.

The river provinces may be divided into lower and upper, the dividing-line being at Ichang near the gorges of the Yang-tse. Hupeh and Hunan, Kiangsi and Anhwei occupy the lower reach; Szechuen, Kweichau, and Yünnan, the upper one. The first two form one viceregal district, with a population exceeding that of any European country excepting Russia.

Hupeh signifies "north of the lake"; Hunan, "south of the lake" — the great lake of Tungting lying between the two. Hupeh has been open to trade and residence for over forty years; but the sister province was long hermetically sealed against the footprints of the white man. Twenty or even ten years ago to venture within its limits would have cost a European his life. Its capital, Changsha, was the seat of an anti-foreign propaganda from which issued masses of foul literature; but the lawless hostility of the people has been held in check by the judicious firmness of the present viceroy, and that city is now the seat of numerous mission bodies which are vying with each other in their efforts to diffuse light and knowledge. It is also open to commerce as a port of trade.

One of the greatest distinctions of the province is its production of brave men, one of the bravest of whom was the first Marquis Tseng who, at the head of a patriotic force from his native province, recaptured the city of Nanking and put an end to the chaotic government of the Taiping rebels—a service which has ever since been recognised by the Chinese Government in conferring the viceroyalty of Nanking on a native of Hunan.

Lying to the south of the river, is the province of Kiangsi, containing the Poyang Lake, next in size to the Tungting. Above its entrance at Kiukiang rises a lone mountain which bears the name of Kuling. Beautifully situated, and commanding a wide view of lake and river, its sides are dotted with pretty cottages, erected as summer resorts for people from all the inland ports. Here may be seen the flags of many nations, and here the hard-worked missionary finds rest and recreation, without idleness; for he finds clubs for the discussion of politics and philosophy, and libraries which more than supply the absence of his own. Just opposite the entrance to the lake stands the "Little Orphan," a vine-clad rock 200 feet in height, with a small temple on the top. It looks like a fragment torn from the mountain-side and planted in the bosom of the stream. Fancy fails to picture the convulsion of which the "Little Orphan" is the monument.

Farther down is the province of Anhwei which takes its name from its chief two cities, Anking and Weichou. In general resembling Kiangsi, it has two flourishing ports on the river, Anking, the capital, and Wuhu. Of the people nothing noteworthy is to be observed, save that they are unusually turbulent, and their lawless spirit has not been curbed by any strong hand like that of the viceroy at Wuchang.[3] The province is distinguished for its production of great men, of whom Li Hung Chang was one.

---

[3] This was written before the Nanchang riot of March, 1906.

CHAPTER X

PROVINCES OF THE UPPER YANG-TSE

A Perilous Passage — Szechuen — Kweichau, the Poorest Province in China — Yünnan — Tribes of Aborigines

Thus far our voyage of exploration, like one of Cook's tours, has been personally conducted. From this point, however, I must depend upon the experience of others: the guide himself must seek a guide to conduct him through the remaining portions of the empire.

We enter the Upper Yang-tse by a long and tortuous passage through which the "Great River" rushes with a force and a roar like the cataracts of the Rhine, only on a vastly greater scale. In some bygone age volcanic forces tore asunder a mountain range, and the waters of the great stream furrowed out a channel; but the obstructing rocks, so far from being worn away, remain as permanent obstacles to steam navigation and are a cause of frequent shipwrecks. Yet, undeterred by dangers that eclipse Scylla and Charybdis, the laborious Chinese have for centuries past carried on an immense traffic through this perilous passage. In making the ascent their junks are drawn against the current by teams of coolies, tens or hundreds of the latter being harnessed to the tow-lines of one boat and driven like a bullock train in South Africa. Slow and difficult is the ascent, but swift and perilous the downward passage.

Rear View of the Summer Palace, Peking

No doubt engineering may succeed in removing some of the obstacles and in minifying the dangers of this passage. Steam, too, may supply another mode of traction to take the place of these teams of men. A still revolution is in prospect, namely a ship canal or railway. The latter, perhaps, might be made to lift the junks bodily out of the water and transport them beyond the rapids. Two cities, however, would suffer somewhat by this change in the mode of navigation, namely, Ichang at the foot and Chungking at the head of the rapids. The latter is the chief river port of Szechuen, a province having four times the average area.

The great province of Szechuen, if it only had the advantages of a seacoast, would take the lead in importance. As it is, it is deemed sufficiently important, like Chihli, to have a viceroy of its own. The name signifies the "four rivers," and the province has as many ranges of mountains. One of them, the Omeshan, is celebrated for its beauty and majesty. The mountains give the province a great variety of climate, and the rivers supply means of transportation and irrigation. Its people, too, are more uniform in language and character than those of most other regions. Their language partakes of the Northern mandarin. Near the end of the Ming dynasty the whole population is said to have been destroyed in the fratricidal wars of that sanguinary period. The population accordingly is comparatively sparse, and the cities are said to present a new and prosperous aspect. Above Szechuen lie the two provinces of Kweichau and Yünnan, forming one viceroyalty under the name of Yünkwei.

Kweichau has the reputation of being the poorest province in China, with a very sparse population, nearly one-half of whom are aborigines, called *shans*, *lolos*, and *miaotzes*.

Yünnan (signifying not "cloudy south," but "south of the cloudy mountains") is next in area to Szechuen. Its resources are as yet undeveloped, and it certainly has a great future. Its climate, if it may be said to have one, is reputed to be unhealthful, and among its hills are many deep gorges which the Chinese say are full of *chang chi*, "poisonous gases" which are fatal to men and animals—like the Grotto del Cane in Italy. But these gorges and cliffs abound in better things also. They are rich in unexploited coal measures and they contain also many mines of the purest copper ore. The river that washes its borders here bears the name of Kinsha, the river of "golden sands." Some of its rivers have the curious peculiarity of flowing the reverse way, that is, to the west and south instead of toward the eastern sea. The Chinese accordingly call the province "Tiensheng" the country of the "converse streams."

Within the borders of Yünnan there are said to be more than a hundred tribes of aborigines all more or less akin to those of Kweichau and Burma, but each under its own separate chief. Some of them are fine-looking, vigorous people; but the Chinese describe them as living in a state of utter savagery. Missionaries, however, have recently begun work for them; and we may hope that, as for the Karens of Burma, a better day will soon dawn on the Yünnan aborigines.

Entrance to Palace, Peking

The French, having colonies on the border, are naturally desirous of exploiting the provinces of this southern belt, and China is intensely suspicious of encroachment from that quarter.

CHAPTER XI
NORTHWESTERN PROVINCES

Shansi—Shensi—Earliest Known Home of the Chinese—Kansuh

Of the three northwestern provinces, the richest is Shansi. More favoured in climate and soil than the other members of the group, its population is more dense. Divided from Chihli by a range of hills, its whole surface is hilly, but not mountainous. The highlands give variety to its temperature—condensing the moisture and supplying water for irrigation. The valleys are extremely fertile, and of them it may be said in the words of Job, "As for the earth, out of it cometh bread: and underneath it is turned up as it were fire." Not only do the fields yield fine crops of wheat and millet, but there are extensive coal measures of excellent quality. Iron ore also is found in great abundance. Mining enterprises have accordingly been carried on from ancient times, and they have now, with the advent of steam, acquired a fresh impetus. It follows, of course, that the province is prolific of bankers. Shansi bankers monopolise the business of finance in all the adjacent provinces.

Next on the west comes the province of Shensi, from *shen*, a "strait or pass" (not *shan* a "hill"), and *si*, "west."

Here was the earliest home of the Chinese race of which there is any record. On the Yellow River, which here forms the boundary of two provinces, stands the city of Si-ngan where the Chou dynasty set up its throne in the twelfth century B. C. Since that date many dynasties have made it the seat of empire. Their palaces have disappeared; but most of them have left monumental inscriptions from which a connected history might be extracted. To us the most interesting monument is a stone, erected about 800 A. D. to commemorate the introduction of Christianity by some Nestorian missionaries from western Asia.

```The province of Kansuh is comparatively barren. Its boundaries extend far out into regions peopled by Mongol tribes; and the neighbourhood of great deserts gives it an arid climate unfavourable to agriculture. Many of its inhabitants are immigrants from Central Asia and profess the Mohammedan faith. It is almost surrounded by the Yellow River, like a picture set in a gilded frame, reminding one of that river of paradise which "encompasseth the whole land of Havilah where there is gold." Whether there is gold in Kansuh we have yet to learn; but no doubt some grains of the precious metal might be picked up amongst its shifting sands.
```

Temple of Heaven, Peking

CHAPTER XII

OUTLYING TERRITORIES

Manchuria—Mongolia—Turkestan—Tibet, the Roof of the World—Journey of Huc and Gabet.

Beyond the eastern extremity of the Great Wall, bounded on the west by Mongolia, on the north by the Amur, on the east by the Russian seaboard, and on the south by Korea and the Gulf of Pechili, lies the home of the Manchus—the race now dominant in the Chinese Empire. China claims it, just as Great Britain claimed Normandy, because her conquerors came from that region; and now that two of her neighbours have exhausted themselves in fighting for it, she will take good care that neither of them shall filch the jewel from her crown.

That remarkable achievement, the conquest of China by a few thousand semi-civilised Tartars, is treated in the second part of this work.

Manchuria consists of three regions now denominated provinces, Shengking, Kairin, and Helungkiang. They are all under one governor-general whose seat is at Mukden, a city sacred in the eyes of every Manchu, because there are the tombs of the fathers of the dynasty.

The native population of Manchuria having been drafted off to garrison and colonise the conquered country, their deserted districts were thrown open to Chinese settlers. The population of the three provinces is mainly Chinese, and, assimilated in government to those of China, they are reckoned as completing the number of twenty-one. Opulent in grain-fields, forests, and minerals, with every facility for commerce, no part of the empire has a brighter future. So thinly peopled is its northern portion that it continues to be a vast hunting-ground which supplies the Chinese market with sables and tiger-skins besides other peltries. The tiger-skins are particularly valuable as having longer and richer fur than those of Bengal.

Of the Manchus as a people, I shall speak later on.[4] Those remaining in their original habitat are extremely rude and ignorant; yet even these hitherto neglected regions are now coming under the enlightening influence of a system of government schools.

Mongolia, the largest division of Tartary, if not of the Empire, is scarcely better known than the mountain regions of Tibet, a large portion of its area being covered with deserts as uninviting and as seldom visited as the African Sahara. One

[4] Part II. page 140 and 142; part III, pages 267-280

route, however, has been well trodden by Russian travellers, namely, that lying between Kiachta and Peking.

In the reign of Kanghi the Russians were granted the privilege of establishing an ecclesiastical mission to minister to a Cossack garrison which the Emperor had captured at Albazin trespassing on his grounds. Like another Nebuchadnezzar, he transplanted them to the soil of China. He also permitted the Russians to bring tribute to the "Son of Heaven" once in ten years. That implied a right to trade, so that the Russians, like other envoys, in Chinese phrase "came lean and went away fat." But they were not allowed to leave the beaten track: they were merchants, not travellers. Not till the removal of the taboo within the last half-century have these outlying dependencies been explored by men like Richthofen and Sven Hedin. Formerly the makers of maps garnished those unknown regions

"With caravans for want of towns."

Sooth to say, there are no towns, except Urga, a shrine for pilgrimage, the residence of a living Buddha, and Kiachta and Kalgan, terminal points of the caravan route already referred to.

Kiachta is a double town—one-half of it on each side of the Russo-Chinese boundary—presenting in striking contrast the magnificence of a Russian city and the poverty and filth of a Tartar encampment. The whole country is called in Chinese "the land of grass." Its inhabitants have sheepfolds and cattle ranches, but neither fields nor houses, unless tents and temporary huts may be so designated. To this day, nomadic in their habits, they migrate from place to place with their flocks and herds as the exigencies of water and pasturage may require.

Lines of demarcation exist for large tracts belonging to a tribe, but no minor divisions such as individual holdings. The members of a clan all enjoy their grazing range in common, and hold themselves ready to fight for the rights of their chieftain. Bloody feuds lasting for generations, such as would rival those of the Scottish clans, are not of infrequent occurrence. Their Manchu overlord treats these tribal conflicts with sublime indifference, as he does the village wars in China.

Peking: Gate of University, Imperial Hill in the Background

The Mongolian chiefs, or "princes" as they are called, are forty-eight in number. The "forty-eight princes" is a phrase as familiar to the Chinese ear as the "eighteen provinces" is to ours. Like the Manchus they are arranged in groups under eight banners. Some of them took part in the conquest, but the Manchus are too suspicious to permit them to do garrison duty in the Middle Kingdom, lest the memories of Kublai Khan and his glory should be awakened. They are, however, held liable to military service. Seng Ko Lin Sin ("Sam Collinson" as the

British dubbed him), a Lama prince, headed the northern armies against the Taiping rebels and afterwards suffered defeat at the hands of the British and French before the gates of Peking.

In the winter the Mongol princes come with their clansmen to revel in the delights of Cambalu, the city of the great Khan, as they have continued to call Peking ever since the days of Kublai, whose magnificence has been celebrated by Marco Polo. Their camping-ground is the Mongolian Square which is crowded with tabernacles built of bamboo and covered with felt. In a sort of bazaar may be seen pyramids of butter and cheese, two commodities that are abominations to the Chinese of the south, but are much appreciated by Chinese in Peking as well as by the Manchus. One may see also mountains of venison perfectly fresh; the frozen carcasses of "yellow sheep" (really not sheep, but antelopes); then come wild boars in profusion, along with badgers, hares, and troops of live dogs—the latter only needing to be wild to make them edible. This will give some faint idea of Mongolia's contribution to the luxuries of the metropolis. Devout Buddhist as he is, the average Mongol deems abstinence from animal food a degree of sanctity unattainable by him.

Mongols of the common classes are clad in dirty sheepskins. Their gentry and priesthood dress themselves in the spoils of wolf or fox—more costly but not more clean. Furs, felt, and woollen fabrics of the coarsest texture may also be noticed. Raiment of camel's hair, strapped with a leathern girdle after the manner of John the Baptist, may be seen any day, and the wearers are not regarded as objects of commiseration.

Their camel, too, is wonderfully adapted to its habitat. Provided with two humps, it carries a natural saddle; and, clothed in long wool, yellow, brown or black, it looks in winter a lordly beast. Its fleece is never shorn, but is shed in summer. At that season the poor naked animal is the most pitiable of creatures. In the absence of railways and carriage roads, it fills the place of the ship of the desert and performs the heaviest tasks, such as the transporting of coals and salt. Most docile of slaves, at a word from its master it kneels down and quietly accepts its burden.

At Peking there is a lamasary where four hundred Mongol monks are maintained in idleness at the expense of the Emperor. Their manners are those of highwaymen. They have been known to lay rough hands on visitors in order to extort a charitable dole; and, if rumour may be trusted, their morals are far from exemplary.

Peking: Imperial Lecture room in the Old University Building

My knowledge of the Mongols is derived chiefly from what I have seen of them in Peking. I have also had a glimpse of their country at Kalgan, beyond the Great Wall. A few lines from a caravan song by the Rev. Mark Williams give a picture of a long journey by those slow coaches:

"Inching along, we are inching along,

At the pace of a snail, we are inching along,
Our horses are hardy, our camels are strong,
We all shall reach Urga by inching along.

"The things that are common, all men will despise;
But these in the desert we most highly prize.
For water is worth more than huge bags of gold
And argols than diamonds of value untold."

—*A Flight for Life*, Pilgrim Press, Boston.

Politically Turkestan is not Mongolia, but Tamerlane, though born there, was a Mongol. His descendants were the Moguls of India. At different epochs peoples called Turks and Huns have wandered over the Mongolian plateau, and Mongols have swept over Turkestan. To draw a line of demarcation is neither easy nor important. In the Turkestan of to-day the majority of the people follow the prophet of Mecca. Russia has absorbed most of the khanates, and has tried more than once to encroach on portions belonging to China. In one instance she was foiled and compelled to disgorge by the courage of Viceroy Chang, a story which I reserve for the sequel. The coveted region was Ili, and Russia's pretext for crossing the boundary was the chronic state of warfare in which the inhabitants existed.

Tibet is the land of the Grand Lama. Is it merely tributary or is it a portion of the Chinese Empire? This is a question that has been warmly agitated during the last two years—brought to the front by Colonel Younghusband's expedition and by a treaty made in Lhasa. Instead of laying their complaints before the court of Peking, the Indian Government chose to settle matters on the spot, ignoring the authority of China. Naturally China has been provoked to instruct her resident at Lhasa to maintain her rights.

A presumptive claim might be based on the fact, that the Grand Lama took refuge at Urga, where he remained until the Empress Dowager ordered him to return to his abandoned post. China has always had a representative at his court; but his function would appear to be that of a political spy rather than an overseer, governor, or even adviser. Chinese influence in Tibet is nearly *nil*. For China to assert authority by interference and to make herself responsible for Tibet's shortcomings would be a questionable policy, against which two wars ought to be a sufficient warning. She was involved with France by her interference in Tongking and with Japan by interference in Korea. Too much intermeddling in Tibet might easily embroil her with Great Britain.

In one sense the Buddhist pope may justly claim to be the highest of earthly potentates. No other sits on a throne at an equal elevation above the level of the sea. Like Melchizedeck, he is without father or mother—each occupant of the throne being a fresh incarnation of Buddha. The signs of Buddhaship are known only to the initiated; but they are supposed to consist in the recognition of places, persons, and apparel. These lamas never die of old age.

Peking: Old Examination Hall, Stalls for Students, and Watch-tower

Old University, Peking

While in other parts of the Empire polygamy prevails for those who can afford it, in Tibet polyandry crops up. Which is the more offensive to good morals we need not decide; but is it not evident that Confucianism shows its weakness on one side as Buddhism does on the other? A people that tolerates either or both hardly deserves to be regarded as civilised.

The Chinese call Tibet the "roof of the world," and most of it is as barren as the roof of a house. Still the roof, though producing nothing, collects water to irrigate a garden. Tibet is the mother of great rivers, and she feeds them from her eternal snows. On her highlands is a lake or cluster of lakes which the Chinese describe as *Sing Su Hai*, the "sea of stars." From this the Yellow River takes its rise and perhaps the Yang-tse Kiang. A Chinese legend says that Chang Chien poled a raft up to the source of the Yellow River and found himself in the Milky Way, *Tienho*, the "River of Heaven."

Fifty years ago two intrepid French missionaries, Huc and Gabet, made their way to Lhasa, but they were not allowed to remain there. The Chinese residents made them prisoners, under pretext of giving them protection, and sent them to the seacoast through the heart of the empire. They were thus enabled to see the vast interior at a time when it was barred alike to traveller and missionary. Of this adventurous journey Huc's published "Travels" is the immortal monument.

We have thus gone over China and glanced at most of her outlying dependencies. The further exploration of Tibet we may postpone until she has made good her claims to dominion in that mountain region. The vastness of the Chinese Empire and the immensity of its population awaken in the mind a multitude of questions to which nothing but history can give an adequate reply. We come therefore to the oracle whose responses may perhaps be less dubious than those of Delphi.

PART II
HISTORY IN OUTLINE FROM THE EAR-
LIEST TIMES TO THE EIGHTEENTH
CENTURY

CHAPTER XIII

ORIGIN OF THE CHINESE

*Parent Stock a Migratory People—They Invade China from the Northwest
and Colonise the Banks of the Yellow River and of the Han—Their Conflicts with the Aborigines—Native Tribes Absorbed by Conquerors*

That the parent stock in which the Chinese nation had its origin was a small
migratory people, like the tribes of Israel, and that they entered the land of promise from the northwest is tolerably certain; but to trace their previous wanderings
back to Shinar, India, or Persia would be a waste of time, as the necessary data are
lacking. Even within their appointed domain the accounts of their early history are
too obscure to be accepted as to any extent reliable.

They appear to have begun their career of conquest by colonising the banks
of the Yellow River and those of the Han. By slow stages they moved eastward
to the central plain and southward to the Yang-tse Kiang. At that early epoch,
between 3000 and 2000 B. C., they found the country already occupied by various
wild tribes whom they considered as savages. In their early traditions they describe these tribes respectively by four words: those of the south are called *Man* (a
word with the silk radical); those on the east, *Yi* (with the bow radical); those on
the north, *Tih* (represented by a dog and fire); and those on the west, *Jung* ("warlike, fierce," the symbol for their ideograph being a spear). Each of these names
points to something distinctive. Some of these tribes were, perhaps, spinners of
silk; some, hunters; and all of them, formidable enemies.

The earliest book of history opens with conflicts with aborigines. There can be
no question that the slow progress made by the invaders in following the course of
those streams on which the most ancient capitals of the Chinese were subsequently located was owing to the necessity of fighting their way. Shun, the second sovereign of whose reign there is record (2200 B. c.), is said to have waged war with San
Miao, three tribes of *miaotze* or aborigines, a term still applied to the independent
tribes of the southwest. Beaten in the field, or at least suffering a temporary check,
he betook himself to the rites of religion, making offerings and praying to Shang-ti,
the supreme ruler. "After forty days," it is stated, "the natives submitted."

In the absence of any explanation it may be concluded that during the suspension of hostilities negotiations were proceeding which resulted not in the destruction of the natives, but in their incorporation with their more civilised neighbours.
This first recorded amalgamation of the kind was doubtless an instance of a process of growth that continued for many centuries, resulting in the absorption of all

the native tribes on the north of the Yang-tse and of most of those on the south. The expanding state was eventually composed of a vast body of natives who submitted to their civilised conquerors, much as the people of Mexico and Peru consented to be ruled by a handful of Spaniards.[5]

Peking: Sacred Tablet, Temple of Confucius

[5] To this day, the bulk of the people in those countries show but small traces of Spanish blood. Juarez, the famous dictator, was a pure Indian.

As late as the Christian era any authentic account of permanent conquests in China to the south of the "Great River" is still wanting, though warlike expeditions in that direction were not infrequent. The people of the northern provinces called themselves *Han-jin*, "men of Han" or "sons of Han," while those of the south styled themselves *T'ang-jin*, "men of T'ang." Does not this indicate that, while the former were moulded into unity by the great dynasty which took its name from the river Han (206 B. c.), the latter did not become Chinese until the brilliant period of the T'angs, nearly a thousand years later? Further confirmation need not be adduced to show that the empire of the Far East contemporary with, and superior in civilisation to, ancient Rome, embraced less than the eighteen provinces of China Proper. Of the nine districts into which it was divided by Ta-yü, 2100 B. C. not one was south of the "Great River."

CHAPTER XIV

THE MYTHICAL PERIOD

Account of Creation—P'an-ku, the Ancient Founder—The Three Sovereigns—The Five Rulers, the Beginnings of Human Civilisation—The Golden Age—Yau, the Unselfish Monarch—Shun, the Paragon of Domestic Virtues—Story of Ta-yü—Rise of Hereditary Monarchy

Unlike the Greeks and Hindoos, the Chinese are deficient in the sort of imagination that breeds a poetical mythology. They are not, however, wanting in that pride of race which is prone to lay claim to the past as well as to the future. They have accordingly constructed, not a mythology, but a fictitious history which begins with the creation of the world.

How men and animals were made they do not say; but they assert that heaven and earth were united in a state of chaos until a divine man, whom they call P'an-ku, the "ancient founder," rent them asunder. Pictures show him wielding his sledge-hammer and disengaging sun and moon from overlying hills—a grotesque conception in strong contrast with the simple and sublime statement, "God said, 'Let there be light' and there was light." P'an-ku was followed by a divine being named Nü-wa, in regard to whom it is doubtful whether to speak in the feminine or in the masculine gender. Designated queen more frequently than king, it is said of her that, a portion of the sky having fallen down (probably owing to the defective work of her predecessor), she rebuilt it with precious stones of many colours. *Lien shih pu tien,* "to patch the sky with precious stones," is a set phrase by which the Chinese indicate that which is fabulous and absurd.

Instead of filling the long interval between the creation of the world and the birth of history with gods and fairies, the Chinese cover that period by three sovereigns whom they call after their favourite triad, heaven, earth, and man, giving them the respective titles Tién-hwang, Ti-hwang, and Jin-hwang. Each of these reigned eighteen thousand years; but what they reigned over is not apparent. At all events they seem to have contributed little to the comfort of their people; for at the close of that long period the wretched inhabitants of the empire—the only country then known to exist on earth—had no houses, no clothes, no laws, and no letters.

Hankow: Mouth of the Han

Now come five personages who, in accordance with Chinese historical propriety, are likewise invested with imperial dignity and are called Wu-ti, "the five rulers." Collectively they represent the first appearance of the useful arts, the rude beginnings of human civilisation. One of these rulers, noticing that birds constructed nests, taught his people to build huts, from which he is called the "nest builder." Another was the Prometheus of his day and obtained fire, not, however, by stealing it from the sun, but by honestly working for it with two pieces of wood which he rubbed together. The third of these rulers, named Fuhi, appears to have been the teacher of his people in the art of rearing domestic animals; in other words, the initiator of pastoral life, and possibly the originator of sacrificial offerings. The fourth in order introduced husbandry. As has been stated in a previous chapter (see page 36), he has no name except Shin-nung, "divine husbandman"; and under that title he continues to be worshipped at the present day as the Ceres of China. The Emperor every spring repairs to his temple to plough a few furrows by way of encouragement to his people. The last of the five personages is called the "yellow ruler," whether from the colour of his robes, or as ruler of the yellow race, is left in doubt. He is credited with the invention of letters and the cycle of sixty years, the foundation of Chinese chronology (2700 B. C.).

Unlike the long twilight which precedes the dawn in high latitudes, the semi-mythical age was brief, covering no more than two reigns, those of Yao and Shun. Confucius regarded these as included in the "five rulers." To make room for them, he omits the first two; and he seldom refers to the others, but appears to accept them as real personages. He is no critic; but he has shown good sense in drawing the line no further back. He has made the epoch of these last a golden age (2356-2206) which is not the creation of a poet, but the conception of a philosopher who wished to have an open space on which to build up his political theories. He found, moreover, in these primitive times some features by which he was greatly fascinated. The simplicity and freedom which appeared to prevail in those far-off days were to him very attractive.

It is related that Yao, the type of an unselfish monarch, while on a tour of inspection in the disguise of a peasant, heard an old man singing this song to the notes of his guitar:

> "I plough my ground and eat my own bread,
> I dig my well and drink my own water:
> What use have I for king or court?"

Yao returned to his palace, rejoicing that the state of his country was such that his people were able to forget him.

Another feature which the Chinese hold up in bold relief is the fact that in those days the occupancy of the throne was not hereditary. Yao is said to have reigned a hundred years. When he was growing old he saw with grief that his son showed no signs of being a worthy successor. Setting him aside, therefore, he asked his ministers to recommend someone as his heir. They all agreed in nominating Shun. "What are his merits?" asked the King. "Filial piety and fraternal kindness," they replied. "By these virtues he has wrought a reform in a family noted for perverseness." The King desiring to know the facts, they related the following story:

"Shun's father is an ill-natured, blind man. He has a cruel stepmother and a selfish, petulant younger brother. This boy, the pet of his parents, treated Shun with insolence; and the father and mother joined in persecuting the elder son. Shun, without showing resentment, cried aloud to Heaven and obtained patience to bear their harshness. By duty and affection he has won the hearts of all three." "Bring him before me," said the King; "I have yet another trial by which to test his virtues." Yao made him his son-in-law, giving him his two daughters at once. He wished to see whether the good son and brother would also be a good husband and father—an example for his people in all their domestic relations. Shun accepted the test with becoming resignation and comported himself to the satisfaction of the old king, who raised him to the throne. After a reign of fifty years, partly as Yao's associate, Shun followed the example of his father-in-law. Passing by his own son, he left the throne to Ta-yü or Yü, a man who had been subjected to trials far more serious than that of having to live in the same house with a pair of pretty princesses.

A question discussed in the school of Mencius, many centuries later, may be cited here for the light it throws on the use made by Chinese schoolmen of the examples of this period. "Suppose," said one of his students, "that Shun's father had killed a man, would Shun, being king, have allowed him to be condemned?" "No," replied the master; "he would have renounced the throne and, taking his father on his shoulders, he would have fled away to the seaside, rejoicing in the consciousness of having performed the duty of a filial son." Shun continues to be cited as the paragon of domestic virtues, occupying the first place in a list of twenty-four who are noted for filial piety.

The trial by which the virtues of Ta-yü were proved was an extraordinary feat of engineering—nothing less than the subduing of the waters of a deluge. "The waters," said the King, "embosom the high hills and insolently menace heaven itself. Who will find us a man to take them in hand and keep them in place?" His ministers recommended one Kun. Kun failed to accomplish the task, and Shun, who in this case hardly serves for the model of a just ruler, put him to death. Then the task was imposed on Ta-yü, the son of the man who had been executed. After nine years of incredible hardships he brought the work to a successful termination. During this time he extended his care to the rivers of more than one province, dredging, ditching, and diking. Three times he passed his own door and, though he heard the cries of his infant son, he did not once enter his house. The son of a criminal who had suffered death, a throne was the meed of his diligence and ability.

A temple in Hanyang, at the confluence of two rivers, commemorates Ta-yü's exploit, which certainly throws the labours of Hercules completely into the shade. On the opposite side of the river stands a pillar, inscribed in antique hieroglyphics, which professes to record this great achievement. It is a copy of one which stands on Mount Hang; and the characters, in the tadpole style, are so ancient that doubts as to their actual meaning exist among scholars of the present day. Each letter is accordingly accompanied by its equivalent in modern Chinese. The stone purports to have been erected by Ta-yü himself—good ground for suspicion—but it has been proved to be a fabrication of a later age, though still very ancient.[6]

---

[6] Dr. Hänisch of Berlin has taken great pains to expose the imposture.

Class in Girls' School, Episcopal Mission, Wuchang

In the two preceding reigns the sovereign had always consulted the public good rather than family interest—a form of monarchy which the Chinese call elective, but which has never been followed, save that the Emperor exercises the right of choice among his sons irrespective of primogeniture. The man who bears the odium of having departed from the unselfish policy of Yao and Shun is this same Ta-yü. He left the throne to his son and, as the Chinese say, "made of the empire a family estate."

This narrative comes from the *Shu-King* or "Book of History," the most venerated of the Five Classics edited by Confucius; but the reader will readily perceive that it is no more historical than the stories of Codrus or Numa Pompilius.

In the reign of Yao we have an account of astronomical observations made with a view to fixing the length of the year. The King tells one man to go to the east and another to the west, to observe the culmination and transit of certain stars. As a result he says they will find that the year consists of 366 days, a close approximation for that epoch. The absurdity of this style, which attributes omniscience to the prince and leaves to his agents nothing but the task of verification, should not be allowed to detract from the credit due to their observations. The result arrived at was about the same as that reached by the Babylonians at the same date (2356 B. c.)

Other rulers who are credited with great inventions probably made them in the same way. Whether under Fuhi or Hwang-ti, Ts'ang-kié is recognised as the Cadmus of China, the author of its written characters; and Tanao, a minister of Hwang-ti, is admitted to be the author of the cycle of sixty. Both of those emperors may be imagined as calling up their ministers and saying to one, "Go and invent the art of writing," and to the other, "Work out a system of chronology."

Freshman Class, Boone School, Wuchang

Boone School Picnic, Wuchang

In the same way, the inception of the culture of the silkworm and the discovery of the magnetic needle are attributed to the predecessors of Yao, probably on the principle that treasure-trove was the property of the King and that if no claimant for the honour could be found it must be attributed to some ancient monarch. The production of silk, as woman's work, they profess to assign to the consort of one of those worthies—a thing improbable if not impossible, her place of residence being in the north of China. Their picture-writing tells a different tale. Their word for a southern barbarian, compounded of "silk" and "worm," points to the south as the source of that useful industry, much as our word "silk," derived from *sericum*, points to China as its origin.

CHAPTER XV
THE THREE DYNASTIES

The House of Hia—Ta-yu's Consideration for His Subjects—Kié's Excesses—The House of Shang—Shang-tang, the Founder, Offers Himself as a Sacrificial Victim, and Brings Rain—Chou-sin Sets Fire to His Own Palace and Perishes in the Flames—The House of Chou

The Hia, Shang and Chou dynasties together extend over the twenty-two centuries preceding the Christian Era. The first occupies 440 years; the second, 644; and the last, in the midst of turmoil and anarchy, drags out a miserable existence of 874 years. They are grouped together as the San Tai or San Wang, "the Three Houses of Kings," because that title was employed by the founder of each. Some of their successors were called *Ti*; but *Hwang-ti*, the term for "emperor" now in use, was never employed until it was assumed by the builder of the Great Wall on the overthrow of the feudal states and the consolidation of the empire, 240 B. C.

THE HOUSE OF HIA, 2205-1766 B. C.
(17 kings, 2 usurpers)

Unlike most founders of royal houses, who come to the throne through a deluge of blood, Ta-yü, as has been shown in the last chapter, climbed to that eminence through a deluge of water. Like Noah, the hero of an earlier deluge, he seems to have indulged, for once at least, too freely in the use of wine. A chapter in the "Book of History," entitled "A Warning Against Wine," informs us that one Yiti having made wine presented it to his prince. Ta-yü was delighted with it, but discontinued its use, saying that in time to come kings would lose their thrones through a fondness for the beverage. In China "wine" is a common name for all intoxicating drinks. That referred to in this passage was doubtless a distillation from rice or millet.

In the discharge of his public duties Ta-yü showed himself no less diligent than in contending with the waters. He hung at his door a bell which the poorest of his subjects might ring and thus obtain immediate attention. It is said that when taking a bath, if he heard the bell he sometimes rushed out without adjusting his raiment and that while partaking of a meal, if the bell rang he did not allow himself time to swallow his rice.

Prior to laying down his toilsome dignity Ta-yü caused to be cast nine brazen tripods, each bearing an outline map or a description of one of the provinces of the empire. In later ages these were deemed preeminently the patent of imperial power. On one occasion a feudal prince asked the question, "How heavy are these tripods?" A minister of state, suspecting an intention to remove them and usurp the power, replied in a long speech, proving the divine commission of his master, and asked in conclusion, "Why then should you inquire the weight of these tripods?"

Of the subsequent reigns nothing worth repetition is recorded except the fall of the dynasty. This, however, is due more to the meagreness of the language of that day than to the insignificance of the seventeen kings. Is it not probable that they were occupied in making good their claim to the nine provinces emblazoned on the tripods?

Kié, the last king, is said to have fallen under the fascination of a beautiful woman and to have spent his time in undignified carousals. He built a mountain of flesh and filled a tank with wine, and to amuse her he caused 3,000 of his courtiers to go on all fours and drink from the tank like so many cows.

THE SHANG DYNASTY, 1766-1122 B. C.
(28 kings)

The founder of this dynasty was Shang-tang, or Cheng-tang, who to great valour added the virtues of humanity and justice. Pitying the oppressions of the people, he came to them as a deliverer; and the frivolous tyrant was compelled to retire into obscurity. A more remarkable exhibition of public spirit was the offering of himself as a victim to propitiate the wrath of Heaven. In a prolonged famine, his prayers having failed to bring rain, the soothsayers said that a human victim was required. "It shall be myself," he replied; and, stripping off his regal robes, he laid himself on the altar. A copious shower was the response to this act of devotion.

The successor of Shang-tang was his grandson T'ai-kia, who was under the tutelage of a wise minister named I-yin. Observing the indolence and pleasure-loving disposition of the young man, the minister sent him into retirement for three years that he might acquire habits of sobriety and diligence. The circumstance that makes this incident worth recording is that the minister, instead of retaining the power in his own family, restored the throne to its rightful occupant.

Another king of this house, by name P'an-keng, has no claim to distinction other than that of having moved his capital five times. As we are not told that he was pursued by vindictive enemies, we are left to the conjecture that he was escaping from disastrous floods, or, perhaps under the influence of a silly superstition, was in quest of some luckier site.

Things went from bad to worse, and finally Chou-sin surpassed in evil excesses the man who had brought ruin upon the House of Hia. The House of Shang of course suffered the same fate. An ambitious but kind-hearted prince came forward to succour the people, and was welcomed by them as a deliverer. The tyrant, seeing that all was lost, arrayed himself in festal robes, set fire to his own palace, and, like another Sardanapalus, perished in the flames.

He and Kié make a couple who are held up to everlasting execration as a warning to tyrannical princes. Like his remote predecessor, Chou-sin is reputed to have been led into his evil courses by a wicked woman, named Ta-ki. One suspects that neither one nor the other stood in need of such prompting. According to history, bad kings are generally worse than bad queens. In China, however, a woman is considered out of place when she lays her hand on the helm of state. Hence the tendency to blacken the names of those famous court beauties.

If Mencius may be believed, the tyrants themselves were not quite so profligate as the story makes them. He says, "Dirty water has a tendency to accumulate in the lowest sinks"; and he warns the princes of his time not to put themselves in a position in which future ages will continue to heap opprobrium on their memory.

Of the wise founders of this dynasty it is said that they "made religion the basis of education," as did the Romans, who prided themselves on devotion to their gods. In both cases natural religion degenerated into gross superstition. In the number of their gods the Chinese have exceeded the Romans; and they refer the worship of many of them to the Shang dynasty.

The following dynasty, that of Chou (35 sovereigns, 1122-249 B. C.) merits a separate chapter.

Pagoda at Wuchang

CHAPTER XVI

HOUSE OF CHOU

Wen-wang, the founder—Rise and Progress of Culture—Communistic Land Tenure—Origin of the term "Middle Kingdom"—Duke Chou and Cheng wang, "The Completer"—A Royal Traveller—Li and Yu, two bad kings

The merciful conqueror who at this time rescued the people from oppression was Wu-wang, the martial king. He found, it is said, the people "hanging with their heads downward" and set them on their feet. On the eve of the decisive battle he harangued his troops, appealing to the Deity as the arbiter, and expressing confidence in the result. "The tyrant," he said, "has ten myriads of soldiers, and I have but one myriad. His soldiers, however, have ten myriads of hearts, while my army has but one heart."

When the battle had been fought and won he turned his war-horses out to pasture and ordained that they should be forever free from yoke and saddle. Could he have been less humane in the treatment of his new subjects?

The credit of his victory he gave to ten wise counsellors, one of whom was his mother. History, however, ascribes it in a large degree to his father, Wen-wang, who was then dead, but who had prepared the way for his son's triumph.

Wen-wang, the Beauclerc of the Chous, is one of the most notable figures in the ancient history of China. A vassal prince, by wise management rather than by military prowess he succeeded in enlarging his dominions so that he became possessor of two-thirds of the empire. He is applauded for his wisdom in still paying homage to his feeble chief. The latter, however, must have regarded him with no little suspicion, as Wen-wang was thrown into prison, and only regained his liberty at the cost of a heavy ransom. Wen-wang apparently anticipated a mortal struggle; for it is related that, seeing an old man fishing, he detected in him an able general who had fled the service of the tyrant. "You," said he, "are the very man I have been looking for"; and, taking him up into his chariot, as Jehu did Jonadab, he rejoiced in the assurance of coming victory. The fisherman was Kiang Tai Kung, the ancestor of the royal House of Ts'i in Shantung. Though eighty-one years of age he took command of the cavalry and presided in the councils of his new master.

Fitting it was that the Beauclerc, Wen-wang should be the real founder of the new dynasty; for now for the first time those pictured symbols become living blossoms from which the fruits of learning and philosophy are to be gathered. The rise and progress of a generous culture is the chief characteristic of the House of Chou. Besides encouraging letters Wen-wang contributed much to the new literature. He is known as a commentator in the *Yih-King,* "Book of Changes," pronounced by Confucius the profoundest of the ancient classics—a book which he never understood.

The Little Orphan, Province of Kiangsi

In theory there was under this and the preceding dynasty no private ownership of land. The arable ground was laid out in plots of nine squares, thus:

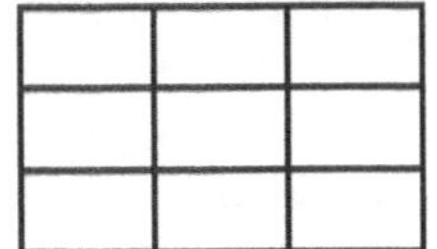

Eight of these were assigned to the people to cultivate for themselves; and the middle square was reserved for the government and tilled by the joint labour of all. The simple-hearted souls of that day are said to have prayed that the rains might first descend on the public field and then visit their private grounds.

In later years this communistic scheme was found not to work perfectly, owing, it is said, to the decay of public virtue. A statesman, named Shangyang, converted the tenure of land into fee simple—a natural evolution which was, however, regarded as quite too revolutionary and earned for him the execrations of the populace.

The charming simplicity of the above little diagram would seem to have suggested the arrangement of fiefs in the state, in which the irregular feudality of former times became moulded into a symmetrical system. The sovereign state was in the centre; and those of the feudal barons were ranged on the four sides in successive rows. The central portion was designated *Chung Kwoh*, "Middle Kingdom," a title which has come to be applied to the whole empire, implying, of course, that all the nations of the earth are its vassals.

Laid out with the order of a camp and ruled with martial vigour, the new state prospered for a few reigns. At length, however, smitten with a disease of the heart the members no longer obeyed the behests of the head. Decay and anarchy are written on the last pages of the history of the House of Chou.

The martial king died young, leaving his infant heir under the regency of his brother, the Duke of Chou. The latter, who inherited the tastes and talents of Wenwang, was avowedly the character which the great Sage took for his pattern. With fidelity and ability he completed the pacification of the state. The credit of that achievement inured to his ward, who received the title of *Cheng-wang*, "The Completer."

Accused of scheming to usurp the throne, the Duke resigned his powers and withdrew from the court. The young prince, opening a golden casket, found in it a prayer of his uncle, made and sealed up during a serious illness of the King, imploring Heaven to accept his life as a ransom for his royal ward. This touching proof of devotion dispelled all doubt; and the faithful duke was recalled to the side of the now full-grown monarch.

Even during the minority of his nephew the Duke never entered his presence in other than full court costume. On one occasion the youthful king, playing with a younger brother, handed him a palm leaf saying, "This shall be your patent of nobility. I make you duke of such and such a place." The regent remonstrated, whereupon the King excused himself by saying, "I was only in sport." The Duke replied, "A king has no right to indulge in such sports," and insisted that the younger lad receive the investiture and emoluments. He was also, it is said, so careful of the sacred person that he never left on it the mark of his rod. When the little king deserved chastisement, the guardian always called up his own son, Pechin, and thrashed him soundly. One pities the poor fellow who was the innocent substitute more than one admires the scrupulous and severe regent. The Chinese have a proverb which runs, "Whip an ass and let a horse see it."

Entrance to the Ichang Gorge (Gorges of the Yang-tse Kiang)

Wuchang Gorge (Gorges of the Yang-tse Kiang)

Early morning at Windbox Gorge (Gorges of the Yang-tse Kiang)

Lower entrance to Niuchang Gorge (Gorges of the Yang-tse Kiang)

What shall be said of the successors of Cheng-wang? To account for the meagre chronicles of previous dynasties one may invoke the poverty of a language not yet sufficiently mature for the requirements of history; but for the seeming insignificance of the long line of Chous, who lived in the early bloom, if not the rich fruitage, of the classic period, no such apology is admissible.

Some there were, doubtless, who failed to achieve distinction because they had no foreign foe to oppose, no internal rebellion to suppress. Others, again, were so hampered by system that they had nothing better to do than to receive the homage of vassals. So wearied was one among them, Mu-wang, the fifth in succession, with those monotonous ceremonies that he betook himself to foreign travel as a relief from ennui, or perhaps impelled by an innate love of adventure. He delighted in horses; and, yoking eight fine steeds to his chariot, he set off to see the world. A book full of fables professes to record the narrative of his travels. He had, it says, a magic whip which possessed the property of compressing the surface of the earth into a small space. To-day Chinese envoys, with steam and electricity at command, are frequently heard to exclaim: "Now at last we have got the swift steeds and the magic whip of Mu-wang."

Two other kings, Li and Yu, are pointed at with the finger of scorn as examples of what a king ought not to be. The latter set aside his queen and her son in favour of a concubine and her son; and so offended was high heaven by this unkingly conduct that the sun hid his face in a total eclipse. This happened 775 B. C.; and it furnishes the starting-point for a reliable chronology. For her amusement the king caused the signal-fires to be lighted. She laughed heartily to see the great barons rush to the rescue and find it was a false alarm; but she did not smile when, not long after this, the capital was attacked by a real foe, the father of her injured rival. The signal-fires were again lighted; but the barons, having once been deceived by the cry of "Wolf," took care not to expose themselves again to derision.

The other king has not been lifted into the fierce light that beats upon a throne by anything so tragic as a burning palace; but his name is coupled with that of the former as a synonym of all that is weak and contemptible.

The story of the House of Chou is not to be disposed of in a few paragraphs, like the accounts of the preceding dynasties, because it was preëminently the formative period of ancient China; the age of her greatest sages, and the birthday of poetry and philosophy. I shall therefore devote a chapter to the sages and another to the reign of anarchy before closing the Book of Chou.

CHAPTER XVII
THE SAGES OF CHINA

*Confucius—Describes Himself as Editor, not Author—"Model Teacher of
All Ages"—Mencius—More Eloquent than his Great Master—Lao-tse,
the Founder of Taoism*

I shall not introduce the reader to all who justly bear the august title of sage;
for China has had more and wiser sages than any other ancient country. Some of
them may be referred to in the sequel; but this chapter I shall devote chiefly to the
two who by universal consent have no equals in the history of the Empire—Confucius and Mencius. These great men owe much of their fame to the learned Jesuits
who first brought them on the stage, clad in the Roman toga, and made them cit-
izens of the world by giving them the euphonious names by which they are pop-
ularly known. Stripped of their disguise they appear respectively as K'ung Fu-tse
and Meng-tse. Exchanging the *ore rotunda* of Rome for the sibillation of China, they
never could have been naturalised as they are now.

CONFUCIUS

Born in the year 549 B. C., Confucius was contemporaneous with Isaiah and
Socrates. Of a respectable but not opulent family he had to struggle for his education—a fact which in after years he was so far from concealing that he ascribed to
it much of his success in life. To one who asked him, "How comes it that you are
able to do so many things," he replied, "I was born poor and had to learn." His
schoolmasters are unknown; and it might be asked of him, as it was of a greater
than Confucius, "How knoweth this man letters, having never learned?"

Of his self-education, which continued through life, he gives the following
concise account: "At fifteen I entered on a life of study; at thirty I took my stand as a
scholar; at forty my opinions were fixed; at fifty I knew how to judge and select; at
sixty I never relapsed into a known fault; at seventy I could follow my inclinations
without going wrong." Note how each stage marks an advance towards moral
excellence. Mark also that this passage gives an outline of self-discipline. It says
nothing of his books or of his work as a statesman and a reformer.

He is said to have had, first and last, three thousand disciples. Those longest
under instruction numbered twelve. They studied, not with lectures and textbooks,
as in modern schools, but by following his footsteps and taking the impress of his
character, much as Peter and John followed the steps and studied the life of Christ.
Some of them followed Confucius when, bent on effecting a political as well as

an ethical reform, he travelled from court to court among the petty principalities. They have placed it on record that once, when exposed to great peril, he comforted them by saying, "If Heaven has made me the depositary of these teachings, what can my enemies do against me?" Nobly conscious of a more than human mission, so pure were his teachings that, though he taught morals, not religion, he might fairly, with Socrates, be allowed to claim a sort of inspiration.

Tibetan Tope, Palace Grounds, Peking

The one God, of whom he knew little, he called Heaven, and he always spoke of Heaven with the profoundest reverence. When neglected or misunderstood he consoled himself by saying, "Heaven knows me." During a serious illness a disciple inquired if he should pray for him, meaning the making of offerings at some temple. Confucius answered, "I have long prayed," or "I have long been in the habit of praying."

In letters he described himself as an "editor, not an author," meaning that he had revised the works of the ancients, but had published nothing of his own. Out of their poetry he culled three hundred odes and declared that "purity of thought" might be stamped on the whole collection. Into a confused mass of traditional ceremonies be brought something like order, making the Chinese (if a trifle too ceremonious) the politest people on earth. Out of their myths and chronicles he extracted a trustworthy history, and by his treatment of vice he made princes tremble, lest their heads should be exposed on the gibbet of history. He gave much time to editing the music of the ancients, but his work in that line has perished. This, however, cannot be regarded as a very great loss, in view of the rude condition in which Chinese music is still found. However deficient his knowledge of the art, his passion for music was extraordinary. After hearing a fine performance "he was unable for three months to enjoy his food." A fifth task was the editing of the *Yih-King*,[7] the book of divination compiled by Wen-wang. How thoroughly he believed in it is apparent from his saying, "Should it please Heaven to grant me five or ten years to study this book, I would not be in danger of falling into great errors." He meant that he would then be able to shape his conduct by the calculation of chances.

Great as were his labours in laying the foundation of literary culture, the impression made by his personal intercourse and by his collected sayings has been ten-fold more influential. They form the substance of the Four Books which, from a similar numerical coincidence, the Chinese are fond of comparing with our Four Gospels. Confucius certainly gives the Golden Rule as the essence of his teaching. True, he puts it in a negative form, "Do not unto others what you would not have them do to you"; but he also says, "My doctrine is comprehended in two words, *chung* and *shu*." The former denotes fidelity; the latter signifies putting oneself in the place of another, but it falls short of that active charity which has changed the face of the world.

It were easy to point out Confucius' limitations and mistakes; yet on the whole his merits were such that his people can hardly be blamed for the exaggerated honours which they show to his memory. They style him the "model teacher of all ages," but they do not invoke him as a tutelary deity, nor do they represent him by an image. Excessively honorific, their worship of Confucius is not idolatry.

---

[7] This and the preceding are the Five Classics, which, like the five books of Moses, lie at the root of a nation's religion and learning.

Monument of Ta-yu

MENCIUS

A hundred years later Mencius was born, and received his doctrine through the grandson of the Sage. More eloquent than his great master, more bold in rebuking the vices of princes, he was less original. One specimen of his teaching must suffice. One of the princes asking him, "How do you know that I have it in me to become a good ruler?" he replied, "I am told that, seeing the extreme terror of an ox that was being led to the altar, you released it and commanded a sheep to be offered in its stead. The ox was before your eyes and you pitied it; the sheep was not before your eyes and you had no pity on it. Now with such a heart if you would only think of your people, so as to bring them before your eyes, you might become the best of rulers."

Mencius lost his father in his infancy, but his mother showed rare good sense in the bringing up of her only child. Living near a butcher, she noticed that the boy mimicked the cries of the pigs. She then removed to the gate of a cemetery; but, noticing that the child changed his tune and mocked the wailing of mourners, she struck her tent and took up her abode near a high school. There she observed with joy that he learned the manners and acquired the tastes of a student. Perceiving, however, that he was in danger of becoming lazy and dilatory, she cut the warp of her web and said, "My son, this is what you are doing with the web of life."

The tomb of each of these sages is in the keeping of one of his descendants, who enjoys the emoluments of a hereditary noble. Mencius himself says of the master whom he never saw, "Since men were born on earth there has been no man like Confucius."

LAO-TSE

I cannot close this chapter without a word or two on Lao-tse, the founder of Taoism. He bore the family name of *Li*, "plum-tree," either from the fact that his cottage was in a garden or possibly because, like the Academics, he placed his school in a grove of plum-trees. The name by which he is now known signifies "old master," probably because he was older than Confucius. The latter is said to have paid him a visit to inquire about rites and ceremonies; but Lao-tse, with his love of solitude and abstract speculation, seems not to have exerted much influence on the mind of the rising philosopher. In allusion to him, Confucius said, "Away from men there is no philosophy—no *tao*."

Less honoured by the official class, Lao-tse's influence with the masses of China has been scarcely less than that of his younger rival. Like the other two sages he, too, has to-day a representative, who enjoys an official status as high priest of the Taoist sect. Chang Tien-shi dwells in a stately palace on the summit of the Tiger and Dragon Mountain, in Kiangsi, as the head of one of the three religions. But, alas! the sublime teachings of the founder of Taoism have degenerated into a contemptible mixture of jugglery and witchcraft.

Snapshot of Dr. Martin and Some of His Professors ...

The Great Wall of China

Not till five centuries later did Buddhism enter China and complete the triad of religions—a triad strangely inharmonious; indeed one can scarcely conceive of three creeds more radically antagonistic.

CHAPTER XVIII
THE WARRING STATES

Five Dictators—Diplomacy and Strategy—A Brave Envoy—Heroes Reconciled—Ts'in Extinguishes the House of Chou

In the first half of the Chou dynasty the machinery moved with such regularity that Confucius could think of no form of government more admirable, saying, "The policy of the future may be foretold for a hundred generations—it will be to follow the House of Chou." The latter half was a period of misrule and anarchy.

Ambitions and jealousies led to petty wars. The King being too feeble to repress them, these petty wars grew into vast combinations like the leagues of modern Europe. Five of the states acquired at different times such a preponderance that their rulers are styled *Wu Pa*, the "five dictators." One of these, Duke Hwan of western Shantung, is famous for having nine times convoked the States-General. The dictator always presided at such meetings and he was recognised as the real sovereign—as were the mayors of the palace in France in the Merovingian epoch, or the shoguns in Japan during the long period in which the Mikado was called the "spiritual emperor."

The legitimate sovereign still sat on his throne in the central state; but he complained that his only function was to offer sacrifices. The Chinese dictatorship was not hereditary, or the world might have witnessed an exact parallel to the duplicate sovereignty in Japan, where one held the power and the other retained the title for seven hundred years.

In China the shifting of power from hand to hand made those four centuries an age of diplomacy. Whenever some great baron was suspected of aspiring to the leadership, combinations were formed to curb his ambitions; embassies sped from court to court; and armies were marshalled in the field. Envoys became noted for courage and cunning, and generals acquired fame by their skill in handling large bodies of soldiers. Diplomacy became an art, and war a science.

An international code to control the intercourse of states began to take shape; but the diplomat was not embarrassed by a multiplicity of rules. In negotiations individual character counted for more than it does at the present day; nor must it be supposed that in the absence of our modern artillery there was no room for generalship. On the contrary, as battles were not decided by the weight of metal, there was more demand for strategy.

All this was going on in Greece at this very epoch: and, as Plutarch indulges in parallels, we might point to compeers of Themistocles and Epaminondas. The cause which in the two countries led to this state of things was the existence of a family of states with a common language and similar institutions; but in the Asiatic empire the theatre was vastly more extensive, and the operations in politics and war on a grander scale.

To the honour of the Chinese it must be admitted that they showed themselves more civilised than the Greeks. The Persian invasion was provoked by the murder of ambassadors by the Athenians. Of such an act there is no recorded instance among the warring states of China. It was reserved for our own day to witness in Peking that exhibition of Tartar ferocity. The following two typical incidents from the voluminous chronicles of those times may be appropriately presented here:

A BRAVE ENVOY

The Prince of Ts'in, a semi-barbarous state in the northwest, answering to Macedonia in Greece, had offered to give fifteen cities for a kohinoor, a jewel belonging to the Prince of Chao (not Chou). Lin Sian Ju was sent to deliver the jewel and to complete the transaction. The conditions not being complied with, he boldly put the jewel into his bosom and returned to his own state. That he was allowed to do so—does it not speak as much for the morality of Ts'in as for the courage of Lin? The latter is the accepted type of a brave and faithful envoy.

HEROES RECONCILED

Jealous of his fame, Lien P'o, a general of Chao, announced that he would kill Lin at sight. The latter took pains to avoid a meeting. Lien P'o, taxing him with cowardice, sent him a challenge, to which Lin responded, "You and I are the pillars of our state. If either falls, our country is lost. This is why I have shunned an encounter." So impressed was the general with the spirit of this reply that he took a rod in his hand and presented himself at the door of his rival, not to thrash the latter, but to beg that he himself might be castigated. Forgetting their feud the two joined hands to build up their native state much as Aristides and Themistocles buried their enmity in view of the war with Persia.

As the Athenian orators thundered against Macedon so the statesmen of China formed leagues and counterplots for and against the rising power of the northwest. The type of patient, shrewd diplomacy is Su Ts'in who, at the cost of incredible hardships in journeying from court to court, succeeded in bringing six of the leading states into line to bar the southward movement of their common foe. His machinations were all in vain, however; for not only was his ultimate success thwarted by the counterplots of Chang Yee, an equally able diplomatist, but his reputation, like that of Parnell in our own times, was ruined by his own passions. The rising power of Ts'in, like a glacier, was advancing by slow degrees to universal sway. In the next generation it absorbed all the feudal states. Chau-siang subjugated Tung-chou-Kiun, the last monarch of the Chou dynasty, and the House of Chou was exterminated by Chwang-siang, who, however, enjoyed the supreme power for only three years (249-246 B. C).

CHAPTER XIX

THE HOUSE OF TS'IN, 246-206 B. C. (2 EMPERORS)

*Ts'in Shi-hwang-ti, "Emperor First"—The Great Wall—The Centralised
Monarchy—The title Hwang-ti—Origin of the name China—Burning
of the Books—Expedition to Japan—Revolution Places the House of Han
on the Throne*

"Viewed in the light of philosophy," says Schiller, "Cain killed Abel because
Abel's sheep trespassed on Cain's cornfield." From that day to this farmers and
shepherds have not been able to live together in peace. A monument of that eternal conflict is the Great Wall of China. Like the Roman Wall in North Britain, to
compare great things with small, its object was not to keep out the Tartars but to
reënforce the vigilance of the military pickets. That end it seems to have accomplished for a long time. It was, the Chinese say, the destruction of one generation
and the salvation of many. We shall soon see how it came to be a mere geographical expression. For our present purpose it may also be regarded as a chronological
landmark, dividing ancient from mediæval China.

With the House of Chou the old feudal divisions disappeared forever. The
whole country was brought under the direct sway of one emperor who, for the first
time in the history of the people, had built up a dominion worthy of that august
title. This was the achievement of Yin Cheng, the Prince of Ts'in. He thereupon
assumed the new style of Hwang-ti. Hwangs and Tis were no novelty; but the
combination made it a new coinage and justified the additional appellation of "the
First," or Shi-hwang-ti. Four imperishable monuments perpetuate his memory:
the Great Wall, the centralised monarchy, the title *Hwang-ti*, and the name of China
itself—the last derived from a principality which under him expanded to embrace
the empire. Where is there another conqueror in the annals of the world who has
such solid claims to everlasting renown? Alexander overthrew many nations; but
he set up nothing permanent. Julius Cæsar instituted the Roman Empire; but its
duration was ephemeral in comparison with that of the empire founded by Shi-
hwang-ti, the builder of the Wall.

Though Shi-hwang-ti completed it, the wall was not the work of his reign
alone. Similarly the triumphs of his arms and arts were due in large measure to
his predecessors, who for centuries had aspired to universal sway. Conscious of
inferiority in culture, they welcomed the aid and rewarded the services of men of
talent from every quarter. Some came as penniless adventurers from rival or hostile states and were raised to the highest honours.

Six great chancellors stand conspicuous as having introduced law and order into a rude society, and paved the way for final success. Every one of these was a "foreigner." The princes whom they served deserve no small praise for having the good sense to appreciate them and the courage to follow their advice. Of some of these it might be said, as Voltaire remarked of Peter the Great, "They civilised their people, but themselves were savages." The world forgets how much the great czar was indebted for education and guidance to Le Fort, a Genevese soldier of fortune. Pondering that history one is able to gauge the merits of those foreign chancellors, perhaps also to understand what foreigners have done for the rulers of China in our day.

Shi-hwang-ti was the real founder of the Chinese Empire. He is one of the heroes of history; yet no man in the long list of dynasties is so abused and misrepresented by Chinese writers. They make him a bastard, a debauchee, and a fool. To this day he is the object of undying hatred to every one who can hold a pen. Why? it may be asked. Simply because he burned the books and persecuted the disciples of Confucius. Those two things, well-nigh incredible to us, are to the Chinese utterly incomprehensible.

Li-Sze, a native of Yen, was his chancellor, a genius more daring and far-sighted than any of the other five. The welding together of the feudal states into a compact unity was his darling scheme, as it was that of his master. "Never," he said, "can you be sure that those warring states will not reappear, so long as the books of Confucius are studied in the schools; for in them feudalism is consecrated as a divine institution." "Then let them be burned," said the tyrant.

The adherents of the Sage were ejected from the schools, and their teachings proscribed. This harsh treatment and the search for their books naturally gave rise to counterplots. "Put them to death," said the tyrant; and they went to the block, not like Christian marytrs for religious convictions, but like the Girondists of France for political principles. Their followers offer the silly explanation that the books were destroyed that the world might never know that there had been other dynasties, and the scholars slaughtered or buried alive to prevent the reproduction of the books.

The First Hwang-ti did not confine his ambition to China. He sent a fleet to Japan; and those isles of the Orient came to view for the first time in the history of the world. The fleet carried, it is said, a crew of three thousand lads and lasses. It never returned; but the traditions of Japan affirm that it arrived, and the islanders ascribe their initiation into Chinese literature to their invasion by that festive company—a company not unlike that with which Bacchus was represented as making the conquest of India. Their further acquaintance with China and its sages was obtained through Korea, which was long a middle point of communication between the two countries. It was, in fact, from the Shantung promontory, near to Korea, that this flotilla of videttes was dispatched.

What was the real object of that strange expedition? Chinese authors assert that it was sent in search of the "elixir of life," but do they not distort everything in the history of the First Hwang-ti? The great monarch was, in fact, a devout believer in the fables of Taoism, among which were stories of the Islands of the Blest, and of a fountain of immortality, such as eighteen centuries later stimulated the researches of Ponce de Leon. The study of alchemy was in full blast among the Chinese at that time. It probably sprang from Taoism; but, in my opinion, the ambitious potentate, sighing for other worlds to conquer, sent that jolly troop as the vanguard of an army.

In spite, however, of elixirs of life and fountains of youth, death put an end to his conquests when he had enjoyed the full glories of imperial power for only twelve years. His son reigned two years; and the first of the imperial dynasties came to an end—overturned by a revolution which placed the House of Han on the vacant throne.

CHAPTER XX

THE HOUSE OF HAN, 206—B. C.—220 A. D. (24 EMPERORS, 2 USURPERS)

Liu-pang Founds Illustrious Dynasty—Restoration of the Books—A Female Reign—The Three Religions—Revival of Letters—Sze-ma Ts'ien, the Herodotus of China—Conquests of the Hans

The burning of the books and the slaughter of the scholars had filled the public mind with horror. The oppressions occasioned by the building of the Great Wall had excited a widespread discontent; and Liu-pang, a rough soldier of Central China, took advantage of this state of things to dispossess the feeble heir of the tyrant. He founded a dynasty which is reckoned among the most illustrious in the annals of the Empire. It takes the name of Han from the river on the banks of which it rose to power. When Liu-pang was securely seated on the throne one of his ministers proposed that he should open schools and encourage learning. "Learning," exclaimed the Emperor, "I have none of it myself, nor do I feel the need of it. I got the empire on horseback." "But can you govern the empire on horseback? That is the question," replied the minister. To conciliate the favour of the learned, the Emperor not only rescinded the persecuting edicts, but caused search to be made for the lost books, and instituted sacrificial rites in honour of the Sage.

Old men were still living who had committed those books to memory in boyhood. One such, Fu-seng by name, was noted for his erudition; and from his capacious memory a large portion of the sacred canon was reproduced, being written from his dictation. The copies thus obtained were of course not free from error. Happily a somewhat completer copy, engraved on bamboo tablets, was discovered in the wall of a house belonging to the Confucian family. Yet down to the present day the Chinese classics bear traces of the tyrant's fire. Portions are wanting and the lacunæ are always ascribed to the "fires of Ts'in." The first chapter of the Great Study closes with the pregnant words, "The source of knowledge is in the study of things." Not a syllable is added on that prolific text. A note informs the reader that there was a chapter on the subject, but that it has been lost. Chinese scholars, when taxed with the barrenness of later ages in every branch of science, are wont to make the naïve reply, "Yes, and no wonder—how could it be otherwise when the Sage's chapter on that subject has been lost?"

After the second reign, that of Hwei-ti, we have the first instance in Chinese history of a woman seizing the reins of government. The Empress Lu made herself supreme, and such were her talents that she held the Empire in absolute subjection for eight years. Like Jezebel she "destroyed all the seed royal," and filled the various offices with her kindred and favourites. At her death they were butchered without mercy, and a male heir to the throne was proclaimed. His posthumous title *Wen-ti*, meaning the "learned" or "patron of letters," marks the progress made by the revival of learning.

One might imagine that these literary emperors would have been satisfied with the recovery of the Confucian classics; but no, a rumour reached them that "there are sages in the West." The West was India. An embassy was sent, 66 A. D., by Ming-ti to import books and bonzes. The triad of religions was thus completed.

Totally diverse in spirit and essence, the three religions could hardly be expected to harmonise or combine. Confucianism exalts letters, and lays stress on ethics to the neglect of the spiritual world. Taoism inculcates physical discipline; but in practice it has become the mother of degrading superstition—dealing in magic and necromancy. Buddhism saps the foundations of the family and enjoins celibacy as the road to virtue. Metempsychosis is its leading doctrine, and to "think on nothing" its mental discipline. It forbids a flesh diet and deprecates scholarship. Through imperial patronage it acquired a footing in China, but it was long before it felt at home there. As late as the eighth century Han Yu, the greatest writer of the age, ridiculed the relics of Buddha and called on his people to "burn their books, close their temples, and make laity of their monks."

Yet Buddhism seems to have met a want. It has fostered a sympathy for animal life, and served as a protest against the Sadducean tenets of the lettered class. It long ago became so rooted in the minds of the illiterate, who form nine-tenths of the population, that China may be truly described as the leading Buddhist country of the globe. [8]

[8] THE APOTHEOSIS OF MERCY

A LEGEND OF KUANYIN PUSA—IN NORTHERN BUDDHISM

Two images adorn this mountain shrine,
Not marble chiselled out by Grecian art,
But carved from wood with Oriental skill.
In days of yore adored by pilgrim throngs,
They languish now without a worshipper.

High up a winding flight of stony steps
See Gautama upon his lotus throne!
More near the gate, her lovely face downcast,
Sits Mercy's Goddess, pity in her eye,
To greet the weary climbers and to hear
Their many-coloured tales of woe and want.

The Buddha, in sublime repose, sees not
His prostrate worshippers; and they to him
No prayer address, save hymns of grateful praise. [A]
'Twas he who for a blinded world sought out
The secret of escape from misery;
The splendour of a royal court resigned,
He found in poverty a higher realm!
Yet greater far the victory, when he broke

Buddhist monasteries are to be seen on every hand. They are often subsidised by the state; and even at the tomb of Confucius a temple was erected called the "Hall of the Three Religions." In it the image of Buddha is said to have occupied the seat of honour, but prior to the date of my visit it had been demolished.

Each of these religions has a hierarchy: that of Confucius with a lineal descendant of the Sage at its head; that of Lao-tse with Chang Tien-shi, the arch-magician, as its high priest; and, higher than all, that of Buddha with the Grand Lama of Tibet.

Under the house of Han a beginning was made in the institution of civil ser-

> The chain of Fate and spurned the wheel of change.
> To suffering humanity he says,
> "Tread in my steps: You, too, may find release."
>
> Like him, the Pusa was of princely birth,
> But not like him did she forsake a throne,
> Nor yet like him did she consent to see
> Nirvana's pearly gates behind her close.
> A field for charity her regal state.
> Her path with ever-blooming flowers she strewed,
> Her sympathy to joy a relish gave,
> To sorrows manifold it brought relief,
> Forgetting self she lived for others' weal
> Till higher than Meru her merit rose.[B]
>
> At length a Voice celestial smote her ear.
> "Nirvana's portal to thee open stands,
> The crown of Buddhaship is thine by right.
> No wave of care that shore can ever reach,
> No cry of pain again thine ear assail;
> But fixed in solitary bliss thou'lt see
> The circling ages rolling at thy feet!"
>
> "Shall I then have no tidings of mankind?
> Such heaven a throne of glittering ice would be.
> That changeless bliss to others thou may'st give.
> Happiest am I th' unhappy to upraise.
> Oh for a thousand hands[C] the task to ply!
> To succour and relieve be mine," she said,
> "Bought though it be by share of suffering.
> Turn then the wheel,[D] and back to earth again."
>
> From out the blue came down the Voice once more:
> "Thy great refusal wins a higher prize;
> A kingdom new thy charity hath gained.[E]
> And there shalt thou, the Queen of Mercy, reign,
> Aloof from pain or weakness of thine own,
> With quickened sense to hear and power to save."
>
> Fair image thou! Almost I worship thee,
> Frail shadow of a Christ that hears and feels!

W. A. P. M.

PEARL GROTTO, NEAR PEKING, August 8, 1906.

vice examinations—a system which has continued to dominate the Chinese intellect down to our time; but it was not fully developed until the dynasty of T'ang. Belles-lettres made a marked advance. The poetry of the period is more finished than that of the Chous. Prose composition, too, is vigorous and lucid. The muse of history claims the place of honour. Sze-ma Ts'ien, the Herodotus of China, was born in this period. A glory to his country, the treatment Sze-ma Ts'ien received at the hands of his people exposes their barbarism. He had recommended Li Ling as a suitable commander to lead an expedition against the Mongols. Li Ling surrendered to the enemy, and Sze-ma Ts'ien, as his sponsor, was liable to suffer death in his stead. Being allowed an alternative, he chose to submit to the disgrace of emasculation, in order that he might live to complete his monumental work—a memorial better than sons and daughters. A pathetic letter of the unfortunate general, who never dared to return to China, is preserved amongst the choice specimens of prose composition.

Not content with the Great Wall for their northern limit nor with the "Great River" for their southern boundary, the Hans attempted to advance their frontiers in both directions. In the north they added the province of Kansuh, and in the other direction they extended their operations as far south as the borders of Annam; but they did not make good the possession of the whole of the conquered territory. Szechuen and Hunan were, however, added to their domain. The latter seems to have served as a penal colony rather than an integral portion of the Empire. A poem by Kiayi, an exiled statesman (200 B. c.), is dated from Changsha, its capital.[9]

In the south the savage tribes by which the Chinese were opposed made a deep impression on the character of the people, but left no record in history. Not so with the powerful foe encountered in the north. Under the title of Shanyu, he was a forerunner of the Grand Khan of Tartary—claiming equality with the emperors of China and exchanging embassies on equal terms. His people, known as the Hiunghu, are supposed to have been ancestors of the Huns.

---

[9] See "Chinese Legends and Other Poems," by W. A. P. Martin.

CHAPTER XXI

THE THREE KINGDOMS, THE NAN-PEH CHAO, AND THE SUI DYNASTY, 214-618 A. D.

The States of Wei, Wu, and Shuh—A Popular Historical Romance—Chu-koh Liang, an Inventive Genius—The "three P's," Pen, Paper, Printing—The Sui Dynasty

After four centuries of undisputed sway, the sceptre is seen ready to fall from the nerveless hands of feeble monarchs. Eunuchs usurp authority, and the hydra of rebellion raises its many heads. Minor aspirants are easily extinguished; but three of them survive a conflict of twenty years, and lay the foundation of short-lived dynasties.

The noble structure erected by the Ts'ins and consolidated by the Hans began to crumble at the beginning of its fifth century of existence. In 221 A. D. its fragments were removed to three cities, each of which claimed to be the seat of empire. The state of Wei was founded by Tsao Tsao, with its capital at Lo-yang, the seat of the Hans. He had the further advantage, as mayor of the palace, of holding in his power the feeble emperor Hwan-ti, the last of the house of Han. The state of Wu, embracing the provinces of Kiangsu, Kiangsi, and Chehkiang, was established by Siun Kien, a man of distinguished ability who secured his full share of the patrimony. The third state was founded by Liu Pi, a scion of the imperial house whose capital was at Chingtu-fu in Szechuen. The historian is here confronted by a problem like that of settling the apostolic succession of the three popes, and he has decided in favour of the last, whom he designates the "Later Han," mainly on the ground of blood relationship.

Authority for this is found in the dynastic history; but reference may also be made to a romance which deals with the wars of those three states. Composed by Lo Kwan-chung and annotated by Kin Sheng Tan, it is the most popular historical novel in the whole range of Chinese literature. Taking the place of a national epic, its heroes are not of one type or all on one side, but its favourites are found among the adherents of Liu Pi. It opens with a scene in which Liu, Kwan, and Chang, like the three Tells on Grütli, meet in a peach-garden and take vows of brotherhood—drinking of a loving-cup tinged with the blood of each and swearing fidelity to their common cause. Of the three brothers the first, Liu Pi, after a long struggle, succeeds in founding a state in western China. The second, Kwan Yü, is the beau-ideal of patriotic courage. In 1594 he was canonised as the god of war. The gifted author has, therefore, the distinction, beyond that of any epic poet of the West, of having created for his countrymen their most popular deity. Chang-fi, the youngest of the three brothers, is the inseparable henchman of the Chinese Mars. He wields a spear eighteen feet in length with a dash and impetuosity which no enemy is able to withstand.

Other characters are equally fixed in the public mind. Tsao Tsao, the chief antagonist of Liu Pi, is not merely a usurper: he is a curious compound of genius, fraud, and cruelty. Another conspicuous actor is Lü Pu, an archer able to split a reed at a hundred paces, and a horseman who performs prodigies on the field of battle. He begins his career by shooting his adopted father, like Brutus perhaps, not because he loved Tung Choh less, but China more.

All these and others too numerous to mention may be seen any day on the boards of the theatre, an institution which, in China at least, serves as a school for the illiterate.[10]

Liu Pi succeeds, after a struggle of twenty years, in establishing himself in the province of Szechuen; but he enjoys undisturbed dominion in his limited realm for three years only, and then transmits his crown to a youthful son whom he commends to the care of a faithful minister. The youth when an infant has been rescued from a burning palace by the brave Chang-fi, who, wrapping the sleeping child in his cloak and mounting a fleet charger, cut his way through the enemy. On reaching a distant point the child was still asleep. The witty annotator adds the remark, "He continued to sleep for thirty years."

The minister to whom the boy had been confided, Chu-koh Liang, is the most versatile and inventive genius of Chinese antiquity. As the founder of the house of Chou discovered in an old fisherman a counsellor of state who paved his way to the throne, so Liu Pi found this man in a humble cottage where he was hiding himself in the garb of a peasant, *San Ku Mao Lu*, say the Chinese. He "three times visited that thatched hovel" before he succeeded in persuading its occupant to commit himself to his uncertain fortunes. From that moment Chu-koh Liang served him as eyes and ears, teeth and claws, with a skill and fidelity which have won the applause of all succeeding ages. Among other things, he did for Liu Pi what Archimedes did for Dionysius. He constructed military engines that appeared so wonderful that, as tradition has it "he made horses and oxen out of wood."

Entrusted by his dying master with the education of the young prince, he has left two papers full of wise counsels which afford no little help in drawing the line between fact and fiction. Unquestionably Chu-koh Liang was the first man of his age in intellect and in such arts and sciences as were known to his times. Yet no one invention can be pointed to as having been certainly derived from Chu-koh Liang. The author of the above-mentioned romance, who lived as late as the end of the thirteenth century, constantly speaks of his use of gunpowder either to terrify the enemy or to serve for signals; but it is never used to throw a cannon-ball. It probably was known to the Chinese of that date, as the Arab speaks of gunpowder

[10] The stage is usually a platform on the open street where an actor may be seen changing his rôle with his costume, now wearing the mask of one and then of another of the contending chieftains, and changing his voice, always in a falsetto key, to produce something like variety.

under the designation of "Chinese snow," meaning doubtless the saltpetre which forms a leading ingredient. The Chinese had been dabbling in alchemy for many centuries, and it is scarcely possible that they should have failed to hit on some such explosive. It is, however, believed on good authority that they never made use of cannon in war until the beginning of the fifteenth century.

There are, however, three other inventions or improvements of the known arts, which deserve notice in this connection, namely, the "three Ps"—pen, paper and printing—all preëminently instruments of peaceful culture. The pen in China is a hair pencil resembling a paint-brush. It was invented by Mung-tien in the third century B. c. Paper was invented by Tsai Lun, 100 B. C., and printing by Fungtao in the tenth century of the present era. What is meant by printing in this case is, however, merely the substitution of wood for stone, the Chinese having been for ages in the habit of taking rubbings from stone inscriptions. It was not long before they divided the slab into movable characters and earned for themselves the honour of having anticipated Gutenberg and Faust. Their divisible types were never in general use, however, and block printing continues in vogue; but Western methods are rapidly supplanting both.

The three states were reunited under the Tsin dynasty, 265 A. D. This lasted for a century and a half and then, after a succession of fifteen emperors, went down in a sea of anarchy, from the froth of which arose more than half a score of contending factions, among which four were sufficiently prominent to make for themselves a place in history. Their period is described as that of the Nan-peh Chao, "Northern and Southern Kingdoms." The names of the principals were Sung, Wei, Liang and Chin. The first only was Chinese, the others belonging to various branches of the Tartar race. The chiefs of the Liang family were of Tibetan origin—a circumstance which may perhaps account for their predilection for Buddhism. The second emperor of that house, Wu Ti, became a Buddhist monk and retired to a monastery where he lectured on the philosophy of Buddhism. He reminds one of Charles the Fifth, who in his retirement amused himself less rationally by repairing watches and striving, in vain, to make a number of them keep identical time.

It may be noted that behind these warring factions there is in progress a war of races also. The Tartars are forever encroaching on the Flowery Land. Repulsed or expelled, they return with augmented force; and even at this early epoch the shadow of their coming conquest is plainly visible.

In the confused strife of North and South the preponderance is greatly on the side of the Tartars. The pendulum of destiny then begins to swing in the other direction. Yan Kien, a Chinese general in the service of a Tartar principality, took advantage of their divisions to rally a strong body of his countrymen by whose aid he cut them off in detail and set up the Sui dynasty, The Tartars have always made use of Chinese in the invasion of China; and if the Chinese were always faithful to their own country no invader would succeed in conquering them.

Though the Sui dynasty lasted less than thirty years (589-618, three reigns), it makes a conspicuous figure on account of two events: (1) a victorious expedition in the north which reached the borders of Turkestan, and (2) the opening of canals between the Yellow River and the Yang-tse Kiang. The latter enterprise only hastened the fall of the house. It was effected by forced labour; and the discontented people were made to believe, as their historians continue to assert, that its chief object was to enable a luxurious emperor to display his grandeur to the people of many provinces. We shall see how the extension of those canals precipitated the overthrow of the Mongols as we have already seen how the completion of the Great Wall caused the downfall of the house of Ts'in.

Yang-ti, the second emperor of the Sui dynasty, though not wanting in energy, is notorious for his excesses in display and debauch. He is reported to have hastened his accession to the throne by the murder of his father. A peaceful end to such a reign would have been out of keeping with the course of human events. Li Yuen, one of his generals, rose against him, and he was assassinated in Nanking.

By wisdom and courage Li Yuen succeeded in setting up a new dynasty which he called *T'ang* (618 A. D.): After a long period of unrest, it brought to the distracted provinces an era of unwonted prosperity; it held the field for nearly three hundred years, and surpassed all its predecessors in splendour.

CHAPTER XXII

THE T'ANG DYNASTY, 618-907 A. D. (20 EMPERORS)

An Augustan Age — A Pair of Poets — The Coming of Christianity — The Empress Wu — System of Examinations

I have seen a river plunge into a chasm and disappear. After a subterranean course of many miles it rose to the surface fuller, stronger than before. No man saw from whence it drew its increment of force, but the fact was undeniable. This is just what took place in China at this epoch.

It is comforting to know that during those centuries of turmoil the Chinese were not wholly engrossed with war and rapine. The T'ang dynasty is conspicuously the Augustan Age. Literature reappears in a more perfect form than under the preceding reigns. The prose writers of that period are to the present day studied as models of composition, which cannot be affirmed of the writers of any earlier epoch. Poetry, too, shone forth with dazzling splendour. A galaxy of poets made their appearance, among whom two particular stars were Tufu and Lipai, the Dryden and Pope of Chinese literature.

The following specimen from Lipai who is deemed the highest poetical genius in the annals of China, may show, even in its Western dress, something of his peculiar talent:

ON DRINKING ALONE BY MOONLIGHT[11]

Here are flowers and here is wine,
But where's a friend with me to join
Hand in hand and heart to heart
In one full cup before we part?

Rather than to drink alone,
I'll make bold to ask the moon
To condescend to lend her face
The hour and the scene to grace.

Lo, she answers, and she brings
My shadow on her silver wings;
That makes three, and we shall be.
I ween, a merry company

The modest moon declines the cup,

---

[11] From "Chinese Legends and Other Poems," by W. A. P. MARTIN.

> But shadow promptly takes it up,
> And when I dance my shadow fleet
> Keeps measure with my flying feet.
>
> But though the moon declines to tipple
> She dances in yon shining ripple,
> And when I sing, my festive song,
> The echoes of the moon prolong.
>
> Say, when shall we next meet together?
> Surely not in cloudy weather,
> For you my boon companions dear
> Come only when the sky is clear.

The second emperor, Tai-tsung, made good his claims by killing two of his brothers who were plotting against him. Notwithstanding this inauspicious beginning he became an able and illustrious sovereign. The twenty-three years during which he occupied the throne were the most brilliant of that famous dynasty.

At Si-ngan in Shensi, the capital of the T'angs, is a stone monument which records the introduction of Christianity by Nestorians from Syria. Favoured by the Emperor the new faith made considerable headway. For five hundred years the Nestorian churches held up the banner of the Cross; but eventually, through ignorance and impurity, they sank to the level of heathenism and disappeared. It is sad to think that this early effort to evangelise China has left nothing but a monumental stone.

At the funeral of Tai-tsung his successor, Kao-tsung, saw Wu, one of his father's concubines, who pleased him so much that, contrary to law, he took her into his own harem. Raised to the rank of empress and left mother of an infant son, she swayed the sceptre after Kao-tsung's death for twenty-one years. Beginning as regent she made herself absolute.

A system of civil service examinations which had sprung up with the revival of learning under the Hans was now brought to maturity. For good or for evil it has dominated the mind of the Empire for twelve centuries. Now, however, the leaders of thought have begun to suspect that it is out of date. The new education requires new tests; but what is to hinder their incorporation in the old system? To abolish it would be fraught with danger, and to modify it is a delicate task for the government of the present day.

That the scholar should hold himself in readiness to serve the state no less than the soldier was an acknowledged principle. It was reserved for the statesmen of T'ang to make it the mainspring of the government. To them belongs the honour of constructing a system which would stimulate literary culture and skim the cream of the national talent for the use of the state. It had the further merit of occupying the minds of ambitious youth with studies of absorbing interest, thus diverting them from the dangerous path of political conspiracy.

Never was a more effective patronage given to letters. Without founding or endowing schools the state said: "If you acquire the necessary qualifications, we shall see that your exertions are duly rewarded. Look up to those shining heights—see the gates that are open to welcome you, the garlands that wait to crown your triumphant course!"

Annual examinations were held in every country; and the degree of S. T. (*Siu-tsai*), equivalent to A. B., was conferred on 3 per cent. of the candidates. To fail was no disgrace; to have entered the lists was a title to respect. Once in three years the budding talent of the province convened in its chief city to compete for the second degree. This was H. L. (*Hiao Lien*, "Filial and Honest"), showing how ethical ideas continued to dominate the literary tribunals. It is now *Chu-jin*, and denotes nothing but promotion or prize man. The prize, a degree answering to A. M., poetically described as a sprig of the *Olea fragrans*, was the more coveted as the competitors were all honour men of the first grade, and it was limited to one in a hundred. Its immediate effect is such social distinction that it is said poor bachelors are common, but poor masters are rare.

If the competition stopped here it would be an Olympic game on a grander scale. But there are loftier heights to be climbed. The new-made masters from all the provinces proceed to the imperial capital to try their strength against the assembled scholars of the Empire. Here the prizes are three in a hundred. The successful student comes forth a Literary Doctor—a *Tsin-shi*, "fit for office." To all such is assured a footing, high or low, on the official ladder.

But another trial remains by which those who are good at the high leap may at a single bound place themselves very near the top. This final contest takes place in the palace—nominally in the presence of the Emperor, and the questions are actually issued by him. Its object is to select the brightest of the doctors for chairs in the Hanlin Academy—an institution in which the humblest seat is one of exalted dignity. How dazzling the first name on that list! The *Chuang Yuen* or senior wrangler takes rank with governors and viceroys. An unfading halo rests on the place of his birth. Sometimes in travelling I have seen a triumphal arch proclaiming that "Here was born the laureate of the Empire." Such an advertisement raises the value of real estate; and good families congregate in a place on which the sun shines so auspiciously. A laureate who lived near me married his daughter to a viceroy, and her daughter became consort to the Emperor Tungchi.

What then are the objections to a regulation which is so democratic that it makes a nobleman of every successful scholar and gives to all the inspiration of equal opportunity? They are, in a word, that it has failed to expand with the growing wants of the people. The old curriculum laid down by Confucius, "Begin with poetry; make etiquette your strong point; and finish off with music," was not bad for his day, but is utterly inadequate for ours, unless it be for a young ladies seminary. The Sage's chapter on experiment as the source of knowledge—a chapter which might have anticipated the *Novum Organum*—having been lost, the statesmen of the T'ang period fell into the error of leaving in their scheme no place for original research. This it was that made the mind of China barren of discoveries for twelve centuries. It was like putting a hood on the keen-eyed hawk and permitting him to fly at only such game as pleased his master.

The chief requirement was superficial polish in prose and verse. The themes were taken exclusively from books, the newest of which was at that time over a thousand years old. To broach a theory not found there was fatal; and to raise a question in physical science was preposterous. Had anyone come forward with a new machine he might have been rewarded; but no such inventor ever came because the best minds in the Empire were trained to trot blindfold on a tread-mill in which there was no possibility of progress. Had the mind of the nation been left free and encouraged to exert its force, who can doubt that the country that produced the mariner's compass might have given birth to a Newton or an Edison?

After Wu none of the monarchs of this dynasty calls for notice. The last emperor was compelled to abdicate; and thus, after a career of nearly three centuries bright with the light of genius and prolific of usages good and bad that set the fashion for after ages, this great house was extinguished.

CHAPTER XXIII

THE SUNG DYNASTY, 960-1280 A. D. (18 EMPERORS)

*The Five Philosophers—Wang Ngan-shi, Economist—The Kin Tartars—
The Southern Sungs—Aid of Mongols Invoked to Drive Out the
Kins—Mongols Exterminate Sungs*

On the fall of the house of T'ang, a score of factions contended for the succession. During the fifty-three years preceding the establishment of the Sungs, no less than five of them rose to temporary prominence sufficient to admit of being dubbed a "dynasty." Collectively they are spoken of as the "Five Dynasties" (907-960).

Their names are without exception a repetition of those of former dynasties, Liang, T'ang, Ts'in, Han, Chou with the prefix "Later"—suggesting that each claimed to be a lineal successor of some previous imperial family. Their struggles for power, not more instructive than a conflict of gladiators, are so devoid of interest that the half-century covered by them may be passed over as a blank. It may, however, be worth while to remind the reader that as the House of Han was followed by the wars of the "Three Kingdoms," and that of Ts'in by a struggle of North and South under four states, so the House of T'ang was now succeeded by five short-lived "dynasties," with a mean duration of scarcely more than ten years. The numerical progression is curious; but it is more important to notice a historical law which native Chinese writers deduce from those scenes of confusion. They state it in this form: "After long union the empire is sure to be divided; after long disruption it is sure to be reunited."

So deep an impression has this historical generalisation made on the public mind that if the empire were now to be divided between foreign nations, as it has been more than once, the people would confidently expect it to be reintegrated under rulers of their own race.

The undivided Sung dynasty held sway from 960 to 1127; that of the southern Sungs from 1127 to 1280. The founder of the house was Chao-kwang-yun, an able leader of soldiers and an astute politician. So popular was he with his troops that they called him to the throne by acclamation. He was drunk, it is said, when his new dignity was announced, and he had no alternative but to wear the yellow robe that was thrown on his shoulders. Undignified as was his debut, his reign was one continued triumph. After a tenure of seventeen years, he left his successor in possession of nearly the whole of China Proper together with a fatal legacy of lands on the north.

The two main features of the Sung period are the rise of a great school of philosophy and the constant encroachment of the Tartars. The two Chengs being brothers, the names of the five leading philosophers fall into an alliterative line of four syllables, *Cheo, Cheng, Chang, Chu*. Acute in speculation and patient in research, they succeeded in fixing the interpretation of the sacred books, and in establishing a theory of nature and man from which it is heresy to dissent. The rise of their school marks an intellectual advance as compared with the lettered age of the T'angs. It was an age of daring speculation; but, as constantly happens in China, the authority of these great men was converted into a bondage for posterity. The century in which they flourished (1020-1120) is unique in the history of their country as the age of philosophy. In Europe it was a part of the Dark Ages; and at that time the Western world was convulsed by the Crusades.

The most eminent of the five philosophers was Chu Fu-tse. Not the most original, he collected the best thoughts of all into a system; and his erudition was such that the whole range of literature was his domain. Chu Hi, the Coryphæus of mediæval China, stands next in honour after that incomparable pair, Confucius and Mencius. Contemporary with the earlier members of this coterie appeared Wang Ngan-shi, an economist, of rare originality. His leading principle was the absorption by the state of all industrial enterprises—state ownership of land, and in general a paternal system to supersede private initiative. So charming was the picture presented in his book "The Secret of Peace" (still extant) that the Emperor gave him *carte blanche* to put his theory into practice. In practical life however it was a failure—perhaps because he failed to allow for the strength or weakness of materials and instruments. His book is a Chinese Utopia, nearly akin to those of Plato and Sir John More.

In the northeast beyond the Wall were two Tartar kingdoms, one of which was the Kin or "Golden Horde"—remote ancestors of the Manchu dynasty. A constant menace to the settled population of the "inner land," they obtained possession of Peking in 1118. For a time they were kept at bay by a money payment which reminds one of the *Danegeld* paid by our forefathers to the sea-robbers of northern Europe. Payments not being punctual, the Tartars occupied portions of the northern provinces, and pushed their way as far south as K'ai-fung-fu, the capital of the Empire. The Emperor retired to Nanking, leaving in command his son, who, unable to resist the Tartars, made a disgraceful peace. A heavy ransom was paid to avert the sacking of the city; and all the region on the north of the Yellow River passed under Tartar sway.

Repenting of their hard bargain, the Chinese provoked a renewal of hostilities, which resulted in a heavier downfall. The capital surrendered after a severe siege, and the Emperor with his court was carried into captivity. The next emperor acknowledged himself a vassal of the Tartars; but peace on such conditions could not be of long duration. An intermittent warfare was kept up for more than a century, in the course of which Nanking was pillaged, and the court fell back successively on Hangchow and Wenchow. When there was no longer a place of safety on the mainland the wretched fugitives sought refuge on an island. Fitting out a fleet the Tartars continued the pursuit; but more used to horses than ships, the fleet was annihilated, and the expiring dynasty obtained a new lease of life.

This was about 1228. The Mongols under Genghis Khan and his successors had carried everything before them in the northwest. Thirsting for revenge, the Chinese appealed for aid to this new power — and the Mongols found an opportunity to bag two birds instead of one. As a Chinese fable puts it: "A sea-bird failing to make a breakfast on a shellfish was held in its grip until a fisherman captured both."

The Kins were driven back into Manchuria; and the Chinese without asking leave of their allies reoccupied their old capital. But the revival of the Sungs was no part of the Mongol programme. The Sungs declining to evacuate K'ai-fung-fu and to cede to the Mongols the northern half of the empire, the latter resolved on a war of extermination. After a bitter struggle of fifteen years, the infant emperor and his guardians again committed their fortunes to the sea. The Mongols, more lucky than the other Tartars, were victorious on water as well as on land; and the last scion of the imperial house drowned himself to escape their fury (1280).

CHAPTER XXIV

THE YUEN OR MONGOL DYNASTY, 1280-1368 (10 EMPERORS)

Kublai Khan—First Intercourse of China with Europe—Marco Polo—The Grand Canal

Parts of China had been frequently overrun by foreign conquerors; but the Mongols were the first to extend their sway over the whole country. The subjugation of China was the work of Kublai, grandson of Genghis, who came to the throne in 1260, inheriting an empire more extensive than Alexander or Cæsar had dreamed of. In 1264 the new khan fixed his court at Peking and proceeded to reduce the provinces to subjection. Exhausted and disunited as they were the task was not difficult, though it took fifteen years to complete. Ambition alone would have been sufficient motive for the conquest, but his hostility was provoked by perfidy—especially by the murder of envoys sent to announce his accession. "Without good faith," says Confucius, "no nation can exist."

By the absorption of China the dominions of Kublai were made richer, if not greater in extent, than those of his grandfather, while the splendour of his court quite eclipsed that of Genghis Khan.

Unknown to the ancient Romans, China was revealed to their mediæval successors by the Mongol conquest. In 1261 two Venetian merchants, Nicolo and Matteo Polo, made their way to Bokhara, whence, joining an embassy from India, they proceeded to Kublai's capital at Xanadu (or Shangtu) near the site of Peking. They were the first white men the Grand Khan had ever seen, and he seems to have perceived at once that, if not of superior race, they were at least more advanced in civilisation than his own people; for, besides intrusting them with letters to the Pope, he gave them a commission to bring out a hundred Europeans to instruct the Mongols in the arts and sciences of the West.

In 1275 they returned to Peking without other Europeans, but accompanied by Marco Polo, the son of Nicolo. They were received with more honour than on their first visit, and the young man was appointed to several positions of trust in the service of the monarch. After a sojourn of seventeen years, the three Polos obtained permission to join the escort of a Mongol princess who was going to the court of Persia. In Persia they heard of the death of their illustrious patron, and, instead of returning to China, turned their faces homeward, arriving at Venice in 1295.

Having been captured by the Genoese, Marco Polo while in prison dictated his wonderful story. At first it was looked on as a romance and caused its author to receive the sobriquet of "Messer Millione"; but its general accuracy has been fully vindicated.

The chief effect of that narrative was to fire the imagination of another Italian and lead him by steering to the west to seek a short cut to the Eldorado. How strange the occult connection of sublunary things! The Mongol Kublai must be invoked to account for the discovery of America! The same story kindled the fancy of Coleridge, in the following exquisite fragment, which he says came to him in a vision of the night:

> "In Xanadu did Kubla Khan
> A stately pleasure-dome decree:
> Where Alph, the sacred river, ran
> Through caverns measureless to man,
> Down to a sunless sea."

> —*Kubla Khan.*

Still another Italian claims mention as having made some impression on the court of Kublai. This was Corvino, a missionary sent by the Pope; but of his church, his schools, and his convents, there were left no more traces than of his predecessors, the Nestorians.

The glory of Kublai was not of long duration. The hardy tribes of the north became enervated by the luxury and ease of their rich patrimony. "Capua captured Hannibal." Nine of the founder's descendants followed him, not one of whom displayed either vigour or statesmanship.

Their power ebbed more suddenly than it rose. Shun-ti, the last of the house, took refuge behind the Great Wall from the rising tide of Chinese patriotism; and after a tenure of ninety years, or of two centuries of fluctuating dominion, reckoning from the rise of Genghis Khan, the Yuen dynasty came to an untimely end.

The magnificent waterway, the Grand Canal, remains an imperishable monument of the Mongol sway. As an "alimentary canal" it was needed for the support of the armies that held the people in subjection; and the Mongols only completed a work which other dynasties had undertaken. A description of it from personal observation is given in Part I of this work (page 31). It remains to be said that the construction of the Canal, like that of the Great Wall, was a leading cause of the downfall of its builders. Forced labour and aggravated taxation gave birth to discontent; rebellion became rife, and the Mongols were too effeminate to take active measures for its suppression.

Ming Tombs

Watch-tower at Yungloh's Tomb

CHAPTER XXV

THE MING DYNASTY, 1368-1644 A. D.
(16 EMPERORS)

Humble Origin of the Founder—Nanking and Peking as Capital—First Arrival of European Ships—Portuguese, Spaniards, and Dutch Traders—Arrival of Missionaries—Tragic End of the Last of the Mings

Humble as was the origin of the founder of the House of Han, spoken of as *Pu-i*, "A peasant clothed in homespun," that of the Father of the Mings was still more obscure. A novice or servant (*sacrificulus*) in a Buddhist monastery, Chu Yuen Chang felt called to deliver his people from oppression. At first regarded as a robber chief, one of many, his rivals submitted to his leadership and the people accepted his protection. Securing possession of Nanking, a city of illustrious memories and strong natural defences, he boldly proclaimed his purpose. After twenty years of blood and strategy, he succeeded in placing the Great Wall between him and the retreating Mongols. Proud of his victory he assumed for the title of his reign *Hungwu*, "Great Warrior," and chose *Ming*, "Luminous," for that of his dynasty.

Leaving his son, the Prince of Yen, at Peking, to hold the Tartars in check, Hungwu spent the remaining years of his reign at his original capital, and then left the sceptre to his grandson. The Prince of Yen, uncle of the youthful emperor, feeling the slight implied in his father's choice, raised an army and captured Nanking. A charred corpse being shown to him as that of the emperor, he caused it to be interred with becoming rites, and at once assumed the imperial dignity, choosing for his reigning title *Yungloh*, "Perpetual Joy." He also removed the seat of government to Peking, where it has remained for five centuries. The "Thesaurus of Yungloh," a digest of Chinese literature so extensive as to form a library in itself, remains a monument to his patronage of letters.

A tragic episode in the history of the Mings was the capture of the next emperor by the Mongols, who, however, failed to take Peking. It was easier to make a new emperor than to ransom the captive. His brother having been proclaimed, the Tartars sent their captive back, hoping that a war between the brothers would weaken their enemy. Retiring into private life he appeared to renounce his claim; but after the death of his brother he once more occupied the throne. What a theme for a romance!

Great Britain was described by a Roman as "almost cut off from the whole world" because it was not accessible by land. China had long been cut off from the Western world because it was not accessible by sea. The way to India was opened by Diaz and Gama in 1498; and the first Portuguese ships appeared at Canton in 1511. Well-treated at first, others came in greater numbers. Their armaments were so formidable as to excite suspicion; and their acts of violence kindled resentment. Under these combined motives a massacre of the foreign traders was perpetrated, and Andrade, a sort of envoy at Peking, was thrown into prison and beheaded. The trading-posts were abolished except at Macao, where the Portuguese obtained a footing by paying an annual rent.

After the Portuguese came the Spaniards, who appear to have been satisfied with the Philippine archipelago, rather than provoke a conflict with the Portuguese. The Chinese they had little reason to dread, as the superiority of their arms would have enabled them to seize portions of the seacoast, though not to conquer the Empire as easily as they did the Mexicans and Peruvians. Perhaps, too, they were debarred by the same authority which divided the Western continent between the two Iberian powers. The Chinese becoming too numerous at Manila, the Spaniards slaughtered them without mercy, as if in retaliation for the blood of their cousins, or taking a hint from the policy of China.

In 1622 the Dutch endeavoured to open trade with China, but their advances being rejected, doubtless through secret opposition from the Portuguese, they seized the Pescadores, and later established themselves on Formosa, whence they were eventually expelled by Koxinga, a Chinese freebooter.

The church founded by Corvino at Peking perished in the overthrow of the Mongols. The Portuguese traders disapproved of missions, as tending to impose restraint on their profligacy and to impart to China the strength that comes from knowledge. The narrow policy of the Mings, moreover, closed the door against the introduction of a foreign creed. Yet it is strange that half a century elapsed before any serious attempt was made to give the Gospel to China. In 1552 St. Francis Xavier, the apostle of the Indies, arrived at Macao. He and his fellow Jesuits were indirect fruits of the Protestant Reformation—belonging to an order organised for the purpose of upholding and extending the power of the Holy See. After wonderful success in India, the Straits, and Japan, Xavier appeared in Chinese waters, but he was not allowed to land. He expired on the island of Shang-chuen or St. John's, exclaiming "O rock, rock, when wilt thou open?"

Ricci, who came in 1580, met with better success: but it cost him twenty years of unceasing effort to effect an entrance to Peking. Careful to avoid giving offence, and courtly in manners, his science proved to be the master-key. Among the eminent men who favoured his mission was Sü of Shanghai, whom he baptised by the name of Paul. Not only did he help Ricci to translate Euclid for a people ignorant of the first elements of geometry, but he boldly came to the defence of missionaries when it was proposed to expel them. His memorial in their favour is one of the best documents in the defence of Christianity. Among the converts to the Christian faith there are no brighter names than Paul Sü and his daughter Candida.

The Ming dynasty compares favourably in point of duration with most of the imperial houses that preceded it; but long before the middle of its third century it began to show signs of decay. In Korea it came into collision with the Japanese, and emerged with more credit than did its successor from a war with the same foe, which began on the same ground three centuries later. In the northeast the Mings were able to hold the Manchus at bay, notwithstanding an occasional foray; but a disease of the heart was sapping the vigour of the dynasty and hastening its doom. Rebellion became rife; and two of the aspirants to the throne made themselves masters of whole provinces. One depopulated Szechuen; the other ravaged Shansi and advanced on Peking. Chungchen, the last of the Mings, realising that all was lost, hanged himself in his garden on the Palatine Hill, after stabbing his daughter, as a last proof of paternal affection (1643).

Arch of Five Spears, Tombs of the Ming Dynasty, Peking

CHAPTER XXVI

THE TA-TS'ING DYNASTY, 1644—

The Manchus, Invited to Aid in Restoring Order, Seat their Own Princes on the Throne — the Traitor, General Wu San-kwei — Reigns of Shunchi and Kanghi — Spread of Christianity — A Papal Blunder — Yung-cheng Succeeded by Kieñlung, who Abdicates Rather than Reign Longer than his Grandfather — Era of Transformation

The Manchus had been preparing for some generations for a descent on China. They had never forgotten that half the Empire had once been in the possession of their forefathers, the Kin Tartars; and after one or two abortive attempts to recover their heritage they settled themselves at Mukden and watched their opportunity. It came with the fall of the Mings.

Wu San-kwei, a Chinese general whose duty it was to keep them in bounds, threw open the gate of the Great Wall and invoked their assistance to expel the successful rebel. His family had been slaughtered in the fall of the capital; he thirsted for revenge, and without doubt indulged the hope of founding a dynasty. The Manchus agreed to his terms, and, combining their forces with his, advanced on Peking. Feeling himself unable to hold the city, the rebel chief burnt his palace and retreated, after enjoying the imperial dignity ten days.

General Wu offered to pay off his mercenaries and asked them to retire beyond the Wall. Smiling at his simplicity, they coolly replied that it was for him to retire or to enter their service. It was the old story of the ass and the stag. An ass easily drove a stag from his pasture-ground by taking a man on his back; but the man remained in the saddle. Forced to submit, the General employed his forces to bring his people into subjection to their hereditary enemy. Rewarded with princely rank, and shielded by the reigning house, he has escaped the infamy which he deserved at the hands of the historians. A traitor to his country, he was also a traitor to his new masters. He died in a vain attempt at counter-revolution.

The new dynasty began with Shunchi, a child of six years, his uncle the Prince Hwai acting as regent. Able and devoted, this great man, whom the Manchus call Amawang, acquitted himself of his task in a manner worthy of the model regent, the Duke of Chou. His task was not an easy one. He had to suppress contending factions, to conciliate a hostile populace, and to capture many cities which refused to submit. In seven years he effected the subjugation of the eighteen provinces, everywhere imposing the tonsure and the "pigtail" as badges of subjection. Many a myriad of the Chinese forfeited their heads by refusing to sacrifice their glossy locks; but the conquest was speedy, and possession secure.

The success of the Manchus was largely due to the fact that they found the empire exhausted by internal strife and came as deliverers. The odium of overturning the Ming dynasty did not rest on them. While at Mukden they had cultivated the language and letters of the "Inner land" and they had before them, for guidance or warning, the history of former conquests.

They have improved on their predecessors, whether Kins or Mongols; and with all their faults they have given to China a better government than any of her native dynasties.

Shunchi (1644-1662) passed off the stage at the age of twenty-four and left the throne to a son, Kanghi (1662-1723), who became the greatest monarch in the history of the Empire. During his long reign of sixty-one years, Kanghi maintained order in his wide domain, corrected abuses in administration, and promoted education for both nationalities. It is notable that the most complete dictionary of the Chinese language bears the imprimatur of Kanghi, a Tartar sovereign.

For his fame in the foreign world, Kanghi is largely indebted to the learned missionaries who enjoyed his patronage, though he took care to distinguish between them and their religion. The latter had been proscribed by the regents, who exercised supreme power during his minority. Their decree was never revoked; and persecution went on in the provinces, without the least interference from the Emperor. Still his patronage of missionaries was not without influence on the status of Christianity in his dominions. It gained ground, and before the close of his reign it had a following of over three hundred thousand converts. Near the close of his reign he pointedly condemned the foreign faith, and commanded the expulsion of its propagators, except a few, who were required in the Board of Astronomy.

The favourable impression made by Ricci had been deepened by Schaal and Verbiest. The former under Shunchi reformed the calendar and obtained the presidency of the Astronomical Board. He also cast cannon to aid the Manchu conquest. The latter did both for Kanghi, and filled the same high post. Schaal employed his influence to procure the building of two churches in Peking. Verbiest made use of his to spread the faith in the provinces. The Church might perhaps have gained a complete victory, had not dissensions arisen within her own ranks. Dominicans and Franciscans entering the field denounced their forerunners for having tolerated heathen rites and accepted heathen names for God. After prolonged discussions and contradictory decrees the final verdict went against the Jesuits. In this decision the Holy See seems not to have been guided by infallible wisdom.

Kanghi, whose opinion had been requested by the Jesuits, asserted that by *Tien* and *Shang-ti* the Chinese mean the Ruler of the Universe, and that the worship of Confucius and of ancestors is not idolatry, but a state or family ceremony. By deciding against his views, the Pope committed the blunder of alienating a great monarch, who might have been won by a liberal policy. The prohibition of the cult of ancestors—less objectionable in itself than the worship of saints—had the effect of arming every household against a faith that aimed to subvert their family altars.

The dethronement of *Shang-ti* (a name accepted by most Protestant missionaries) and the substitution of *Tien Chu*, could not fail to shock the best feelings of devout people. *Tien Chu*, if not a new coinage, was given by papal fiat an artificial value, equivalent to "Lord of all"—whereas it had previously headed a list of divisional deities, such as Lord of Heaven, Lord of Earth, Lord of the Sea, etc.

What wonder that for two centuries Christianity continued to be a prohibited creed! The ground thus lost by a papal blunder it has never regained. The acceptance of *Tien* and *Shang-ti* by Protestants might perhaps do something to retrieve the situation, if backed by some form of respect for ancestors.

Kanghi was succeeded by his son Yungcheng (1722-1736), who was followed by Kienlung (1736-1796), during whose reign the dynasty reached the acme of splendour. Under Kienlung, Turkestan was added to the empire. The Grand Lama of Tibet was also enrolled as a feudatory; but he never accepted the laws of China, and no doubt considered himself repaid by spiritual homage. No territory has since been added, and none lost, if we except the cession of Formosa to Japan and of Hong Kong to Great Britain. The cessions of seaports to other powers are considered as temporary leases.

After a magnificent reign of sixty years, Kienlung abdicated in favour of his fifth son, Kiak'ing, for the whimsical reason that he did not wish to reign longer than his grandfather. In Chinese eyes this was sublime. Why did they not enact a law that no man should surpass the longevity of his father?

As to Kiak'ing, who occupied the throne for twenty-four years, weak and dissolute is a summary of his character.

The next four reigns came under the influence of new forces. They belong to the era of transformation, and may properly be reserved for Part III.

PART III
CHINA IN TRANSFORMATION

CHAPTER XXVII

THE OPENING OF CHINA, A DRAMA IN FIVE ACTS—GOD IN HISTORY

Prologue—Act 1, the Opium War—(Note on the Taiping Rebellion)—Act 2, the "Arrow" War—Act 3, War with France—Act 4, War with Japan— Act 5, the Boxer War

PROLOGUE

If one were asked to name the most important three events that took place in Asia in the last century, he could have no hesitation in pointing to the extension of the Indian Empire and the renovation of Japan as two of them. But where would he look for the third? Possibly to some upheaval in Turkey, Persia, or Asiatic Russia. In my opinion, however, China is the only country whose history supplies the solution of the problem. The opening of that colossal empire to unrestricted intercourse with other countries was not a gradual evolution from within—it was the result of a series of collisions between the conservatism of the extreme Orient and the progressive spirit of the Western world.

Each of those collisions culminated in a war, giving rise to a cloud of ephemeral literature, in which a student might easily lose his way, and which it would require the lifetime of an antediluvian to exhaust. I think, therefore, that I shall do my readers a service if I set before them a concise outline of each of those wars, together with an account of its causes and consequences. Not only will this put them on their guard against misleading statements; it will also furnish them with a syllabus of the modern history of China in relation to her intercourse with other nations.

During the past seven decades the Chinese Empire has been no less than five times in conflict with foreign powers; and on each occasion her policy has undergone a modification more or less extensive. Taking these five conflicts seriatim— without touching on those internal commotions whose rise and fall resembles the tides of the ocean—I shall ask my readers to think of the Flowery Land as a stage on which, within the memory of men now living, a tragedy in five acts has been performed. Its subject was the Opening of China; and its first act was the so-called Opium War (1839-42). Prior to 1839 the Central Empire, as the Chinese proudly call their country, with a population nearly equal to that of Europe and America combined, was hermetically sealed against foreign intercourse, except at one point, viz., the "Factories" at Canton.

This state of things is depicted with a few masterstrokes in a popular work in Chinese entitled "Strange Stories of an Idle Student." The first of these tales describes a traveller meeting in the mountains an old man, in the costume of a former dynasty, whose family had there sought a refuge from the anarchy that preceded the fall of the imperial house. This old fellow had not even heard of the accession of the Manchu conquerors; and though he was eager for information, he disappeared without giving any clue to the Sleepy Hollow in which he was hiding. The author no doubt intended a quiet satire on the seclusion of China, that had nothing to ask of the outside world but to be let alone.

Another of the sketches, which is no satire, but a cautionary hint—perhaps an unconscious prophecy—is entitled "The Magic Carpet of the Red-haired," a vulgar designation for Europeans, in contrast with the Chinese, who style themselves the "Black-haired race." During the former dynasty, it says, a ship arrived from some unknown country, and those aboard desired to engage in commerce. Their request was refused; but when they asked permission to dry their goods on shore, requiring for that purpose no more ground than they could cover with a carpet, their petition was readily granted. The carpet was spread, and the goods were exposed to the sun; then, taking the carpet by its four corners, they stretched it so that it covered several acres. A large body of armed men then planted themselves on it, and striking out in every direction took possession of the country. This elastic carpet reminds one of Dido's bull's hide, which covered space enough for the foundation of Carthage.

ACT 1. THE OPIUM WAR, 1839-1842

The Tartars, who began their conquest in 1644, were naturally suspicious of other foreigners who had secured a foothold in India, where the Great Mogul, a scion of their own race, still held nominal sway. The trading-posts, which the Chinese emperors had permitted foreigners to open as far north as Ningpo, were closed, and only one point of tangency was allowed to remain—the above-mentioned Factories at Canton, a spot, as we shall see, large enough to admit of the spreading of a "magic carpet." Foreign trade was at that time insignificant, in comparison with the enormous expansion which it has now attained. It was mainly in the hands of the British, as it still continues to be; and no small part of it consisted in opium from the poppy-fields of India. Though under the ban of prohibition, this drug was smuggled into every bay and inlet, with scarcely a pretence of concealment. With the introduction of the vicious opium habit the British had nothing to do; but they contrived to turn it to good account.

The Emperor Tao Kwang, moved, it is said, by the unhappy fate of one of his sons who had fallen a victim to the seductive poison, resolved at all hazards to put a stop to a traffic so ruinous to his people. Commissioner Lin, a native of Foochow, was transferred from the viceroyalty of Wuchang to that of Canton and clothed with plenary powers for the execution of this decree. To understand the manner in which he undertook to execute the will of his master it must be remembered that diplomatic intercourse had as yet no existence in China, because she considered herself as sustaining to foreign nations no other relation than that of a suzerain to a vassal. Her mandarins scorned to hold direct communication with any of the superintendents of foreign commerce—receiving petitions and sending mandates through the hong merchants, thirteen native firms which had purchased a monopoly of foreign trade.

In 1834 Lord Napier was appointed to the humble position of superintendent of British trade in China, He arrived at Macao on July 15 of that year, and announced his appointment by a letter to the prefect, which was handed for transmission to the commander of the city gate of Canton—a barrier which no foreigner was permitted to pass. The letter was returned through the brokers without any answer other than a line on the cover informing the "barbarian eye" (consul) that the document was "tossed back" because it was not superscribed with the character *pin* (or *ping*), which signifies a "humble petition."

This was the beginning of sorrows for China as well as for poor Napier, who, failing in his efforts to communicate with the mandarins on equal terms, retired to the Portuguese settlement of Macao and died of disappointment. The eminent American statesman, John Quincy Adams, speaking in later years of the war that ensued, declared that its cause was not opium but a *pin*, i. e., an insolent assumption of superiority on the part of China.

The irrepressible conflict provoked by these indignities was precipitated in 1839 by the action of the new viceroy, who undertook to effect a summary suppression of the traffic in opium. One morning shortly after his arrival, the foreigners at Canton, who were always locked up at night for their own safety, awoke to find themselves surrounded by a body of soldiers and threatened with indiscriminate slaughter unless they surrendered the obnoxious drug, stored on their opium hulks, at an anchorage outside the harbour.

While they were debating as to what action to take, Captain Charles Elliot, the new superintendent, came up from Macao and bravely insisted on sharing the duress of his countrymen. Calling the merchants together he requested them to surrender their opium to him, to be used in the service of the Queen as a ransom for the lives of her subjects, assuring them that Her Majesty's Government would take care that they should be properly indemnified. Twenty thousand chests of opium were handed over to the viceroy (who destroyed the drug by mixing it with quicklime in huge vats); and the prisoners were set at liberty.

The viceroy fondly imagined that the incident was closed, and flattered himself that he had gained an easier victory than he could have done by sending his junks against the armed ships of the smugglers. Little did he suspect that he had lighted a slow-match, that would blow up the walls of his own fortress and place the throne itself at the mercy of the "barbarian."

A strong force was despatched to China to exact an indemnity, for which the honour of the Crown had been pledged, and to punish the Chinese for the cutthroat fashion in which they had sought to suppress a prohibited trade. The proud city of Canton averted a bombardment by paying a ransom of $6,000,000; islands and seaports were occupied by British troops as far north as the River Yang-tse; and Nanking, the ancient capital, was only saved from falling into their hands by the acceptance of such conditions of peace as Sir Henry Pottinger saw fit to impose.

Those conditions were astonishingly moderate for a conqueror who, unembarrassed by the interests of other powers, might have taken the whole empire. They were, besides payment for the destroyed drug, the opening of five ports to British trade, and the cession to Great Britain of Hong Kong, a rocky islet which was then the abode of fishermen and pirates, but which to-day claims to outrank all the seaports of the world in the amount of its tonnage. Not a word, be it noted, about opening up the vast interior, not a syllable in favour of legalising the opium traffic, or tolerating Christianity.

So much for the charge that this war, which bears a malodorous name, was waged for the purpose of compelling China to submit to the continuance of an immoral traffic. That a smuggling trade would go on with impunity was no doubt foreseen and reckoned on by interested parties; but it is morally certain that if the Chinese had understood how to deal with it they might have rid themselves of the incubus without provoking the discharge of another shot.

Here ends the first act, in 1842; and in it I may claim a personal interest from the fact that my attention was first turned to China as a mission field by the boom of British cannon in the Opium War.

China was not opened; but five gates were set ajar against her will. For that she has to thank the pride and ignorance of emperor and viceroy which betrayed them into the blunder of dealing with British merchants as a policeman deals with pickpockets. For the first time in her history she was made aware of the existence of nations with which she would have to communicate on a footing of equality.

The moderation and forbearance of Pottinger in refraining from demanding larger concessions, and in leaving the full consequences of this war to be unfolded by the progress of time, may fairly challenge comparison with the politic procedure of Commodore Perry in dealing with Japan in 1854. One may ask, too, would Japan have come to terms so readily if she had not seen her huge neighbour bowing to superior force?

An important consequence of the Opium War was the outbreak of rebellions in different parts of the Empire. The prestige of the Tartars was in the dust. Hitherto deemed invincible, they had been beaten by a handful of foreigners. Was not this a sure sign that their divine commission had been withdrawn by the Court of Heaven? If so, might it not be possible to wrest the sceptre from their feeble grasp, and emancipate the Chinese race?

Private ambition was kindled at the prospect, and patriotism was invoked to induce the people to make common cause. Three parties entered the field: the Tai-pings of the South, the "Red-haired" on the seacoast, and the Nienfi in the north. Neither of the latter two deserves notice; but the first-named made for themselves a place in history which one is not at liberty to ignore, even if their story were less romantic than it is. It will be convenient to introduce here the following note on the Tai-ping rebellion.

THE TAI-PING REBELLION

In 1847 a young man of good education and pleasing manners, named Hung Siu-tsuen, presented himself at the American Baptist mission in Canton, saying he had seen their sacred book and desired instruction. This he received from the Rev. Issachar Roberts; and he was duly enrolled as a catechumen. Without receiving the sealing ordinance, or taking his instructor into confidence, Siu-tsuen returned to his home at Hwa-hien and began to propagate his new creed. His talents and zeal won adherents, whom he organised into a society called *Shang-ti-hwui*, "the Church of the supreme God." Persecution transformed it into a political party, to which multitudes were attracted by a variety of motives.

Following the early Church, in the absence of any modern model, his converts expected and received spiritual gifts. Shall we describe such manifestations as hysteria, hypnotism, or hypocrisy? Their fanaticism was contagious, especially after their flight to the mountains of Kwangsi. There Siu-tsuen boldly raised the flag of rebellion and proclaimed that he had a divine call to restore the throne to the Chinese race, and to deliver the people from the curse of idolatry. In this twofold crusade he was ably seconded by one Yang, who possessed all the qualities of a successful hierophant. Shrewd and calculating, Yang was able at will to bring on cataleptic fits, during which his utterances passed for the words of the Holy Ghost.

The new empire which they were trying to establish, they called *Tai-ping Tien-kwoh*, "The Kingdom of Heaven and the reign of peace." Hung was emperor, to be saluted with *Wansue!* (Japanese, *Banzai!*) "10,000 years!" Yang as prince-premier was saluted with "9,000 years," nine-tenths of a banzai. He was the medium of communication with the Court of Heaven; and all their greater movements were made by command of Shang-ti, the Supreme Ruler.

On one occasion Yang went into a trance and declared that Shang-ti was displeased by something done by his chief, and required the latter to receive a castigation on his naked shoulders. The chief submitted, whether from credulity or from policy it might not be easy to say; but thereby the faith of his followers seems to have been confirmed rather than shaken. Nor did Yang take advantage of his chief's disgrace to usurp his place or to treat him as a puppet.

Through Yang it was revealed that they were to leave their mountain fortress and strike for Nanking, which had been made the capital on the expulsion of the Mongols, and which was destined to enjoy the same dignity on the overthrow of the Manchus. That programme, one of unexampled daring, was promptly put into execution. Descending into the plains of Hunan, like a mountain torrent they swept everything before them and began their march towards the central stronghold fifteen hundred miles distant. Striking the "Great River" at Hankow, they pillaged the three rich cities Wuchang, Hanyang, and Hankow, and, seizing all the junks, committed themselves to its current without a doubt as to the issue of their voyage.

Nanking was carried by assault despite the alleged impregnability of its ramparts, and despite also a garrison of 25,000 Manchus. These last must have fought with the fury of despair; for they well knew what fate awaited them. Not one was spared to tell the tale—this was in 1853. There the Tai-pings held their ground for ten years; and it is safe to affirm that without the aid of foreign missionaries they never would have been dislodged.

The second part of their enterprise—the expulsion of the Manchus from Peking—ended in defeat. A strong detachment was sent north by way of the Grand Canal. At first they met with great success—no town or city was able to check their progress, which resembled Napoleon's invasion of Russia. At the beginning of winter they were met by a strong force under the Mongol prince Sengkolinsin; then came the more dreaded generals—January and February. Unable to make headway, they went into winter quarters, and committed the blunder of dividing themselves between two towns, where they were besieged and cut off in detail.

In the meantime the eyes of the world were turned toward Nanking. Ships of war were sent to reconnoitre and Consul T. T. Meadows, who accompanied the *Hermes*, made a report full of sympathy; but the failure of their expedition to the north deterred the nation from any formal recognition of the Tai-ping government.

Missionaries were attracted by their profession of Christianity. Among others, I made an unsuccessful attempt to reach them. Unable to induce my boatmen to run the blockade, I returned home and took up the pen in their defence. My letters were well received, but they did not prevent soldiers of fortune, like the American Frederick G. Ward and Colonel Gordon of the British army, throwing their swords into the scale.

Two Sabbatarians hearing that the rebels observed Saturday for their day of rest, posted off to confirm them in that ancient usage. Learning at an outpost that the seeming agreement with their own practice grew out of a mistake in reckoning, they did not continue their journey.

A missionary who actually penetrated to the rebel headquarters was the Rev. Issachar Roberts, the first instructor of the rebel chief. The latter had sent him a message inviting him to court. His stay was not long. He found that his quondam disciple had substituted a new mode of baptism, neither sprinkling nor immersion, but washing the pit of the stomach with a towel dipped in warm water! Who says the Chinese are not original? It is probable that Roberts's dispute lay deeper than a mere ceremony. Professing a New Testament creed, the rebel chief shaped his practice on Old Testament examples—killing men as ruthlessly as David, and, like Solomon, filling his harem with women. A remonstrance on either head was certain to bring danger; it was said indeed that Roberts's life was threatened.

Some queer titles were adopted by the Tai-pings. As stated above, the premier was styled "Father of 9,000 years"; other princes had to content themselves with 7,000, 6,000, etc.—or seven-tenths and six-tenths of a "Live forever!" Christ was the "Heavenly Elder Brother"; and the chief called himself "Younger Brother of Jesus Christ." These designations might excite a smile; but when he called Yang, his adviser, the "Holy Ghost," one felt like stopping one's ears, as did the Hebrews of old. The loose morals of the Tai-pings and their travesty of sacred things horrified the Christian world; and Gordon no doubt felt that he was doing God a service in breaking up a horde of blasphemers and blackguards.

Gordon's victory won an earldom for Li Hung Chang; but the Chinese conferred no posthumous honours on Gordon as they did on Ward, who has a temple and is reckoned among the gods of the empire.

The Tai-pings were commonly called Changmao, "long-haired" rebels, because they rejected the tonsure and "pigtail" as marks of subjection. They printed at Nanking, by what they called "Imperial authority," an edition of the Holy Scriptures. At one time Lord Elgin, disgusted by the conduct of the Peking Government, proposed to make terms with the court at Nanking. The French minister refused to coöperate, partly because the rebels had not been careful to distinguish between the images in Roman Catholic chapels and those in pagan temples, but chiefly from an objection to the ascendency of Protestant influence, coupled with a fear of losing the power that comes from a protectorate of Roman Catholic missions. How different would have been the future of China had the allied powers backed up the Tai-pings against the Manchus!

ACT 2. THE "ARROW" WAR, 1857-1860

Of the second act in this grand drama on the world's wide stage, a vessel, named the *Arrow*, was, like opium in the former conflict, the occasion, not the cause. The cause was, as before, pride and ignorance on the part of the Chinese, though the British are not to be altogether exonerated. Their flag was compromised; and they sought to protect it. Fifteen years of profitable commerce had passed, during which China had been a double gainer, receiving light and experience in addition to less valuable commodities, when Viceroy Yeh seized the lorcha *Arrow*, on a charge of piracy. Though owned by Chinese, she was registered in Hong Kong, and sailed under the British flag. Had the viceroy handed her over to a British court for trial, justice would no doubt have been done to the delinquents, and the two nations would not have been embroiled; but, haughty as well as hasty, the viceroy declined to admit that the British Government had any right to interfere with his proceedings. Unfortunately (or fortunately) British interests at Canton were in the hands of Consul Parkes, afterward Sir Harry Parkes, the renowned plenipotentiary at Peking and Tokio.

Sir John Bowring was governor of Hong Kong, with the oversight of British interests in the Empire. A gifted poet, and an enthusiastic advocate of universal peace, he was a man who might be counted on, if in the power of man, to hold the dogs of war in leash. But he, too, had been consul at Canton and he knew by experience the quagmire in which the best intentions were liable to be swamped.

Parkes, whom I came to know as Her Britannic Majesty's minister in Peking, was the soul of honour, as upright as any man who walked the earth. But with all his rectitude, he, like the Viceroy Yeh, was irascible and unyielding. When the viceroy refused his demand for the rendition of the *Arrow* and her crew, he menaced him with the weight of the lion's paw. Alarmed, but not cowed, the viceroy sent the prisoners in fetters to the consulate, instead of replacing them on board their ship; nor did he vouchsafe a word of courtesy or apology. Parkes, too fiery to overlook such contemptuous informality, sent them back, much as a football is kicked from one to another; and the viceroy, incensed beyond measure, ordered their heads to be chopped off without a trial.

Here was a Gordian knot, which nothing but the sword could loose. War was provoked as before by the rashness of a viceroy. The peace-loving governor did not choose to swallow the affront to his country, nor did the occupant of the Dragon Throne deign to interfere; looking on the situation with the same sublime indifference with which the King of Persia regarded the warlike preparations of the younger Cyrus, when he supposed, as Xenophon tells us, that he was only going to fight out a feud with a neighbouring satrap. How could China be opened; how was a stable equilibrium possible so long as foreign powers were kept at a distance from the capital of the Empire?

In three months the haughty viceroy was a prisoner in India, never to return, and his provincial capital was held by a garrison of British troops. On this occasion the old blunder of admitting the city to ransom was not repeated, else Canton might have continued to be a hotbed of seditious plots and anti-foreign hostilities. Parkes knew the people, and he knew their rulers also. He was accordingly allowed to have his own way in dealing with them. The viceroy being out of the way, he proposed to Pehkwei, the Manchu governor, to take his place and carry on the provincial government as if the two nations were at peace. Strange to say, the governor did not decline the task. That he did not was due to the fact that he disapproved the policy of the viceroy, and that he put faith in the assurance that Great Britain harboured no design against the reigning house or its territorial domain.

To the surprise of the Chinese, who in their native histories find that an Asiatic conqueror always takes possession of as much territory as he is able to hold, it soon became evident that the Queen of England did not make war in the spirit of conquest. Her premier, Lord Palmerston, invited the coöperation of France, Russia, and the United States, in a movement which was expected to issue advantageously to all, especially to China. France, at that time under an ambitious successor of the great Napoleon, seized the opportunity to contribute a strong contingent, with the view of checkmating England and of obtaining for herself a free hand in Indo-China, possibly in China Proper also. For assuming a hostile attitude towards China, she found a pretext in the judicial murder of a missionary in Kwangsi, just as Germany found two of her missionaries similarly useful as an excuse for the occupation of Kiao-Chao in 1897. No wonder the Chinese have grown cautious how they molest a missionary; but they needed practical teaching before they learned the lesson.

Unable to take a morsel of China as long as his powerful ally abstained from territorial aggrandisement, Louis Napoleon subsequently employed his troops to enlarge the borders of a small state which the French claimed in Annam, laying the foundation of a dominion which goes far to console them for the loss of India. America and Russia, having no wrongs to redress, declined to send troops, but consented to give moral support to a movement for placing foreign relations with China on a satisfactory basis.

In the spring of 1858, the representatives of the four powers met at the mouth of the Peiho, coöperating in a loose sort of concert which permitted each one to carry on negotiations on his own account. As interpreter to the Hon. W. B. Reed, the American minister, I enjoyed the best of opportunities for observing what went on behind the scenes, besides being a spectator of more than one battle.

Palatine Hill, Peking, Scene of the Suicide of the Last of the Mings

The neutrals, arriving in advance of the belligerents, opened negotiations with the Viceroy of Chihli, which might have added supplementary articles, but must have left the old treaties substantially unchanged. The other envoys coming on the stage insisted that the viceroy should wear the title and be clothed with the powers of a plenipotentiary. When that was refused, as being "incompatible with the absolute sovereignty of the Emperor," they stormed the forts and proceeded to Tientsin where they were met by men whose credentials were made out in due form, though it is doubtful if their powers exceeded those of the crestfallen viceroy. A pitiful artifice to maintain their affectation of superiority was the placing of the names of foreign countries one space lower than that of China in the despatch announcing their appointment. When this covert insult was pointed out they apologised for a clerical error, and had the despatches rectified.

The allies were able to dictate their own terms; and they got all they asked for, though, as will be seen, they did not ask enough. The rest of us got the same, though we had struck no blow and shed no blood. One article, known as "the most-favoured-nation clause" (already in the treaty of 1844), was all that we required to enable us to pick up the fruit when others shook the tree.

Four additional seaports were opened, but Tienstin, where the treaties were drawn up, was not one of them. I remember hearing Lord Elgin, whose will was absolute, say that he was not willing to have it thrown open to commerce, because in that case it would be used to overawe the capital—just as if *overaweing* were not the very thing needed to make a bigoted government enter on the path of progress. Never did a man in repute for statesmanship show himself more shortsighted. His blunder led to the renewal of the war, and its continuance for two more years.

The next year when the envoys came to the mouth of the river, on their way to Peking to exchange ratified copies of their treaties, they found the forts rebuilt, the river closed, and access to the capital by way of Tientsin bluntly refused. In taking this action, the Chinese were not chargeable with a breach of faith; but the allies, feeling insulted at having the door shut in their faces, decided to force it open. They had a strong squadron; but their gunboats were no match for the forts. Some were sunk; others were beached; and the day ended in disastrous defeat. Though taking no part in the conflict the Americans were not indifferent spectators. Hearing that the British admiral was wounded, their commodore, the brave old Tatnall, went through a shower of bullets to express his sympathy, getting his boat shattered and losing a man on the way. When requested to lend a helping hand, he exclaimed "Blood is thicker than water;" and, throwing neutrality to the winds, he proceeded to tow up a flotilla of British barges. His words have echoed around the world; and his act, though impolitic from the viewpoint of diplomacy, had the effect of knitting closer the ties of two kindred nations.

Seeing the repulse of the allies, the American minister, the Hon. J. E. Ward, resolved to accept an offer which they had declined, namely, to proceed to the capital by land under a Chinese escort. His country was pledged in the treaty, of which he was the bearer, to use her good offices on the occurrence of difficulties with other powers. Without cavilling at the prescribed route or mode of conveyance, he felt it his duty to present himself before the Throne as speedily as possible in the hope of averting a threatened calamity. For him, it was an opportunity to do something great and good; for China, it was the last chance to ward off a crushing blow. But so elated were the Chinese by their unexpected success that they were in no mood to accept the services of a mediator. The Emperor insisted that he should go on his knees like the tribute-bearer from a vassal state. "Tell them," said Mr. Ward, "that I go on my knees only to God and woman"—a speech brave and chivalrous, but undignified for a minister and unintelligible to the Chinese. With this he quitted the capital and left China to her fate. He was not the first envoy to meet a rude rebuff at the Chinese court. In 1816 Lord Amherst was not allowed to see the "Dragon's Face" because he refused to kneel. At that date England was not in a position to punish the insult; but it had something to do with the war of 1839. In 1859 it was pitiful to see a power whose existence was hanging in the scales alienate a friend by unseemly insolence.

The following year (1860) saw the combined forces of two empires at the gates of Peking. The summer palace was laid in ashes to punish the murder of a company of men and officers under a flag of truce; and it continues to be an unsightly ruin. The Emperor fled to Tartary to find a grave; and throne and capital were for the first time at the mercy of an Occidental army. On the accession of Hien-feng, in 1850, an old counsellor advised him to make it his duty to "restore the restrictions all along the coast." His attempt to do this was one source of his misfortunes. Supplementary articles were signed within the walls, by which China relinquished her absurd pretensions, abandoned her long seclusion, and, at the instance of France, threw open the whole empire to the labours of Christian missions. They had been admitted by rescript to the Five Ports, but no further.

Thus ends the second act of the drama; and a spectator must be sadly deficient in spiritual insight if he does not perceive the hand of God overruling the strife of nations and the blunders of statesmen.

ACT 3. WAR WITH FRANCE

The curtain rises on the third act of the drama in 1885. Peking was open to residence, and I had charge of a college for the training of diplomatic agents.

I was at Pearl Grotto, my summer refuge near Peking, when I was called to town by a messenger from the Board of Foreign Affairs. The ministers informed me that the French had destroyed their fleet and seized their arsenal at Foochow. "This," they said, "is war. We desire to know how the non-combatants of the enemy are to be treated according to the rules of international law." I wrote out a brief statement culled from text-books, which I had myself translated for the use of the Chinese Government; but before I had finished writing a clerk came to say that the Grand Council wished to have it as soon as possible, as they were going to draw up a decree on the subject. The next day an imperial decree proclaimed a state of war and assured French people in China that if they refrained from taking part in any hostile act they might remain in their places, and count on full protection. Nobly did the government of the day redeem its pledge. Not a missionary was molested in the interior; and two French professors belonging to my own faculty were permitted to go on with the instruction of their classes.

There was not much fighting. The French seized Formosa; and both parties were preparing for a trial of strength, when a seemingly unimportant occurrence led them to come to an understanding. A small steamer belonging to the customs service, employed in supplying the wants of lighthouses, having been taken by the French, Sir Robert Hart applied to the French premier, Jules Ferry, for its release. This was readily granted; and an intimation was at the same time given that the French would welcome overtures for a settlement of the quarrel. Terms were easily agreed upon and the two parties resumed the *status quo ante bellum*.

So far as the stipulations were concerned neither party had gained or lost anything, yet as a matter of fact France had scored a substantial victory. She was henceforward left in quiet possession of Tongking, a principality which China had regarded as a vassal and endeavoured to protect.

ACT 4. WAR WITH JAPAN

China had not thoroughly learned the lesson suggested by this experience; for ten years later a fourth act in the drama grew out of her unwise attempt to protect another vassal.

In 1894 the Japanese, provoked by China's interference with their enterprises in Korea, boldly drew the sword and won for themselves a place among the great powers. I was in Japan when the war broke out, and, being asked by a company of foreigners what I thought of Japan's chances, answered, "The swordfish can kill the whale."

Not merely did the islanders expel the Chinese from the Korean peninsula, but they took possession of those very districts in Manchuria from which they have but yesterday ousted the Russians. Peking itself was in danger when Li Hung Chang was sent to the Mikado to sue for peace. Luckily for China a Japanese assassin lodged a bullet in the head of her ambassador; and the Mikado, ashamed of that cowardly act, granted peace on easy conditions. China's greatest statesman carried that bullet in his *dura mater* to the end of his days, proud to have made himself an offering for his country, and rejoicing that one little ball had silenced the batteries of two empires.

By the terms of the treaty, Japan was to be left in possession of Port Arthur and Liao-tung. But this arrangement was in fatal opposition to the policy of a great power which had already cast covetous eyes on the rich provinces of Manchuria. Securing the support of France and Germany, Russia compelled the Japanese to withdraw; and in the course of three years she herself occupied those very positions, kindling in the bosom of Japan the fires of revenge, and sowing the seeds of another war.[12]

The effect of China's defeat at the hands of her despised neighbour, was, if possible, more profound than that of her humiliation by the English and French in 1860. She saw how the adoption of Western methods had clothed a small Oriental people with irresistible might; and her wisest statesmen set themselves to work a similar transformation in their antiquated empire. The young Emperor showed

[12] The Russo-Japanese war lies outside of our present programme because China was not a party to it, though it involved her interests and even her existence. The subject will be treated in another chapter.

himself an apt pupil, issuing a series of reformatory edicts, which alarmed the conservatives and provoked a reaction that constitutes the last act in this tremendous drama.

ACT 5. THE BOXER WAR

The fifth act opens with the *coup d'état* of the Empress Dowager, and terminates with the capture of Peking by the combined forces of the civilised world.

Instead of attempting, even in outline, a narrative of events, it will be more useful to direct attention to the springs of action. It should be borne in mind that the late Emperor was the adopted son of the Dowager Empress. After the death of her own son, Tung-chi, who occupied the throne for eleven years under a joint regency of two empresses, his mother cast about for some one to adopt in his stead. With motives not difficult to divine she chose among her nephews an infant of three summers, and gave him the title *Kwangsu*, "Illustrious Successor." When he was old enough to be entrusted with the reins of government, she made a feint of laying down her power, in deference to custom. Yet she exacted of the imperial youth that he visit her at her country palace and throw himself at her feet once in five days—proof enough that she kept her hand on the helm, though she mitted her nephew to pose as steersman. She herself was noted for progressive ideas; and it was not strange that the young man, under the influence of Kang Yuwei, backed by enlightened viceroys, should go beyond his adoptive mother. Within three years from the close of the war he had proclaimed a succession of new measures which amounted to a reversal of the old policy; nor is it likely that she disapproved of any of them, until the six ministers of the Board of Rites, the guardians of a sort of Levitical law, besought her to save the empire from the horrors of a revolution.

For her to command was to be obeyed. The viceroys were her appointees; and she knew they would stand by her to a man. The Emperor, though nominally independent, was not emancipated from the obligations of filial duty, which were the more binding as having been created by her voluntary choice. There was no likelihood that he would offer serious resistance; and it was certain that he would not be supported if he did. Coming from behind the veil, she snatched the sceptre from his inexperienced hand, as a mother takes a deadly weapon from a half-grown boy. Submitting to the inevitable he made a formal surrender of his autocratic powers and, confessing his errors, implored her "to teach him how to govern." This was in September, 1898.

Stripped of every vestige of authority, the unhappy prince was confined, a prisoner of state, in a secluded palace where it was thought he would soon receive the present of a silken scarf as a hint to make way for a worthier successor. That his life was spared was no doubt due to a certain respect for the public sentiment of the world, to which China is not altogether insensible. He having no direct heir, the son of Prince Tuan was adopted by the Dowager as heir-apparent, evidently in expectation of a vacancy soon to be filled. Prince Tuan, hitherto unknown in the politics of the state, became, from that moment, the leader of a reactionary party. Believing that his son would soon be called to the throne by the demise of the Emperor, he put on all the airs of a *Tai-shang Hwang*, or "Father of an Emperor."

Palace where the Emperor was Imprisoned

Here again the *patria potestas* comes in as a factor; and in the brief career of the father of the heir-apparent, it shows itself in its most exaggerated form. Under the influence of the reactionary clique, of which he was acknowledged chief, the Empress Dowager in her new regency was induced to repeal almost everything the Emperor had done in the way of reform. In her edict she said cynically: "It does not follow that we are to stop eating, because we have been choked!" Dislike to foreign methods engendered an ill-concealed hatred of foreigners; and just at this epoch occurred a series of aggressions by foreign powers, which had the effect of fanning that hatred into a flame.

In the fall of 1897 Germany demanded the cession of Kiao-Chao, calling it a lease for 99 years. The next spring Russia under the form of a lease for 25 years obtained Port Arthur for the terminus of her long railway. England and France followed suit: one taking a *lease* of Wei-hai-wei; the other, of Kwang-chou-wan. Though in every case the word "lease" was employed, the Chinese knew the transfer meant permanent alienation.

A hue and cry was raised against what they described as the "slicing of the melon," and in Shantung, where the first act of spoliation had taken place, the Boxers, a turbulent society of long standing, were encouraged to wage open war against native Christians, foreigners and foreign products, including railways, telegraphs, and all sorts of merchandise.

Not until those predatory bands had entered the metropolitan province, with the avowed object of pushing their way to Peking[13] did the legations take steps to strengthen their guards. A small reinforcement of 207 men luckily reached Peking a few days before the railway was wrecked.

With a view to protect the foreign settlement at Tientsin, then threatened by Boxers, the combined naval forces stormed the forts at the mouth of the river, and advanced to that rich emporium. The Court denounced this as an act of war, and ordered all foreigners to leave the capital within twenty-four hours. That meant slaughter at the hands of the Boxers. The foreign ministers protested, and endeavoured by prolonged negotiation to avoid compliance with the cruel order.

On June 20, the German minister, Baron von Ketteler, was on his way to the Foreign Office to obtain an extension of time, when he was shot dead in the street by a man in the uniform of a soldier. His secretary, though wounded, gave the alarm; and all the legations, with all their respective countrymen, took refuge in the British Legation, with the exception of Bishop Favier and his people who, with the aid of forty marines, bravely defended themselves in the new cathedral.

In the evening we were fired on by the Government troops, and from that time we were closely besieged and exposed to murderous attacks day and night for eight weeks, when a combined force under the flags of eight nations carried the walls by storm, just in time to prevent such a massacre as the world has never seen. Massacres on a larger scale have not been a rare spectacle; but never before in the history of the world had any government been seen attempting to destroy

---

[13] On March 30, 1900, the following Boxer manifesto in jingling rhyme, was thrown into the London Mission, at Tientsin. It is here given in a prose version, taken from "A Flight for Life," by the Rev. J. H. Roberts, Pilgrim Press, Boston.

"We Boxers have come to Tientsin to kill an foreign devils, and protect the Manchu dynasty. Above, there is the Empress Dowager on our side, and below there is Junglu. The soldiers of Yulu and Yuhien [governors of Shantung and Chihli] are an our men. When we have finished killing in Tientsin, we shall go to Peking. All the officials high and low will welcome us. Whoever is afraid let him quickly escape for his life."

an entire diplomatic body, every member of whom is made sacred by the law of nations.[14]

On August 14 Gen. Gaseles and his contingent entered the British Legation. The Court, conscious of guilt, fled to the northwest, leaving the city once more at the mercy of the hated foreigner; and so the curtain falls on the closing scene.

What feats of heroism were performed in the course of those eventful weeks; how delicate women rose to the height of the occasion in patient endurance and helpful charity; how international jealousies were merged in the one feeling of devotion to the common good—all this and more I should like to relate for the honour of human nature.

How an unseen power appeared to hold our enemies in check and to sustain the courage of the besieged, I would also like to place on record, to the glory of the Most High; but space fails for dealing with anything but general principles.[15]

---

[14] AN APPEAL FROM THE LION'S DEN

(Written four weeks before the end of the siege, this appeal failed to reach the outside world. It is now printed for the first time. Nothing that I could now write would show the situation with half such vividness. It reveals the scene as with a lightning flash.)

"British Legation, July 16, 1900.

"TO THE CHRISTIAN WORLD

"On the 19th ult. the Chinese declared war on account of the attack on the forts at Taku. Since then we have been shut up in the British Legation and others adjacent, and bombarded day and night with shot and shell. The defence has been magnificent. About 1,000 foreigners (of both sexes) have held their ground against the forces of the Empire. Some thousands of Chinese converts are dependent on us for protection. The City Wall near the legations is held by our men, but the Chinese are forcing them back and driving in our outposts. The mortality in our ranks is very great; and unless relief comes soon we must all perish. Our men have fought bravely, and our women have shown sublime courage. May this terrible sacrifice prove not to be in vain! We are the victims of pagan fanaticism. Let this pagan empire be partitioned among Christian powers, and may a new order of things open on China with a new century!

"The chief asylum for native Christians is the Roman Catholic Cathedral, where Bishop Favier aided by forty marines gives protection to four or five thousand. The perils of the siege have obliterated the lines of creed and nation, making a unity, not merely of Christians, but bringing the Japanese into brotherhood with us. To them the siege is a step toward Christianity."

"(Signed) DR. W. A. P. MARTIN."

[15] See the author's "The Siege in Peking," New York: Fleming H. Revell Company.

The French Cathedral, Peking

On the day following our rescue, at a thanksgiving meeting, which was largely attended, Dr. Arthur Smith pointed out ten instances—most of us agreed that he might have made the number ten times ten—in which the providence of God had intervened on our behalf.

It was a role of an ancient critic that a god should not be brought on the stage unless the occasion were such as to require the presence of a more than human power. *Nec deus intersit nisi dignus vindice nodus.* How many such occasions we have had to notice in the course of this narrative! What a theodicæa we have in the result of all this tribulation! We see at last, a government convinced of the folly of a policy which brought on such a succession of disastrous wars. We see missionaries and native Christians fairly well protected throughout the whole extent of the Empire. We see, moreover, a national movement in the direction of educational reform, which, along with the Gospel of Christ, promises to impart new life to that ancient people.

The following incident may serve to show the state of uncertainty in which we lived during the interregnum preceding the return of the Court.

While waiting for an opportunity to get my "train (the university) on the track," I spent the summer of 1901 at Pearl Grotto, my usual retreat, on the top of a hill over a thousand feet high, overlooking the capital. "The Boxers are coming!" cried my writer and servants one evening about twilight. "Haste—hide in the rocks—they will soon be on us!" "I shall not hide," I replied; and seizing my rifle I rested it on a wall which commanded the approach. They soon became visible at the distance of a hundred yards, waving flambeaux, and yelling like a troop of devils. Happily I reserved my fire for closer range; for leaving the path at that point they betook themselves to the top of another hill where they waved their torches and shouted like madmen. We were safe for the night; and in the morning I reported the occurrence to Mr. O'Conor, the British chargé d'affaires, who was at a large temple at the foot of the hills. "They were not Boxers," he remarked, "but a party we sent out *to look for a lost student.*"

POSTSCRIPT

It is the fashion to speak slightingly of the Boxer troubles, and to blink the fact that the movement which led to the second capture of Peking and the flight of the Court was a serious war. The southern viceroys had undertaken to maintain order in the south. Operations were therefore localised somewhat, as they were in the Russo-Japanese War. It is even said that the combined forces were under the impression that they were coming to the rescue of a helpless government which was doing all in its power to protect foreigners. Whether this was the effect of diplomatic dust thrown in their eyes or not, *it was a fiction.*

How bitterly the Empress Dowager was bent on exterminating the foreigner, may be inferred from her decree ordering the massacre of foreigners and their adherents—a savage edict which the southern satraps refused to obey. A similar inference may be drawn from the summary execution of four ministers of state for remonstrating against throwing in the fortunes of the empire with the Boxer party. China should be made to do penance on her knees for those shocking displays of barbarism. At Taiyuan-fu, forty-five missionaries were murdered by the governor, and sixteen at Paoting-fu. Such atrocities are only possible among a *half-civilised people.*

CHAPTER XXVIII
THE RUSSO-JAPANESE WAR

Russia's Schemes for Conquest—Conflicting Interests in Korea—Hostilities Begin—The First Battles—The Blockade—Dispersion of the Russian Fleet—Battle of Liao-yang—Fall of Port Arthur—Battle of Mukden—The Armada—Battle of Tsushima—The Peace of Portsmouth—The Effect on China

To the Chinese the retrospect of these five wars left little room for those pompous pretensions which appeared to be their vital breath.

Beaten by Western powers and by the new power of the East, their capital taken a second time after forty years' opportunity to fortify it, and their fugitive court recalled a second time to reign on sufferance or during good behaviour, what had they left to boast of except the antiquity of their country and the number of their people? Dazed and paralysed, most of them gave way to a sullen resignation that differed little from despair.

There were, indeed, a few who, before things came to the worst, saw that China's misfortunes were due to folly, not fate. Ignorant conservatism had made her weak; vigorous reform might make her strong. But another war was required to turn the feeling of the few into a conviction of the many. This change was accomplished by a war waged within their borders but to which they were not a party—a war which was not an act in their national drama, but a spectacle for which they furnished the stage. That spectacle calls for notice in the present work on account of its influence on the destinies of China.

For the springs of action it will be necessary to go back three centuries, to the time when Yermak crossed the Ural Mountains and made Russia an Asiatic power. The conquest of Siberia was not to end in Siberia. Russia saw in it a chance to enrich herself at the expense of weaker neighbours. What but that motive led her, in 1858, to demand the Manchurian seacoast as the price of neutrality? What but that led her to construct the longest railway in the world? What but that impelled her to seek for it a second terminus on the Gulf of Pechili?

The occupation of Port Arthur and Liao-tung by the Japanese, in 1895, was a checkmate to Russia's little game; and, supported by France and Germany, she gave her notice to quit. During the Boxer War of 1900, Russia increased her forces in Manchuria to provide for the eventualities of a probable break-up, and after the peace her delay in fulfilling her promise of evacuation was tantamount to a refusal.

Had the Russians confined their attention to Manchuria they might have continued to remain in possession; but another feeble state offered itself as a tempting prize. They set greedy eyes on Korea, made interest with an impoverished court, and obtained the privilege of navigating the Yalu and cutting timber on its banks. This proceeding, though explained by the requirements of railway construction, aroused the suspicion and jealousy of the Japanese. They knew it meant more than seeking an outlet for a lumber industry. They knew it portended vassalage for Korea and ejection for themselves. Had they not made war on China ten years before because they could brook no rival in the peninsula? How could they tolerate the intrusion of Russia? Not merely were their interests in Korea at stake; every advance of Russia in that quarter, with Korea for vassal or ally, was a menace to the existence of Japan.

The Japanese lost no time in entering a protest. Russia resorted to the Fabian policy of delay as before; but she was dealing with a people whose pride and patriotism were not to be trifled with. After protracted negotiations Japan sent an ultimatum in which she proposed to recognise Manchuria as Russia's sphere of influence, provided Russia would recognise Japanese influence as paramount in Korea. For a fortnight or more the Czar vouchsafed no reply. Accustomed to being waited on, he put the paper in his pocket and kept it there while every train on the railway was pouring fresh troops into Manchuria. Without waiting for a formal reply, or deigning to discuss modifications intended to gain time, the Japanese heard the hour strike and cleared for action.

They are reproached for opening hostilities without first formally declaring war. In the age of chivalry a declaration of war was a solemn ceremony. A herald standing on the border read or recited his master's complaint and then hurled a spear across the boundary as an act of defiance. In later times nothing more than a formal announcement is required, except for the information of neutrals and the belligerents' own people. The rupture of relations leaves both parties free to choose their line of action. Japan, the newest of nations, naturally adopted the most modern method.

Recalling her ambassador on February 6, 1904, Japan was ready to strike simultaneous blows at two points. On February 8, Admiral Uriu challenged two Russian cruisers at Chemulpo to come out and fight, otherwise he would attack them in the harbour. Steaming out they fired the first shots of the war, and both were captured or destroyed. A little later on the same day Admiral Togo opened his broadsides on the Russian fleet at Port Arthur, and resumed the attack the following morning. Without challenge or notification of any kind, his attack had the effect of a genuine surprise. The Russians, whether from confidence in their position or contempt for their enemy, were unprepared and replied feebly. They had seven battleships to Togo's six, but the big ships of Japan were supported by a flotilla of torpedo-boats which outnumbered those of Russia. These alert little craft did great execution. Creeping into the harbour while the bombardment kept the enemy occupied they sank two battleships and one armoured cruiser. Other Russian vessels were badly damaged; but, according to Togo's report, on the side of Japan not one vessel was incapacitated for actual service.

Land forces, fully equipped and waiting for this special service, commenced operations without delay and began to cut off communication from the land side while Togo's squadron corked up every inlet from the sea. Alexieff, whose title of viceroy revealed the intentions of Russia in regard to Manchuria, taking alarm at the prospect of a siege, escaped to Harbin near the Siberian frontier—a safer place for headquarters. To screen his flight he made unwarrantable use of an ambulance train of the Red Cross Society. Disagreeing with General Kuropatkin as to the plan of campaign, he resigned the command of the army in April, and Kuropatkin was promoted to the vacant place. Beaten in several engagements on the Liao-tung peninsula, the Russians began to fall back, followed by the Japanese under Field-Marshal Oyama; and the siege of the fortress was prosecuted with unremitting vigour.

By July the Japanese had secured possession of the outer line of forts, and, planting heavy guns on the top of a high hill, they were able to throw plunging shot into the bosom of the harbour. No longer safe at their inner anchorage, the Russian naval officers resolved to attempt to reach Vladivostok, where the combined squadrons might assume the offensive or at least be secure from blockade. Scarcely had they gained the open sea when (on August 10) the Japanese fell on them like a whirlwind and scattered their ships in all directions. A few reëntered the harbour to await their doom; two or three found their way to Vladivostok; two sought refuge at the German port of Tsing-tao; two put into Shanghai; and one continued its flight as far south as Saigon.

One gunboat sought shelter at Chefoo, where I was passing my summer vacation. The Japanese, in hot pursuit, showed no more respect to the neutrality of China than they had shown to Korea. Boarding the fugitive vessel, they summoned the captain to surrender. He replied by seizing the Japanese officer in his arms and throwing himself into the sea. They were rescued; and the Japanese then carried off the boat under the guns of a Chinese admiral. Of this incident in its main features I was an eye-witness. I may add that we were near enough to bear witness to the fact of the siege; for, in the words of Helen Sterling:

> "We heard the boom of guns by day
> And saw their flash by night,
> And almost thought, tho' miles away,
> That we were in the fight.

The Chinese admiral, feeling the affront to the Dragon flag and fearing that he would be called to account, promptly tendered his resignation. He was told to keep his place; and, by way of consoling him for his inaction, the Minister of Marine added, "You are not to blame for not firing on the Japanese. They are fighting our battles—we can't do anything against them." So much for Chinese neutrality in theory and in practice.

Kuropatkin, like the Parthian, "most dreaded when in flight," renouncing any further attempt to break through the cordon which the Japanese had drawn around the doomed fortress, intrenched his forces in and around Liaoyang. His position was strong by nature, and he strengthened it by every device known to a military engineer; yet he was driven from it in a battle which lasted nine days.

The Japanese, though not slow to close around his outposts, were too cautious to deliver their main attack until they could be certain of success. The combat thickened till, on August 24, cannon thundered along a line of forty miles. Outflanked by his assailants, the Russian general, perceiving that he must secure his communications on the north or sustain a siege, abandoned his ground and fell back on Mukden.

In this, the greatest battle of the campaign thus far, 400,000 men were engaged, the Japanese, as usual, having a considerable majority. The loss of life was appalling. The Russian losses were reported at 22,000; and those of Japan could not have been less. Yet Liaoyang with all its horrors was only a prelude to a more obstinate conflict on a more extended arena.

Without hope of succour by land, and without a fleet to bring relief by sea, the Russians defended their fortress with the courage of despair. Ten years before this date the Japanese under Field-marshal Oyama had carried this same stronghold almost by assault. Taking it in the rear, a move which the Chinese thought so contrary to the rules of war that they had neglected their landward defences, they were masters of the place on the morning of the third day.

How different their reception on the present occasion! How changed the aspect! The hills, range after range, were now crowned with forts. Fifty thousand of Russia's best soldiers were behind those batteries, many of which were provided with casemates impenetrable to any ordinary projectile. General Stoessel, a man of science, courage and experience, was in command; and he held General Nogi with a force of sixty or seventy thousand at bay for eleven months. Prodigies of valour were performed on both sides, some of the more commanding positions being taken and retaken three or four times.

When, in September, the besiegers got possession of Wolf Hill, and with plunging shot smashed the remnant of the fleet, they offered generous terms to the defenders. General Stoessel declined the offer, resolving to emulate Thermopylæ, or believing, perhaps, in the possibility of rescue. When, however, he saw the "203 Metre Hill" in their hands and knew his casemates would soon be riddled by heavy shot, in sheer despair he was forced to capitulate. This was on the first day of the new year (1905). His force had been reduced to half its original numbers, and of these no fewer than 14,000 were in hospital.

General Stoessel has been censured for not holding out until the arrival of the armada; but what could the armada have done had it appeared in the offing? It certainly could not have penetrated the harbour, for in addition to fixed or floating mines it would have had to run the gauntlet of Togo's fleet and its doom would have been precipitated. One critic of distinction denounced Stoessel's surrender as "shameful"; but is it not a complete vindication that his enemies applaud his gallant defence, and that his own government was satisfied that he had done his duty.[16]

---

[16] Since writing this I have read the finding of the court-martial. It has the air of an attempt to diminish the national disgrace by throwing blame on a brave commander.

The Russian commander had marked out a new camp at Mukden, the chief city of the province and the cradle of the Manchu dynasty. There he was allowed once more to intrench himself. Was this because the Japanese were confident of their ability to compel him again to retire, or were they occupied with the task of filling up their depleted ranks? If the latter was the cause, the Russians were doing the same; but near to their base and with full command of the sea, the Japanese were able to do it more expeditiously than their enemy. Yet with all their facilities they were not ready to move on his works until winter imposed a suspension of hostilities.

On October 2 Kuropatkin published a boastful manifesto expressing confidence in the issue of the coming conflict—trusting no doubt to the help of the three generals, December, January, and February. Five months later, on March 8, 1905, he sent two telegrams to the Czar: the first said "I am surrounded;" the second, a few hours later, conveyed the comforting intelligence "the army has escaped."

The Japanese, not choosing to encounter the rigours of a Manchurian winter, waited till the advent of spring. The air was mild and the streams spanned by bridges of ice. The manœuvres need not be described here in detail. After more than ten days of continuous fighting on a line of battle nearly two hundred miles long, with scarcely less than a million of men engaged (Japanese in majority as before), the great Russian strategist broke camp and retired in good order. His army had escaped, but it had lost in killed and wounded 150,000. The losses of Japan amounted to 50,000.

The greatest battle of this latest war, the Battle of Mukden was in some respects the greatest in modern history. In length of line, in numbers engaged, and in the resulting casualties its figures are double those of Waterloo. Once more by masterly strategy a rout was converted into a retreat; and the Russian army withdrew to the northwest.

Weary of crawfish tactics the Czar appointed General Lineivitch to the chief command; and the ablest of the Russian generals was relieved of the duty of contriving ways of "escape." To cover the rear of a defeated force is always reckoned a post of honour; but it is not the sort of distinction that satisfies the ambition of a great commander.

By dint of efforts and sacrifices an enormous fleet was assembled for the relief of Port Arthur. It sailed from Cronstadt on August 11, 1905, leaving the Baltic seaports unprotected save by the benevolent neutrality of the German Kaiser, who granted passage through his ship canal, although he knew the fleet was going to wage war on one of his friends.

Part of the fleet proceeded via Suez, and part went round the Cape of Good Hope—to them a name of mockery. The ships moved leisurely, their commanders not doubting that Stoessel would be able to hold his ground; but scarcely had they reached a rendezvous which, by the favour of France, they had fixed in the waters adjacent to Madagascar, when they heard of the fall of Port Arthur. Of the annihilation of the fleet attached to the fortress, and of the destruction of a squadron coming to the rescue from the north they had previously learned. With what dismay did they now hear that the key of the ocean was lost. Almost at the same moment the last of Job's messengers arrived with the heavier tidings that Mukden, the key of the province, had been abandoned by a defeated army—stunning intelligence for a forlorn hope! Should they turn back or push ahead? Anxious question this for Admiral Rozhesvenski and his officers. Too late for Port Arthur, might they not reënforce Vladivostok and save it from a like fate? The signal to "steam ahead" was displayed on the flagship.

Slowly and painfully, its propellers clogged by seaweed, its keels overgrown with barnacles, the grand armada crossed the Indian Ocean and headed northward for the China Sea. On May 27, steering for the Korean channel, it fell into a snare which a blind man ought to have been able to foresee. Togo's fleet had the freedom of the seas. Where could it be, if not in that very channel? Yet on the Russians went:

> "Unmindful of the whirlwind's sway
> That hushed in grim repose
> Expects his evening prey."

The struggle was short and decisive—finished, it is said, in less than one hour. While Togo's battleships, fresh and in good condition, poured shot and shell into the wayworn strangers, his torpedo-boats, greatly increased in number, glided almost unobservedly among the enemy and launched their thunderbolts with fatal effect. Battleships and cruisers went down with all on board. The Russian flagship was disabled, and the admiral, severely wounded, was transferred to the hold of a destroyer. Without signals from their commander the vessels of the whole fleet fought or fled or perished separately; of 18,000 men, 1,000 escaped and 3,000 were made prisoners. What of the other 14,000?

> "Ask of the winds that far around
> With fragments strewed the sea."

The much vaunted armada was a thing of the past; and Tsushima or, as Togo officially named it, the Battle of the Sea of Japan, has taken its place along with Trafalgar and Salamis.

Tired of a spectacle that had grown somewhat monotonous, the world was clamorous for peace. The belligerents, hitherto deaf to every suggestion of the kind, now accepted an invitation from President Roosevelt and appointed commissioners to arrange the terms of a treaty. They met in August, 1905, at Portsmouth, New Hampshire, and after a good deal of diplomatic fencing the sword was sheathed. In the treaty, since ratified, Russia acknowledges Japan's exceptional position in Korea, transfers to Japan her rights in Port Arthur and Liao-tung, and hands over to Japan her railways in Manchuria. Both parties agree to evacuate Manchuria within eighteen months.

Japan was obliged to waive her claim to a war indemnity and to allow Russia to retain half the island of Saghalien. Neither nation was satisfied with the terms, but both perceived that peace was preferable to the renewal of the struggle with all its horrors and uncertainties. For tendering the olive branch and smoothing the way for its acceptance, President Roosevelt merits the thanks of mankind.[17] Besides other advantages Japan has assured her position as the leading power of the Orient; but the greatest gainer will be Russia, if her defeat in the field should lead her to the adoption of a liberal government at home.

Bishop Favier

    "Peace hath her victories,
      No less renowned than war."

The Czar signified his satisfaction by making Witte the head of a reconstruction

[17] Since this was written a Nobel Peace Prize has justly been awarded to the President.

ministry and by conferring upon him the title of Count; and the Mikado showed his entire confidence in Baron Komura, notwithstanding some expressions of disappointment among the people, by assigning him the delicate task of negotiating a treaty with China.

Though the attitude of China had been as unheroic as would have been Menelaus' had the latter declared neutrality in the Trojan war, the issue has done much to rouse the spirit of the Chinese people. Other wars made them feel their weakness: this one begot a belief in their latent strength. When they witnessed a series of victories on land and sea gained by the Japanese over one of the most formidable powers of the West, they exclaimed, "If our neighbour can do this, why may we not do the same? We certainly can if, like them, we break with the effete systems of the past. Let us take these island heroes for our schoolmasters."

That war was one of the most momentous in the annals of history. It unsettled the balance of power, and opened a vista of untold possibilities for the yellow race.

Not slow to act on their new convictions, the Chinese have sent a small army of ten thousand students to Japan—of whom over eight thousand are there now, while they have imported from the island a host of instructors whose numbers can only be conjectured. The earliest to come were in the military sphere, to rehabilitate army and navy. Then came professors of every sort, engaged by public or private institutions to help on educational reform. Even in agriculture, on which they have hitherto prided themselves, the Chinese have put themselves under the teaching of the Japanese, while with good reason they have taken them as teachers in forestry also. Crowds of Japanese artificers in every handicraft find ready employment in China. Nor will it be long before pupils and apprentices in these home schools will assume the rôle of teacher, while Chinese graduates returning from Japan will be welcomed as professors of a higher grade. This Japanning process, as it is derisively styled, may be somewhat superficial; but it has the recommendation of cheapness and rapidity in comparison with depending on teachers from the West. It has, moreover, the immense advantage of racial kinship and example. Of course the few students who go to the fountain-heads of science—in the West—must when they return home take rank as China's leading teachers.

All this inclines one to conclude that a rapid transformation in this ancient empire is to be counted on. The Chinese will soon do for themselves what they are now getting the Japanese to do for them. Japanese ideas will be permanent; but the direct agency of the Japanese people will certainly become less conspicuous than it now is.

To the honour of the Japanese Government, the world is bound to acknowledge that the island nation has not abused its victories to wring concessions from China. In fact to the eye of an unprejudiced observer it appears that in unreservedly restoring Manchuria Japan has allowed an interested neutral to reap a disproportionate share of the profits.

CHAPTER XXIX
REFORM IN CHINA

Reforms under the Empress Dowager—The Eclectic Commission—Recent Reforms—Naval Abortion—Merchant Marine—Army Reform—Mining Enterprises—Railways—The Telegraph—The Post Office—The Customs—Sir Robert Hart—Educational Reform—The Tung-Wen College—The Imperial University—Diplomatic Intercourse—Progressive Viceroys—New Tests for Honours—Legal Reform—Newspapers—Social Reforms—Reading Rooms—Reform in Writing—Anti-foot-binding Society—The Streets.

"When I returned from England," said Marquis Ito, "my chief, the Prince of Chosin, asked me if I thought anything needed to be changed in Japan. I answered, 'Everything.'" These words were addressed in my hearing, as I have elsewhere recorded, to three Chinese statesmen, of whom Li Hung Chang was one. The object of the speaker was to emphasise the importance of reform in China. He was unfortunate in the time of his visit—it was just after the *coup d'état*, in 1898. His hearers were men of light and leading, in sympathy with his views; but reform was on the ebb; a ruinous recoil was to follow; and nothing came of his suggestions.

The Emperor had indeed shown himself inclined to "change everything," but at that moment his power was paralyzed. What vicissitudes he has passed through since that date! Should he come again to power, as now seems probable, may he not, sobered by years and prudent from experience, still carry into effect his grand scheme for the renovation of China. To him a golden dream, will it ever be a reality to his people?

Taught by the failure of a reaction on which she had staked her life and her throne, the Dowager became a convert to the policy of progress. She had, in fact, outstripped her nephew. "Long may she live!" "Late may he rule us!" During her lifetime she could be counted on to carry forward the cause she had so ardently espoused. She grasped the reins with a firm hand; and her courage was such that she did not hesitate to drive the chariot of state over many a new and untried road. She knew she could rely on the support of her viceroys—men of her own appointment. She knew too that the spirit of reform was abroad in the land, and that the heart of the people was with her.

The best embodiment of this new spirit was the High Commission sent out in 1905 to study the institutions of civilized countries east and west, and to report on the adoption of such as they deemed advisable. The mere sending forth of such an embassy was enough to make her reign illustrious. The only analogous mission in the history of China, is that which was despatched to India, in 66 A. D., in quest of a better faith, by Ming-ti, "The Luminous." The earlier embassy borrowed a few sparks to rekindle the altars of their country; the present embassy propose to introduce new elements in the way of political reform. Their first recommendation, if not their first report, reaches me while I write, and in itself is amply sufficient to prove that this High Commission is not a sham designed to dazzle or deceive. The Court *Gazette*, according to the *China Times*, gives the following on the subject:

> "The five commissioners have sent in a joint memorial dealing with what they have seen in foreign countries during the last three months. They report that the wealthiest and strongest nations in the world to-day are governed by constitutional government. They mention the proclamation of constitutional government in Russia, and remark that China is the only great country that has not adopted that principle. As they have carefully studied the systems of England, the United States, Japan, etc., they earnestly request the Throne to issue a decree fixing on five years as the limit within which 'China will adopt a constitutional form of government.'

> "A rescript submits this recommendation to a council of state to advise on the action to be taken."

If that venerable body, consisting of old men who hold office for life, does not take umbrage at the prospect of another tribunal infringing on their domain, we shall have at least the promise of a parliament. And five years hence, if the *congé d'elire* goes forth, it will rend the veil of ages. It implies the conferment on the people of power hitherto unknown in their history. What a commotion will the ballot-box excite! How suddenly will it arouse the dormant intellect of a brainy race! But it is premature to speculate.

In 1868 the Mikado granted his subjects a charter of rights, the first article of which guarantees freedom of discussion, and engages that he will be guided by the will of the people. In China does not the coming of a parliament involve the previous issue of a Magna Charta?

It is little more than eight years since the restoration, as the return of the Court in January, 1902, may be termed. In this period, it is safe te assert that more sweeping reforms have been decreed in China than were ever enacted in a half-century by any other country, if one except Japan, whose example the Chinese profess to follow, and France, in the Revolution, of which Macaulay remarks that "they changed everything—from the rites of religion to the fashion of a shoe-buckle."

Reference will here be made to a few of the more important innovations or ameliorations which, taken together, made the reign of the Empress Dowager the most brilliant in the history of the Empire. The last eight years have been uncommonly prolific of reforms; but the tide began to turn after the peace of Peking in 1860. Since that date every step in the adoption of modern methods was taken during the reign or regency of that remarkable woman, which dated from 1861 to

1908.

As late as 1863 the Chinese Government did not possess a single fighting ship propelled by steam. Steamers belonging to Chinese merchants were sometimes employed to chase pirates; but they were not the property of the state. The first state-owned steamers, at least the first owned by the Central Government, was a flotilla of gunboats purchased that year in England by Mr. Lay, Inspector-General of Maritime Customs. Dissatisfied with the terms he had made with the commander, whom he had bound not to act on any orders but such as the Inspector should approve, the Government dismissed the Inspector and sold the ships.

In the next thirty years a sufficient naval force was raised to justify the appointment of an admiral; but in 1895 the whole fleet was destroyed by the Japanese, and Admiral Ting committed suicide. At present there is a squadron under each viceroy; but all combined would hardly form the nucleus of a navy. That the Government intend to create a navy may be inferred from the establishment of a Naval Board. In view of the naval exploits of Japan, and under the guidance of Japanese, they are certain to develop this feeble plant and to make it formidable to somebody—perhaps to themselves.

Their merchant marine is more respectable. With a fleet of fifty or more good ships the China Merchants' Steam Navigation Company are able by the aid of subsidies and special privileges to compete for a share in the coasting trade; but as yet they have no line trading to foreign ports.

In 1860 a wild horde with matchlocks, bows, and spears, the land army is now supplied in large part with repeating rifles, trained in Western drill, and dressed in uniform of the Western type. The manœuvres that took place near Peking in 1905 made a gala day for the Imperial Court, which expressed itself as more than satisfied with the splendour of the spectacle. The contingent belonging to this province is 40,000, and the total thus drilled and armed is not less than five times that number. In 1907 the troops of five provinces met in Honan. Thanks to railways, something like concentration is coming within the range of possibility. Not deficient in courage, what these raw battalions require to make them effective is confidence in themselves and in their commanders. Lacking in the lively patriotism that makes heroes of the Japanese, these fine big fellows are not machines, but animals. To the mistaken efforts recently made to instil that sentiment at the expense of the foreigner, I shall refer in another chapter. A less objectionable phase of the sentiment is provincialism, which makes it easy for an invader to employ the troops of one province to conquer another. In history these provinces appear as kingdoms, and their mutual wars form the staple subject. What feeling of unity can exist so long as the people are divided by a babel of dialects? More than once have Tartars employed Chinese to conquer China; and in 1900 a fine regiment from Wei-hai-wei helped the British to storm Peking. It may be added they repaid themselves by treating the inhabitants as conquered foes. Everywhere they were conspicuous for acts of lawless violence.

Three great arsenals, not to speak of minor establishments, are kept busy turning out artillery and small arms for the national army, and the Board of Army

Reform has the supervision of those forces, with the duty of making them not provincial, but national. Efforts of this kind, however, are no proof of a reform spirit. Are not the same to be seen all the way from Afghanistan to Dahomey? "To be weak is to be miserable"; and the Chinese are right in making military reorganisation the starting-point of a new policy. Yet the mere proposal of a parliament is a better indication of the spirit of reform than all these armaments.

In the mind of China, wealth is the correlative of strength. The two ideas are combined in the word *Fuchiang*, which expresses national prosperity. Hence the treasures hidden in the earth could not be neglected, when they had given up the follies of geomancy and saw foreigners prospecting and applying for concessions to work mines. At first such applications were met by a puerile quibble as to the effect of boring on the "pulse of the Dragon"—in their eyes not the guardian of a precious deposit, but the personification of "good luck." To find lucky locations, and to decide what might help or harm, were the functions of a learned body of professors of *Fungshui*, a false science which held the people in bondage and kept the mines sealed up until our own day. Gradually the Chinese are shaking off the incubus and, reckless of the Dragon, are forming companies for the exploitation of all sorts of minerals. The Government has framed elaborate regulations limiting the shares of foreigners, and encouraging their own people to engage in mining enterprises.

> "Give up your *Fungshui*;
> It keeps your wealth locked up,"

says a verse of Viceroy Chang.

A similar change has taken place in sentiment as regards railways. At first dreaded as an instrument of foreign aggression, they are now understood to be the best of auxiliaries for national defence. It has further dawned on the mind of a grasping mandarinate that they may be utilised as a source of revenue. If stocks pay well, why should not the Government hold them? "Your railways pay 10 per cent.—that's the sort of railway we want in China," said one of the commissioners at a banquet in England.

It would not be strange if the nationalisation of railways decided on this spring in Japan should lead to a similar movement in China. In a country like America, with 300,000 miles of track, the purchase would be *ultra vires* in more senses than one, but with only 1 per cent. of that mileage, the purchase would not be difficult, though it might not be so easy to secure an honest administration.

Trains from Peking now reach Hankow (600 miles) in thirty-six hours. When the grand trunk is completed, through trains from the capital will reach Canton in three days. Set this over against the three months' sea voyage of former times (a voyage made only once a year), or against the ten days now required for the trip by steamer! What a potent factor is the railroad in the progress of a great country!

The new enterprises in this field would be burdensome to enumerate. Shanghai is to be connected by rail with Tientsin (which means Peking), and with Nanking and Suchow. Lines to penetrate the western provinces are already mapped out; and even in Mongolia it is proposed to supersede the camel by the iron horse on the caravan route to Russia. "Alas! the age of golden leisure is gone—the iron age of hurry-skurry is upon us!" This is the lament of old slow-going China.

When China purchased the Shanghai-Woosung railway in 1876, she was thought to be going ahead. What did we think when she tore up the track and dumped it in the river? An æon seems to have passed since that day of darkness.

The advent of railways has been slow in comparison with the telegraph. The provinces are covered with wires. Governors and captains consult with each other by wire, in preference to a tardy exchange of written correspondence. The people, too, appreciate the advantage of communicating by a flash with distant members of their families, and of settling questions of business at remote places without stirring from their own doors. To have their thunder god bottled up and brought down to be their courier was to them the wonder of wonders; yet they have now become so accustomed to this startling innovation, that they cease to marvel.

The wireless telegraph is also at work—a little manual, translated by a native Christian, tells people how to use it.

Over forty years ago, when I exhibited the Morse system to the astonished dignitaries of Peking, those old men, though heads of departments, chuckled like children when, touching a button, they heard a bell ring; or when wrapping a wire round their bodies, they saw the lightning leap from point to point. "It's wonderful," they exclaimed, "but we can't use it in our country. The people would steal the wires." Electric bells are now common appliances in the houses of Chinese who live in foreign settlements. Electric trolleys are soon to be running at Shanghai and Tientsin. Telephones, both private and public, are a convenience much appreciated. Accustomed as the Chinese are to the instantaneous transmission of thought and speech, they have yet to see the *telodyne*—electricity as a transmitter of force. But will they not see it when the trolleys run? The advent of electric power will mark an epoch.

China's weakness is not due wholly to backwardness in the arts and sciences. It is to be equally ascribed to defective connection of parts and to a lack of communication between places. Hence a sense of solidarity is wanting, and instead there is a predominance of local over national interests. For this disease the remedy is forthcoming—rail and wire are rapidly welding the disjointed members of the Empire into a solid unity. The post office contributes to the same result.

A postal system China has long possessed: mounted couriers for official despatches, and foot messengers for private parties, the Government providing the former, and merchant companies the latter. The modernised post office, now operating in every province, provides for both. To most of the large towns the mails are carried by steamboat or railroad—a marvellous gain in time, compared with horse or foot. The old method was slow and uncertain; the new is safe and expeditious.

That the people appreciate the change is shown by the following figures: In 1904 stamps to the amount of $400,000 (Mexican) were sold; in 1905 the sale rose to $600,000—an advance of 50 per cent. in one year. What may we not expect when the women learn to read, and when education becomes more general among men?

Sir Robert Hart, from whom I had this statement, is the father of China's postal system. Overcoming opposition with patience and prudence, he has given the post office a thorough organisation and has secured for it the confidence of princes and people. Already does the Government look to it as a prospective source of revenue.

To the maritime customs service, Sir Robert has been a foster-father. Provided for by treaty, it was in operation before he took charge, in 1863; but to him belongs the honour of having nursed the infant up to vigorous maturity by the unwearied exertions of nearly half a century. While the post office is a new development, the maritime customs have long been looked upon as the most reliable branch of the revenue service. China's debts to foreign countries, whether for loans or indemnities, are invariably paid from the customs revenue. The Government, though disinclined to have such large concerns administered by foreign agents, is reconciled to the arrangement in the case of the customs by finding it a source of growing income. The receipts for 1905 amounted to 35,111,000 taels = £5,281,000. In volume of trade this shows a gain of 11-1/2 per cent. on 1904; but, owing to a favouring gale from the happy isles of high finance, in sterling value the gain is actually 17 per cent.

To a thoughtful mind, native or foreign, the maritime customs are not to be estimated by a money standard. They rank high among the agencies working for the renovation of China. They furnish an object-lesson in official integrity, showing how men brought up under the influence of Christian morals can collect large sums and pay them over without a particle sticking to their fingers. While the local commissioners have carried liberal ideas into mandarin circles all along the seacoast and up the great rivers into the interior, the Inspector-General (the "I. G." as Sir Robert is usually called) has been the zealous advocate of every step in the way of reform at headquarters.

Another man in his position might have been contented to be a mere fiscal agent, but Sir Robert Hart's fertile brain has been unceasingly active for nearly half a century in devising schemes for the good of China. All the honours and wealth that China has heaped on her trusted adviser are far from being sufficient to cancel her obligations. It was he who prompted a timid, groping government to take the first steps in the way of diplomatic intercourse. It was he who led them to raise their school of interpreters to the rank of a diplomatic college. He it was who made peace in the war with France; and in 1900, after the flight of the Court, he it was who acted as intermediary between the foreign powers and Prince Ching. To some of these notable services I shall refer elsewhere. I speak of them here for the purpose of emphasising my disapproval of an intrigue designed to oust Sir Robert and to overturn the lofty structure which he has made into a light-house for China.

In May, 1906, two ministers were appointed by the Throne to take charge of the entire customs service, with plenary powers to reform or modify *ad libitum*. Sir Robert was not consulted, nor was he mentioned in the decree. He was not dismissed, but was virtually superseded. Britain, America, and other powers took alarm for the safety of interests involved, and united in a protest. The Government explained that it was merely substituting one tribunal for another, creating a dual headship for the customs service instead of leaving it under the Board of Foreign

Affairs, a body already overburdened with responsibilities. They gave a solemn promise that while Sir Robert Hart remained there should be no change in his status or powers; and so the matter stands. The protest saved the situation for the present. Explanation and promise were accepted; but the Government (or rather the two men who got themselves appointed to a fat office) remain under the reproach of discourtesy and ingratitude. The two men are Tieliang, a Manchu, and Tang Shao-yi, a Chinese. The latter, I am told on good authority, is to have £30,000 per annum. The other will not have less. This enormous salary is paid to secure honesty.

In China every official has his salary paid in two parts: one called the "regular stipend," the other, a "solatium to encourage honesty." The former is counted by hundreds of taels; the latter, by thousands, especially where there is a temptation to peculate. What a rottenness at the core is here betrayed!

Peking: Indian Troops at Palace Gate After the Siege

A new development worthy of all praise is the opening, by imperial command, of a school for the training of officials for the customs service. It is a measure which Sir Robert Hart with all his public spirit, never ventured to recommend, because it implies the speedy replacement of the foreign staff by trained natives.

Filling the sky with a glow of hope not unlike the approach of sunshine after an arctic winter, the reform in the field of education throws all others into the shade. By all parties is recognised its supremacy. Its beginning was feeble and unwelcome, implying on the part of China nothing but a few drops of oil to relieve the friction at a few points of contact with the outside world.

The new treaties found China unprovided with interpreters capable of translating documents in foreign languages. Foreign nations agreed to accompany their despatches with a Chinese version, until a competent staff of interpreters should be provided. With a view to meeting this initial want, a school was opened in 1862, in connection with the Foreign Office, and placed under the direction of the Inspector-General of Maritime Customs, by whom I was recommended for the presidency. Professors of English, French, and Russian were engaged; and later on German took a place alongside of the three leading languages of the Western world.

At first no science was taught or expected, but gradually we succeeded in obtaining the consent of the Chinese ministers to enlarge our faculty so as to include chairs of astronomy, mathematics, chemistry, and physics. International law was taught by the president; and by him also the Chinese were supplied with their first text-books on the law of nations. What use had they for books on that subject, so long as they held no intercourse on equal terms with foreign countries? The students trained in that school of diplomacy had to shiver in the cold for many a year before the Government recognised their merits and rewarded them with official appointments. The minister recently returned from London, the ministers now in Germany and Japan, and a minister formerly in France, not to speak of secretaries of legation and consuls, were all graduates of our earlier classes.

In 1898 the young Emperor, taught by defeat at the hands of the Japanese, resolved on a thorough reform in the system of national education. It would never do to confine the knowledge of Western science to a handful of interpreters and attachés. The highest scholars of the Empire must be allowed access to the fountain of national strength. A university was created with a capital of five million taels, and the writer was made president by an imperial decree which conferred on him the highest but one of the nine grades of the mandarinate.

Two or three hundred students were enrolled, among whom were bachelors, masters, and doctors of the civil service examinations. It was launched with a favouring breeze; but the wind changed with the *coup d'état* of the Empress Dowager, and two years later the university went down in the Boxer cyclone. A professor, a tutor, and a student lost their lives. How the cause of educational reform rose stronger after the storm, I relate in a special chapter. It is a far cry from a university for the *élite* to that elaborate system of national education which is destined to plant its schools in every town and hamlet in the Empire. The new education was in fact still regarded with suspicion by the honour men of the old system. They looked on it, as they did on the railway, as a source of danger, a perilous experiment.

As yet the intercourse was one-sided: envoys came; but none were sent. Embassies were no novelty; but they had always moved on an inclined plane, either coming up laden with tribute, or going down bearing commands. Where there was no tribute and no command, why send them? Why send to the very people who had robbed China of her supremacy! It was a bitter pill, and she long refused to swallow it. Hart gilded the dose and she took it. Obtaining leave to go home to get married, he proposed that he should be accompanied by his teacher, Pinchun, a learned Manchu, as unofficial envoy—with the agreeable duty to see and report. It was a travelling commission, not like that of 1905-06, to seek light, but to ascertain whether the representative of a power so humbled and insulted would be treated with common decency.

The old pundit was a poet. All Chinese pundits are poets; but Pinchun had real gifts, and the flow of champagne kindled his inspiration. Everywhere wined and dined, though accredited to no court, he was in raptures at the magnificence of the nations of the West. He lauded their wealth, culture, and scenery in faultless verse; and if he indulged in satire, it was not for the public eye. He was attended by several of our students, to whom the travelling commission was an education. They were destined, after long waiting as I have said, to revisit the Western world, clothed with higher powers.

The impression made on both sides was favourable, and the way was prepared for a genuine embassy. The United States minister, Anson Burlingame, a man of keen penetration and broad sympathies, had made himself exceedingly acceptable to the Foreign Office at Peking. When he was taking leave to return home, in 1867, the Chinese ministers begged his good offices with the United States Government and with other governments as occasion might offer—"In short, you will be our ambassador," they said, with hearty good-will.

Burlingame, who grasped the possibilities of the situation, called at the Customs on his way to the Legation. Hart seized the psychological moment, and, hastening to the *Yamên*, induced the ministers to turn a pleasantry into a reality. The Dowagers (for there were two) assented to the proposal of Prince Kung, to invest Burlingame with a roving commission to all the Treaty powers, and to associate with him a Manchu and a Chinese with the rank of minister. An "œcumenical embassy" was the result. Some of our students were again attached to the suite; reciprocal intercourse had begun; and Burlingame has the glory of initiating it".

In the work of reform three viceroys stand pre-eminent, viz., Li Hung Chang, Yuen Shi Kai and Chang Chitung. Li, besides organising an army and a navy (both demolished by the Japanese in 1895), founded a university at Tienstin, and placed Dr. Tenney at the head of it. Yuen, coming to the same viceroyalty with the lesson of the Boxer War before his eyes, has made the army and education objects of special care. In the latter field he had had the able assistance of Dr. Tenney, and succeeded in making the schools of the province of Chihli an example for the Empire.

Viceroy Chang has the distinction of being the first man (with the exception of Kang Yuwei) to start the emperor on the path of reform. Holding that, to be rich, China must have the industrial arts of the West, and to be strong she must have the sciences of the West, he has taken the lead in advocating and introducing both. Having been called, after the suspension of the Imperial University, to assist this enlightened satrap in his great enterprise, I cannot better illustrate the progress of reform than by devoting a separate chapter to him and to my observations during three years in Central China.

Tests of scholarship and qualifications for office have undergone a complete change. The regulation essay, for centuries supreme in the examinations for the civil service, is abolished; and more solid acquirements have taken its place. It takes time to adjust such an ancient system to new conditions. That this will be accomplished is sufficiently indicated by the fact that in May, 1906, degrees answering to A. M. and Ph. D. were conferred on quite a number of students who had completed their studies at universities in foreign countries. As a result there is certain to be a rush of students to Europe and America, the fountain-heads of science. Forty young men selected by Viceroy Yuen from the advanced classes of his schools were in 1906 despatched under the superintendence of Dr. Tenney to pursue professional studies in the United States. That promising mission was partly due to the relaxation of the rigour of the exclusion laws.

The Chinese assessor of the Mixed Court in Shanghai was dismissed the same year because he had condemned criminals to be beaten with rods—a favourite punishment, in which there is a way to alleviate the blows. Slicing, branding, and other horrible punishments with torture to extort confessions have been forbidden by imperial decree. Conscious of the contempt excited by such barbarities, and desirous of removing an obstacle to admission to the comity of nations, the Government has undertaken to revise its penal code. Wu-ting-fang, so well known as minister at Washington, has borne a chief part in this honourable task. The code is not yet published; but magistrates are required to act on its general principles. When completed it will no doubt provide for a jury, a thing hitherto unknown in China. The commissioners on legal reform have already sent up a memorial, explaining the functions of a jury; and, to render its adoption palatable, they declare that it is an ancient institution, having been in use in China three thousand years ago. They leave the Throne to infer that Westerners borrowed it from China.

The fact is that each magistrate is a petty tyrant, embodying in his person the functions of local governor, judge, and jury, though there are limits to his discretion and room for appeal or complaint. It is to be hoped that lawyers and legal education will find a place in the administration of justice.

Formerly clinging to a foreign flagstaff, the editor of a Chinese journal cautiously hinted the need for some kinds of reform. Within this *lustrum mirabile* the daily press has taken the Empire by storm. Some twenty or more journals have sprung up under the shadow of the throne, and they are not gagged. They go to the length of their tether in discussing affairs of state—notwithstanding cautionary hints. Refraining from open attack, they indulge in covert criticism of the Government and its agents.

Social reforms open to ambitious editors a wide field and make amends for exclusion from the political arena. One of the most influential recently deplored the want of vitality in the old religions of the country, and, regarding their reformation as hopeless, openly advocated the adoption of Christianity. To be independent of the foreigner it must, he said, be made a state church, with one of the princes for a figurehead, if not for pilot.

Another deals with the subject of marriage. Many improvements, he says, are to be made in the legal status of woman. The total abolition of polygamy might be premature; but that is to be kept in view. In another issue he expresses a regret that the Western usage of personal courtship cannot safely be introduced. Those who are to be companions for life cannot as yet be allowed to see each other, as disorders might result from excess of freedom. Such liberty in social relations is impracticable "except in a highly refined and well-ordered state of society." The same or another writer proposes, by way of enlarging woman's world, that she shall not be confined to the house, but be allowed to circulate as freely as Western women but she must hide her charms behind a veil.

Reporting an altercation between a policeman and the driver of one of Prince Ching's carts, who insisted on driving on tracks forbidden to common people, an editor suggests with mild sarcasm that a notice be posted in such cases stating that only "noblemen's carts are allowed to pass." Do not these specimens show a laudable attempt to simulate a free press? Free it is by sufferance, though not by law.

Reading-rooms are a new institution full of promise. They are not libraries, but places for reading and expounding newspapers for the benefit of those who are unable to read for themselves. Numerous rooms may be seen at the street corners, where men are reciting the contents of a paper to an eager crowd. They have the air of wayside chapels; and this mode of enlightening the ignorant was confessedly borrowed from the missionary. How urgent the need, where among the men only one in twenty can read; and among women not one in a hundred!

Reform in writing is a genuine novelty, Chinese writing being a development of hieroglyphics, in which the sound is no index to the sense, and in which each pictorial form must be separately made familiar to the eye. Dr. Medhurst wittily calls it "an occulage, not a language." Without the introduction of alphabetic writing, the art of reading can never become general. To meet this want a new alphabet of fifty letters has been invented, and a society organised to push the system, so that the common people, also women, may soon be able to read the papers for themselves. The author of the system is Wang Chao, mentioned above as having given occasion for the *coup d'état* by which the Dowager Empress was restored to power in 1898.

I close this formidable list of reforms with a few words on a society for the abolition of a usage which makes Chinese women the laughing-stock of the world, namely, the binding of their feet. With the minds of her daughters cramped by ignorance, and their feet crippled by the tyranny of an absurd fashion, China suffers an immense loss, social and economic. Happily there are now indications that the proposed enfranchisement will meet with general favour. Lately I heard mandarins of high rank advocate this cause in the hearing of a large concourse at Shanghai. They have given a pledge that there shall be no more foot-binding in their families; and the Dowager Empress came to the support of the cause with a hortatory edict. As in this matter she dared not prohibit, she was limited to persuasion and example. Tartar women have their powers of locomotion unimpaired. Viceroy Chang denounced the fashion as tending to sap the vigour of China's mothers; and he is reported to have suggested a tax on small feet—in inverse proportion to their size, of course. The leader in this movement, which bids fair to become national, is Mrs. Archibald Little.

The streets are patrolled by a well-dressed and well-armed police force, in strong contrast with the ragged, negligent watchmen of yore. The Chinese, it seems, are in earnest about mending their ways. Their streets, in Peking and other cities, are undergoing thorough repair—so that broughams and rickshaws are beginning to take the place of carts and palanquins. A foreign style of building is winning favour; and the adoption of foreign dress is talked of. When these changes come, what will be left of this queer antique?

CHAPTER XXX

VICEROY CHANG-A LEADER OF REFORM

His Origin—Course as a Student—In the Censorate—He Floors a Magnate—The First to Wake Up—As a Leader of Reform—The Awakening of the Giant

If I were writing of Chang, the Chinese giant, who overtopped the tallest of his fellow-men by head and shoulders, I should be sure of readers. Physical phenomena attract attention more than mental or moral grandeur. Is it not because greatness in these higher realms requires patient thought for due appreciation?

Chang, the viceroy of Hukwang, a giant in intellect and a hero in achievement, is not a commonplace character. If my readers will follow me, while I trace his rise and progress, not only will they discover that he stands head and shoulders above most officials of his rank, but they will gain important side-lights on great events in recent history.

During my forty years' residence in the capital I had become well acquainted with Chang's brilliant career; but it is only within the last three or four years that I have had an opportunity to study him in personal intercourse, having been called to preside over his university and to aid him in other educational enterprises.

Whatever may be thought of the rank and file of China's mandarins, her viceroys are nearly always men of exceptional ability. They are never novices, but as a rule old in years and veterans in experience. Promoted for executive talent or for signal services, their office is too high to be in the market; nor is it probable that money can do much to recommend a candidate. A governor of Kwangsi was recently dismissed for incompetence, or for ill-success against a body of rebels. Being a rich man, he made a free use of that argument which commonly proves effective at Peking. But, so far from being advanced to the viceroyalty, he was not even reinstated in his original rank. The most he was able to obtain by a lavish expenditure was the inspectorship of a college at Wuchang, to put his foot on one of the lower rounds of the official ladder.

Chang was never rich enough to buy official honours, even in the lower grades; and it is one of his chief glories that, after a score of years in the exercise of viceregal power, he continues to be relatively poor.

His name in full is Chang Chi-tung, meaning "Longbow of the Cavern," an allusion to a tradition that one of his ancestors was born in a cave and famed for archery. This was far back in the age of the troglodytes. Now, for many generations, the family has been devoted to the peaceful pursuit of letters. As for Chang himself, it will be seen with what deadly effect he has been able to use the pen, in his hands a more formidable weapon than the longbow of his ancestor.

Chang was born at Nanpi, in the metropolitan province of Chihli, not quite seventy years ago; and that circumstance debarred him from holding the highest viceroyalty in the Empire, as no man is permitted to hold office in his native place. He has climbed to his present eminence without the extraneous aids of wealth and family influence. This implies talents of no ordinary grade; but how could those talents have found a fit arena without that admirable system of literary competition which for so many centuries has served the double purpose of extending patronage to letters and of securing the fittest men for the service of the state.

Crowned with the laurel of A. B., or budding genius, before he was out of his teens, three years later he won the honour of A. M., or, as the Chinese say, he plucked a sprig of the *olea fragrans* in a contest with his fellow-provincials in which only one in a hundred gained a prize. Proceeding to the imperial capital he entered the lists against the picked scholars of all the provinces. The prizes were 3 per cent. of the whole number of competitors, and he gained the doctorate in letters, which, as the Chinese title indicates, assures its possessor of an official appointment. Had he been content to wait for some obscure position he might have gone home to sleep on his laurels. But his restless spirit saw fresh battle-fields beckoning him to fresh triumphs. The three hundred new-made doctors were summoned to the palace to write on themes assigned by the Emperor, that His Majesty might select a score of them for places in the Hanlin Academy. Here again fortune favoured young Chang; the elegance of his penmanship and his skill in composing mechanical verse were so remarkable that he secured a seat on the literary Olympus of the Empire.

His conflicts were not yet ended. A conspicuous advantage of his high position was that it qualified him as a candidate for membership of the Board of Censors. Nor did fortune desert her favourite in this instance. After writing several papers to show his knowledge of law, history, and politics, he came forth clothed with powers that made him formidable to the highest officers of the state—powers somewhat analogous to the combined functions of censor and tribune in ancient Rome.

Before I proceed to show how our "knight of the longbow" employed his new authority, a few words on the constitution of that august tribunal, the Board of Censors, may prove interesting to the reader. Its members are not judges, but prosecuting attorneys for the state. They are accorded a freedom of speech which extends even to pointing out the shortcomings of majesty. How important such a tribunal for a country in which a newspaper press with its argus eyes has as yet no existence! There is indeed a court *Gazette*, which has been called the oldest newspaper in the world; but its contents are strictly limited to decrees, memorials, and appointments. Free discussion and general news have no place in its columns; so that in the modern sense it is not a newspaper.

The court—even the occupant of the Dragon Throne—needs watch-dogs.

Such is the theory; but as a matter of fact these guardians of official morals find it safer to occupy themselves with the aberrations of satellites than to discover spots on the sun. About thirty years ago one of them, Wukotu, resolved to denounce the Empress Dowager for having adopted the late emperor as her son instead of making him her grandson. He accordingly immolated himself at the tomb of the late emperor by way of protesting against the impropriety of leaving him without a direct heir to worship his manes. It is doubtful whether the Western mind is capable of following Wukotu's subtle reasoning; but is it not plain that he felt that he was provoking an ignominious death, and chose rather to die as a hero—the champion of his deceased master?

If a censor succeeds in convicting a single high functionary of gross misconduct his fortune is made. He is rewarded by appointment to some respectable post, possibly the same from which his victim has been evicted. Practical advantage carries the day against abstract notions of æsthetic fitness. Sublime it might be to see the guardians of the common weal striking down the unworthy, with a public spirit untainted by self-interest; but in China (and in some other countries) such machinery requires self-interest for its motive force. Wanting that, it would be like a windmill without wind, merely a fine object in the landscape.

As an illustration of the actual procedure take the case in which Chang first achieved a national reputation. Chunghau, a Manchu of noble family and high in favour at court, had been sent to Russia in 1880 to demand the restoration of Ili, a province of Chinese Turkestan, which the Russians had occupied on pretext of quelling its chronic disorders. Scarcely had he reported the success of his mission, which had resulted in recovering two-thirds of the disputed territory, when Chang came forward and denounced it as worse than a failure. He had, as Chang proved, permitted the Russians to retain certain strategic points, and had given them fertile districts in exchange for rugged mountains or arid plains. To such a settlement no envoy could be induced to consent, unless chargeable with corruption or incompetence.

The unlucky envoy was thrown into prison and condemned to death (but reprieved), and his accuser rose in the official scale as rapidly as if he had won a great battle on land or sea. His victory was not unlike that of those British orators who made a reputation out of the impeachment of Lord Clive or Warren Hastings, save that with him a trenchant pen took the place of an eloquent tongue. I knew Chunghau both before and after his disgrace. In 1859, when an American embassy for the first time entered the gates of Peking, it was Chunghau who was appointed to escort the minister to the capital and back again to the seacoast—a pretty long journey in those days when there was neither steamboat nor railway. During that time, acting as interpreter, I had occasion to see him every day, and I felt strongly attracted by his generous and gentlemanly bearing. The poor fellow came out of prison stripped of all his honours, and with his prospects blighted forever. In a few months he died of sheer chagrin.

The war with Japan in 1894-1895 found Chang established in the viceroyalty of Hukwang, two provinces in Central China, with a prosperous population of over fifty millions, on a great highway of internal traffic rivalling the Mississippi, and with Hankow, the hub of the Empire, for its commercial centre. When he saw the Chinese forces scattered like chaff by the battalions of those despised islanders he was not slow to grasp the explanation. Kang Yuwei, a Canton man, also grasped it, and urged on the Emperor the necessity for reform with such vigour as to prompt him to issue a meteoric shower of reformatory edicts, filling one party with hope and the other with dismay.

Viceroy Chang

Chang had held office at Canton; and his keen intellect had taken in the changed relations of West and East. He perceived that a new sort of sunshine shed its beams on the Western world. He did not fully apprehend the spiritual elements of our civilisation; but he saw that it was clothed with a power unknown to the sages of his country, the forces of nature being brought into subjection through science and popular education. He felt that China must conform to the new order of things, or perish—even if that new order was in contradiction to her ancient traditions as much as the change of sunrise to the west. He saw and felt that knowledge is power, a maxim laid down by Confucius before the days of Bacon; and he set about inculcating his new ideas by issuing a series of lectures for the instruction of his subordinates. Collected into a volume under the title of "Exhortations to Learn,"[18] they were put into the hands of the young Emperor and by his command distributed among the viceroys and governors of the Empire.

What a harvest might have sprung from the sowing of such seed in such soil by an imperial husbandman! But there were some who viewed it as the sowing of dragons' teeth. Those reactionaries induced the Dowager Empress to come out from her retirement and to reassume her abdicated power in order to save the Empire from a threatening conflagration. It was the fable of Phaëton enacted in real life. The young charioteer was struck down and the sun brought back to his proper course instead of rising in the west. The progressive legislation of the two previous years 1897-98 was repealed and then followed two years of a narrow, benighted policy, controlled by the reactionaries under the lead of Prince Tuan, father of the heir-apparent, with a junta of Manchu princes as blind and corrupt as Russian grand dukes. That disastrous recoil resulted in war, not against a single power, but against the whole civilised world, as has been set forth in the account of the Boxer War (see page 172).

Affairs were drifting into this desperate predicament when Chang of the Cavern became in a sense the saviour of his country. This he effected by two actions which called for uncommon intelligence and moral force: (1) By assuring the British Government that he would at all costs maintain peace in Central China; (2) by refusing to obey an inhuman decree from Peking, commanding the viceroys to massacre all foreigners within their jurisdiction—a decree which would be incredible were it not known that at the same moment the walls of the capital were placarded with proclamations offering rewards of 50, 30 and 20 taels respectively for the heads of foreign men, women, and children.

It is barely possible that Chang was helped to a decision by a friendly visit from a British man-of-war, whose captain, in answer to a question about his artillery, informed Chang that he had the bearings of his official residence, and could drop a shell into it with unerring precision at a distance of three miles. He was also aided by the influence of Mr. Fraser, a wide-awake British consul. Fraser modestly disclaims any special merit in the matter, but British missionaries at Hankow give him the credit. They say that, learning from them the state of feeling among the people, he induced the viceroy to take prompt measures to prevent an outbreak. At one time a Boxer army from the south was about to cross the river and destroy the foreign settlement. Chang, when appealed to, frankly confessed that his troops were in sympathy with the Boxers, and that being in arrears of pay they were on the verge of revolt. Fraser found him the money by the help of the Hong Kong

---

[18] Translated by Dr. Woodbridge as "China's Only Hope." Kelly & Walsh, Shanghai.

Bank; the troops were paid; and the Boxers dispersed.

The same problem confronted Liu, the viceroy of Nanking; and it was solved by him in the same way. Both viceroys acted in concert; but to which belongs the honour of that wise initiative can never be decided with certainty. The foreign consuls at Nanking claim it for Liu. Mr. Sundius, now British consul at Wuhu, assures me that as Liu read the barbarous decree he exclaimed, "I shall repudiate this as a forgery," adding "I shall not obey, if I have to die for it." His words have a heroic ring; and suggest that his policy was not taken at second-hand.

A similar claim has been put forward for Li Hung Chang, who was at that time viceroy at Canton. Is it not probable that the same view of the situation flashed on the minds of all three simultaneously? They were not, like the Peking princes, ignorant Tartars, but Chinese scholars of the highest type. They could not fail to see that compliance with that bloody edict would seal their own doom as well as that of the Empire.

Speaking of Chang, Mr. Fraser says: "He had the wit to see that any other course meant ruin." Chang certainly does not hesitate to blow his own trumpet; but I do not suspect him of "drawing the longbow." Having the advantage of being an expert rhymer, he has put his own pretensions into verses which all the school-children in a population of fifty millions are obliged to commit to memory. They run somewhat like this:

> "In Kengtse (1900) the Boxer robbers went mad,
> And Peking became for the third time the prey of fire and sword;
> But the banks of the Great River and the province of Hupei
> Remained in tranquillity."

He adds in a tone of exultation:

> "The province of Hupei was accordingly exempted
> From the payment of an indemnity tax,
> And allowed to spend the amount thus saved
> In the erection of schoolhouses."

In these lines there is not much poetry; but the fact which they commemorate adds one more wreath to a brow already crowned with many laurels, showing how much the viceroy's heart was set on the education of his people.

In the interest of the educational movement, I was called to Chang's assistance in 1902. The Imperial University was destroyed in the Boxer War, and, seeing no prospect of its reëstablishment I was on the way to my home in America when, on reaching Vancouver, I found a telegram from Viceroy Chang, asking me to be president of a university which he proposed to open, and to instruct his junior officials in international law. I engaged for three years; and I now look back on my recent campaign in Central China as one of the most interesting passages in a life of over half a century in the Far East.

Besides instructing his mandarins in the law of nations, I had to give them some notion of geography and history, the two coördinates of time and place, without which they might, like some of their writers, mistake Rhode Island for the Island of Rhodes, and Rome, New York, for the City of the Seven Hills. A book on the Intercourse of Nations and a translation of Dudley Field's "International Code," remain as tangible results of those lectures. But the university failed to materialise.

Within a month after my arrival the viceroy was ordered to remove to Nanking to take up a post rendered vacant by the death of his eminent colleague, Liu. Calling at my house on the eve of embarking he said, "I asked you to come here to be president of a university for two provinces. If you will go with me to Nanking, I will make you president of a university for five provinces," meaning that he would combine the educational interests of the two viceroyalties, and showing how the university scheme had expanded in his fertile brain.

Before he had been a month at that higher post he learned to his intense disappointment that he was only to hold the place for another appointee. After nearly a year at Nanking, he was summoned to Peking, where he spent another year in complete uncertainty as to his future destination. In the meantime the university existed only on paper. In justice to the viceroy I ought to say that nothing could exceed the courtesy and punctuality with which he discharged his obligations to me. The despatch which once a month brought me my stipend was always addressed to me as president of the Wuchang University, though as a matter of fact I might as well have been styled president of the University of Weissnichtwo. In one point he went beyond his agreement, viz., in giving me free of charge a furnished house of two stories, with ten rooms and a garden. It was on the bank of the "Great River" with the picturesque hills of Hanyang nearly opposite, a site which I preferred to any other in the city. I there enjoyed the purest air with a minimum of inconvenience from narrow, dirty streets. To these exceptional advantages it is doubtless due that my health held out, notwithstanding the heat of the climate, which, the locality being far inland and in lat. 30° 30′, was that of a fiery furnace. On the night of the autumnal equinox, my first in Wuchang, the mercury stood in my bedroom at 102°. I was the guest of the Rev. Arnold Foster of the London Missionary Society, whose hospitality was warm in more ways than one.

The viceroy returned from Peking, broken in health; the little strength he had left was given to military preparation for the contingencies of the Russo-Japanese War; and his university was consigned to the limbo of forgotten dreams.

Viceroy Chang has been derided, not quite justly, as possessing a superabundance of initiative along with a rather scant measure of finality, taking up and throwing down his new schemes as a child does its playthings. In these enterprises the paucity of results was due to the shortcomings of the agents to whom he entrusted their management. The same reproach and the same apology might be made for the Empress Dowager who, like the Roman Sybil, committed her progressive decrees to the mercy of the winds without seeming to care what became of them.

Next after the education of his people the development of their material resources has been with Chang a leading object. To this end he has opened cotton-mills, silk-filatures, glass-works and iron-works, all on an extensive scale, with foreign machinery and foreign experts. For miles outside of the gates of Wuchang the banks of the river are lined with these vast establishments. Do they not announce more clearly than the batteries which command the waterway the coming of a new China? Some of them he has kept going at an annual loss. The cotton-mill, for example, was standing idle when I arrived, because in the hands of his mandarins he could not make it pay expenses. A Canton merchant leased it on easy terms, and made it such a conspicuous success that he is now growing rich. It is an axiom in China that no manufacturing or mercantile enterprise can be profitably conducted by a deputation of mandarins.

Chang is rapidly changing the aspect of his capital by erecting in all parts of it handsome school-buildings in foreign style, literally proclaiming from the house-tops his gospel of education. The youth in these schools are mostly clad in foreign dress; his street police and the soldiers in his barracks are all in foreign uniform; and many of the latter have cut off their cues as a sign of breaking with the old régime. In talking with their officers I applauded the prudence of the measure as making them less liable to be captured while running away.

Chang's soldiers are taught to march to the cadence of his own war-songs—which, though lacking the fire of Tyrtæus or Körner, are not ill-suited to arouse patriotic sentiment. Take these lines as a sample:

> "Foreigners laugh at our impotence,
> And talk of dividing our country like a watermelon,
> But are we not 400 million strong?
> If we of the Yellow Race only stand together,
> What foreign power will dare to molest us?
> Just look at India, great in extent
> But sunk in hopeless bondage.
> Look, too, at the Jews, famous in ancient times,
> Now scattered on the face of the earth.
> Then look at Japan with her three small islands,
> Think how she got the better of this great nation,
> And won the admiration of the world.
> What I admire in the Japanese
> Is not their skill in using ship or gun
> But their single-hearted love of country."

Viceroy Chang's mode of dealing with his own malady might be taken as a picture of the shifting policy of a half-enlightened country.

The first doctor he consulted was a Chinese of the old school. Besides administering pills composed of

> "Eye of newt, and toe of frog,
> Wool of bat, and tongue of dog,"

the doctor suggested that one thing was still required to put the patient in harmony with the course of Nature. Pointing to a fine chain of hills that stretches in a waving line across the wide city, he said: "The root of your trouble lies there. That carriage-road that you have opened has wounded the spinal column of the serpent. Restore the hill to its former condition and you will soon get well."

The viceroy filled the gap incontinently, but found himself no better. He then sent for English and American doctors—dismissing them in turn to make way for a Japanese who had him in charge when I left Wuchang. For a paragon of intelligence and courage, how pitiful this relapse into superstition! Did not China after a trial of European methods also relapse during the Boxer craze into her old superstitions? And is she not at this moment taking the medicine of Japan? To Japan she looks for guidance in the conduct of her public schools as well as for the training of her army and navy. To Japan she is sending her sons and daughters in growing numbers. No fewer than eight thousand of her young men, and, what is more significant, one or two hundred of her young women from the best families are now in those islands inhaling the breath of a new life.

Some writers have sounded a note of alarm in consequence of this wholesale surrender on the part of China. But for my part I have no fear of any sinister tendency in the teachings of Japan, whether political or educational. On a memorable occasion twelve years ago, when Marquis Ito was entertained at a banquet in Peking by the governor of the city and the chancellor of the Imperial University, I congratulated him on the fact that "Japan exerts a stronger influence on China than any Western power—just as the moon raises a higher tide than the more distant sun"—implying, what the Japanese are ready enough to admit, that their country shines by borrowed light.

After all, the renovating effect, for which I look to them, will not come so much from their teaching as from their example. "What is to hinder us from doing what those islanders have done?" is an argument oft reiterated by Viceroy Chang in his appeals to his drowsy countrymen. It was, as I have said, largely under his influence that the Emperor was led to adopt a new educational programme twelve years ago. Nor can there be a doubt that by his influence more than that of any other man, the Empress Dowager was induced to reenact and to enlarge that programme.

To show what is going on in this very decade: On September 3, 1905, an edict was issued "abolishing the literary competitive examinations of the old style," and ordering that "hereafter exclusive attention shall be given to the establishment of schools of modern learning throughout the Empire in lieu thereof." The next day a supplementary decree ordained that the provincial chancellors or examiners who, like Othello, found their occupation gone, should have the duty of examining and inspecting the schools in their several provinces; and, to give the new arrangement greater weight, it was required that they "discharge this duty in conjunction with the viceroy or governor of the province."

An item of news that came along with these decrees seemed to indicate that a hitherto frivolous court has at length become thoroughly in earnest on the subject of education. A sum of 300,000 taels appeared in the national budget as the annual expense of a theatrical troupe in attendance on the Court. At the instance of two ministers (Viceroy Yuan and General Tieliang) Her Majesty reduced this to one-third of that amount, ordering that theatricals should be performed twice a week instead of daily; and that the 200,000 taels thus economised shall be set apart for *the use of schools*. How much this resembles the policy of Viceroy Chang who, exempted from raising a war indemnity, set apart an equal amount for the building of schoolhouses! An empire that builds schoolhouses is more certain to make a figure in the world than one that spends its money on batteries and forts.

In addition to adopting the new education there are three items which Chang proclaims as essential to a renovation of Chinese society. In the little book, already cited, he says:

> The crippling of women makes their offspring weak;
> The superstition of *Fungshui* prevents the opening of mines,
> And keeps China poor."

How could the man who wrote this fall back into the folly of *Fungshui?* Is it not possible that he closed that new road in deference to the superstitions of his people? In either case it would be a deplorable weakness; but his country, thanks to his efforts, is now fully committed to progress. She moves, however, in that direction much as her noble rivers move toward the sea—with many a backward bend, many a refluent eddy.

POSTSCRIPT NO. I

In taking leave of this eminent man, who represents the best class of his countrymen, there are two or three incidents, which I mention by way of supplement. In his telegram to Vancouver, besides engaging me to assume the office of president of the proposed university, he asked me to act as his legal and political adviser. In the agreement formally made through the consul in New York, in place of these last-named functions was substituted the duty of instructing his junior mandarins in international law. The reason assigned for the change was that the Peking Government declined to allow *any foreigner* to hold the post of adviser. The objection was represented as resting on general policy, not on personal grounds. If, however, the Peking officials had read my book on the Siege, in which I denounce the treachery of Manchu government and favour the position of China, it is quite conceivable that their objection might have a tinge of personality.

When Viceroy Chang was starting for Peking, I called to see him on board his steamer. He held in his hand a printed report of my opening lecture at the beginning of a new term, and expressed regret that in the hurry of departure he had been unable to find time to attend in person. On that occasion (the previous day) several of his higher officials, including the treasurer, judge, and prefect, after giving me tiffin at the Mandarin Institute, brought sixty junior officials to make their salaam to their instructor. This ceremony performed, I bowed to Their Excellencies, and requested them to leave me with my students. "No," they replied, "we too are desirous of hearing you"; and they took seats in front of the platform.

Viceroy Chang seems to have manifested some jealousy of Sir Robert Hart, in criticising the Inspector-General's proposal for a single tax. He likewise criticised unfavourably the scheme of Professor Jenckes for unifying the currency of the Empire—influenced, perhaps, by the fear that such an *innovation* might impair the usefulness of a costly plant which he has recently erected for minting both silver and copper coin. For the same reason perhaps he objects, as I hear he does, to the proposed engagement of a Cornell professor by the Board of Revenue in the capacity of financial adviser.

With all his foibles, however, he is a true patriot; and his influence has done much to move China in the right direction. O for more men like Chang, the "Long-bow of the Cavern!"

I append a weighty document that is not the less interesting for being somewhat veiled in mystery. I regret that I am not at liberty to disclose its authorship. The report is to be taken as anonymous, being an unpublished document of the secret service. To the reader it is left to divine the nationality and personality of its author. Valuable for the light it throws on a great character in a trying situation, the report gains piquancy and interest from the fact that the veil of official secrecy has to be treated with due respect. My unnamed friend has my thanks and deserves those of my readers.

OFFICIAL INTERVIEWS WITH VICEROY CHANG DURING THE CRISIS OF 1900

"At our interview of 17th June, described at length in my despatch to you of 18th June, the Viceroy explained his determination to maintain order and to afford the protection due under treaty; he also emphasised his desire to be on friendly terms with England.

"Early in June, the three cities of Wuchang, Hanyang and Hankow had been full of rumours of the kidnapping of children and even grown persons by means of hypnotism; and though a concise notification by the Viceroy, that persons spreading such tales would be executed, checked its prevalence here, the scare spread to the country districts and inflamed the minds of the people against foreigners and, in consequence, against converts and missions.

"On the 25th June, the Viceroy, as reported in a separate despatch of 28th June, to Lord Salisbury, sent a special envoy to assure me that H. E. would not accept or act upon any anti-foreign decrees from Peking. At the same time he communicated copy of a telegraphic memorial from himself and seven other high provincial officers insisting on the suppression of the Boxers and the maintenance of peace. This advice H. E. gave me to understand led to the recall of Li Hung Chang to the north as negotiator.

"Distorted accounts of the capture of the Taku forts and the hostilities of the north caused some excitement, but the Viceroy's proclamation of 2nd July, copy of which was forwarded in my despatch of 3rd July to the Foreign Office, and the vigorous police measures taken by His Excellency soon restored calm which, despite occasional rumours, continued until the recent plot and scare reported in my despatch to you of 23rd of August. In the same despatch I described how, in compliance with my wish, H. E. took the unprecedented step of tearing down his proclamation embodying an Imperial Decree which had been taken to imply license to harry converts. To foreigners during the past two months the question of interest has been whether the Viceroy could and would keep his troops in order. The Viceroy himself seemed to be in some doubt until the return of his trusted officers, who were attending the Japanese manœuvres when the northern troubles began. Every now and then reports of disaffection have been industriously circulated, but the drilled troops have never shown any sign of disloyalty.

"A point of H. E.'s policy which has caused considerable suspicion is the despatch of troops northward, At the end of June some 2,000 or 3,000 men passed through Hankow bound for Nyanking where the Governor was said to want a body-guard. They were unarmed and did no mischief beyond invading the Customs and China Merchants' Steam Navigation Company's premises. During July some 5,000 troops, of whom perhaps half were drilled men, went from Hukeang provinces overland to Honan and on to Chihli. They were led by the anti-foreign Treasurer of Hunan; and their despatch was explained by the constitutional duty of succouring the Emperor. Since July I have not heard of any further detachments leaving, though it was said that the total would reach 10,000. Possibly the Viceroy sent the men because he did not feel strong enough to defy Peking altogether, because failure to help the court would have excited popular reprobation, and also in order to get rid of a considerable part of the dangerous 'loafer' class.

"About the 20th July there was a persistent report that the Viceroy was secretly placing guns on the opposite banks of the river. The German military instructors assured me that the report was baseless; and Lieutenant Brandon, H. M. S. *Pique*, thoroughly searched the bank for a distance of three miles in length and breadth, without discovering a trace of a cannon. The only guns in position are the two 5-inch Armstrong M. L. within the walls of Wuchang, and they have been there for a long time and are used 'merely for training purposes.'

"So early as our interview of June 17th, the Viceroy expressed anxiety as to missionaries at remote points in the interior; and I had about that time suggested to the various missions that women and children would be better at a treaty port. The missions themselves preferred to recall all their members, and at the Viceroy's request supplied lists of the stations thus left to the care of the local authorities. Since then, even in Hupeh, there have been a few cases of plundering, especially in the large district of Sin Chan on the Hunan border, while at Hangchow-fu, in Hunan, the London Mission premises were wrecked early in July and for a time throughout the whole province it appeared probable that the Missions would be destroyed. The chief cause of this, as of the riots in Hupeh, was the dissemination of an alleged decree of 26th June praising the Boxers and ordering the authorities to imitate the north in exterminating foreigners. This decree seems to have reached local authorities direct; and those hostile to foreigners acted upon it or let its existence be known to the gentry and people. The chapels in Hunan were all sealed up; and it was understood that all mission and convert property would be confiscated. Towards the end of July, however, the Viceroy and the Hunan Governor issued a satisfactory proclamation, and I have heard no more complaints from that province, the western part of which seems tranquil.

"Besides safeguarding foreign life and property in his own province the Viceroy has frequently been asked to aid missionaries retiring from Kansuh, Shensi,

Shansi, and Honan. In every case H. E. has readily consented. Detailed telegrams have been sent again and again not only to his frontier officers, but to the governors of other provinces with whom H. E. has expostulated, when necessary, in strong terms. Thus, when Honan seemed likely to turn against us, the Viceroy insisted on the publication of favourable decrees, and even went so far as to send his men to establish a permanent escort depot at Ching Tzu Kuan, an important post in Honan where travellers from the north and northwest have to change from cart to boat. Happily the acting Governor of Shensi has coöperated nobly. But the refugees who testify invariably to the marvellous feeling of security engendered by reaching Hupeh, will, I doubt not, agree that they owe their lives to Chang Chi-tung's efforts; for simple inaction on his part would have encouraged the many hostile officers to treat them as Shansi has treated its missionaries.

"At times during the past two anxious months the Viceroy's action in sending troops north, the occurrence of riots at various points, H. E.'s communication of decrees in which the Peking Government sought to gloss over the northern uprising, and his eagerness to make out that the Empress Dowager had not incited the outbreak and had no hostile feeling against foreigners have inevitably made one uneasy. But on looking back one appreciates the skill and constancy with which H. E. has met a most serious crisis and done his duty to Chinese and foreigners alike. It is no small thing for a Chinese statesman and scholar to risk popularity, position, and even life in a far-seeing resistance to the apparent decrees of a court to which his whole training enforces blind loyalty and obedience. His desire to secure the personal safety of the Empress Dowager on account of her long services to the Empire is natural enough; nor need he be blamed for supplying some military aid to his sovereign, even though he may have guessed that it would be used against those foreign nations with whom he himself steadfastly maintains friendship and against whose possible attack he has not mounted an extra gun."

POSTSCRIPT NO.2

TUAN FANG OF THE HIGH COMMISSION

During Chang's long absence, Tuan Fang, Governor of Hupeh, held the seals and exercised the functions of viceroy. He was a Manchu—one of those specimens, admirable but not rare, who, in acquiring the refinement of Chinese culture, lose nothing of the vigour of their own race. "Of their own race," I say, because in language and habits the Manchus are strongly differentiated from their Chinese subjects.

In the Boxer War Governor Tuan established an excellent record. Acting as governor in Shensi, instead of killing missionaries, as did the Manchu governor of the next province, he protected them effectually and sent them safely to Hankow. One day when I was at his house a missionary came to thank him for kindness shown on that occasion.

Mentioning one of my books I once asked him if he had read it. "You never wrote a book that I have not read," was his emphatic reply. He was a pretty frequent visitor at my house, punctually returning all my calls; and when he was transferred to the governorship of Hunan he appeared pleased to have the Yale Mission commended to his patronage. He has a son at school in the United States; and his wife and daughters have taken lessons in English from ladies of the American Episcopal Mission.

Governor Tuan (now viceroy) is a leading member of a commission recently sent abroad to study and report on the institutions of the Western world. Its departure was delayed by the explosion of a bomb in one of the carriages just as the commission was leaving Peking. The would-be assassin was "hoist with his own petard," leaving the public mystified as to the motive of the outrage.

Tuan Fang, Viceroy of Nanking

CHAPTER XXXI

ANTI-FOREIGN AGITATION

American Influence in the Far East — Officials and the Boycott — Interview with President Roosevelt — Riot in a British Concession — Ex-territoriality — Two Ways to an End — A Grave Mistake — The Nan-chang Tragedy — Dangers from Superstition

So far from being new, an anti-foreign spirit is the normal state of the Chinese mind. Yet during the year past it has taken on new forms, directed itself against new objects, and employed new methods. It deserves therefore a conspicuous place among the new developments in the China of the twentieth century.

Where everything is changing, the temper of the people has undergone a change. They have become restless as the sea and fickle as a weather-vane, The friends of yesterday are the enemies of to-day; and a slight or petty annoyance is enough to make them transfer man or country from one to the other category. Murderous outbreaks, rare in the past, have now become alarmingly frequent, so much so that the last year might be described as a year of anti-foreign riots. The past nine months have witnessed four such outbreaks, In four widely separated provinces, venting their fury pretty impartially on people of four nationalities and of all professions, they were actuated by a common hate and indicated a common purpose. That purpose — if they had a purpose — was to compel a readjustment of treaty relations.

America has the distinction of being the target for the first assaults. In treating the subject I accordingly begin with America and the boycott, as set forth in a long extract from an address before the Publishers' League of New York, November 8, 1905, on

AMERICAN INFLUENCE IN THE FAR EAST

"Mr. President and Gentlemen:

"If I were asked to find a *pou sto*, a fulcrum, on which to erect a machine to move the world, I should choose this league of publishers; and the machine would be no other than the power press! I have accepted your invitation not merely from pleasant recollections of your former hospitality, but because new occurrences have taken place which appeal to the patriotism of every good citizen. They are issues that rise above party; they involve our national character and the well-being of another people whom we owe the sacred duties of justice and humanity.

"When I agreed to speak to you of American influence in the Far East, I was not aware that we should have with us a representative of Japan, and I expected to spread myself thinly over two empires. Happy I am to resign one of these empires to Mr. Stevens.

"I shall accordingly say no more about Japan than to advert to the fact that the wise forbearance of Commodore Perry, which, in 1854, induced the Shogun to open his ports without firing a gun, has won the gratitude of the Japanese people; so that in many ways they testify a preference for us and our country. For instance, they call the English language 'Americano,' etc. They were disappointed that their claims against Russia were not backed up by the United States. That, however, caused only a momentary cloud. Beyond this, nothing has ever occurred to mar the harmony of the two peoples who face each other on the shores of the Pacific. Perry's wise initiative was followed by the equal wisdom of Townsend Harris, who, before any other consul or minister had arrived, was invited to Yedda to give advice to the government of the Shogun.

"American influence thus inaugurated has been fostered by a noble army of ministers, consuls, and missionaries. The total absence of massacres and murders[19] makes the history of our intercourse with Japan tame in contrast with the tragic story from China. It speaks the reign of law.

"My acquaintance with Japan dates back forty-six years; and in the meantime I have had pleasant relations with most of the ministers she has sent to China. One of her officials recently gave me a beautiful scarf-pin that speaks volumes for American influence, showing as it does the two flags in friendly union on one flagstaff. I gave him in return the following lines:

> "'To sun and stars divided sway!
> Remote but kindred suns are they,
> In friendly concord here they twine
> To form a new celestial sign.
>
> "'Thou, Orient sun, still higher rise
> To fill with light the Eastern skies!
> And you, ye stars and stripes, unfurled
> Shed glory on the Western world!
>
> "'Our starry flag first woke the dawn
> In the empire of the Rising Sun.
> May no ill chance e'er break the tie,
> And so we shout our loud *banzai!*'

"I now turn to the less cheering theme of American influence in China. It reminds me of the naturalist who took for the heading of a chapter 'Snakes in Iceland,' and whose entire chapter consisted of the words 'There are no snakes in Iceland.' Though formerly blazing like a constellation in the Milky Way, American influence has vanished so completely that you can hardly see it with a microscope. What influence can we presume on when our commodities are shut out, not by legislative action but as a result of popular resentment?

[19] The only missionary killed in the last fifty years was stabbed while grappling with a burglar.

THE BOYCOTT

"True, the latest advices are to the effect that the boycott has broken down. I foresaw and foretold more than two months ago that it could not in the nature of the case be of long duration, that it was a mere *ballon d'essai*—an encouraging proof that Orientals are learning to apply our methods. But is there not a deplorable difference between the conditions under which it is used in the two countries? In one the people all read, and the newspaper is in everybody's hand. The moment a strike or boycott is declared off all hands fall into their places and things go on as usual. In the other the readers are less than one in twenty. Newspapers, away from the open ports, are scarcely known, or if they exist they are subject to the tyranny of the mandarins or the terrorism of the mob. Hence a war may be waged in one province and people in another may scarcely hear of it. Chevaux-de-frise may bar out goods from one port, while they are more or less openly admitted in other ports. Not only so, the hostile feeling engendered by such conflict of interest is not dissipated by sunshine, but rankles and spreads like an epidemic over vast regions unenlightened by newspapers or by contact with foreign commerce.

"Witness the massacre of American missionaries at Lienchow in the Canton province. I am not going to enter into the details of that shocking atrocity, nor to dwell on it further than to point out that although the boycott was ended on September 14, the people in that district were in such a state of exasperation that the missionaries felt themselves in danger fourteen days after that date. In the New York *Sun* of November 5 I find part of a letter from one of the victims, the Reverend Mr. Peale, written exactly one month before the tragedy. Allow me to read it along with an introductory paragraph.

"'PRINCETON, N. J., Nov. 4.—A. Lee Wilson, a student in the Princeton Theological Seminary, received a letter a few days ago from John R. Peale, the missionary who, with his wife, was killed in Lienchow, China, on October 28. The letter was dated September 28, and reached America at the time that Peale and his wife were murdered. It gives a clue to the troubles which led to the death of Peale. The letter says in part:

"'"'The interest in the boycott is vital to the missionaries. Heretofore the Americans always enjoyed special favour, and to fly the American flag meant protection; but it is different now. No personal violence has been attempted, but the people are less cordial and more suspicious. People in China are not asking that their coolies be allowed entrance into the States, but they only ask that the Americans cease treating the Chinese with contempt and allow their merchants and students the same privileges that other foreigners receive."

"'Peale graduated from the Princeton Theological Seminary last May.

"Is it not evident that whatever spark caused the explosion, the nitro-glycerin that made it possible came from the boycott?

"Not only do they boycott ponderables such as figure at the custom-house, but they extend the taboo to things of the head and heart. The leader of the whole movement was formerly an active supporter of the International Institute, an institution which proposes to open gratuitous courses of lectures and to place Chinese men of intelligence on common ground with scholars of the West, He now opposes the International Institute because, forsooth, it is originated and conducted by Dr. Reid, a large-minded American.

"After this, will you be surprised to hear that your own publications, the best text-books for the schools of the Far East, have been put on the *index expurgatorius?* A number of such books were lately returned with the excuse that they were forbidden because they bore the stamp of an American press.

"If I should go on to say that government officials, high and low, look with satisfaction on this assertion of something like national feeling, you might reply, 'National feeling! Yes, it is a duty to cultivate that.' But do we not know how it has been fostered in China? Has not hatred of the foreigner been mistaken for patriotism, and been secretly instigated as a safeguard against foreign aggression? In this instance, however, there is no room to suspect such a motive. The movement is purely a result of provocation on our part; and it is fostered with a view to coercing our government into modifying or repealing our offensive exclusion laws. The Viceroy of Central China, with whom I have spent the last three years, is known as a pioneer of reform—a man who has done more than any other to instruct his people in their duties as well as their rights. When, on the expiration of my engagement, I was about to leave for home, the prefect of Wuchang, a Canton man, addressed me a letter begging me to plead the cause of his people with the President of the United States. That letter was referred to in an interview by the viceroy, and the request which it contained reiterated by him. He gave me a parting banquet, attended by many of his mandarins, and on that occasion the subject came up again and the same request was renewed and pressed on me from all sides. While I promised to exert myself on their behalf, let me give you a specimen of the kind of oil which I poured on their wounded feelings.

"Said I, 'Under the exasperating effect of these petty grievances your people forget what they owe to the United States. They lose sight of the danger of alienating their best friend. In the Boxer War, when Peking was captured by a combined force of eight foreign powers, who but America was the first to introduce a self-denying ordinance forbidding any power to take any portion of the Chinese territory? In this she was backed up by Great Britain; the other powers fell into line and the integrity of the Empire was assured. Again, when China was in danger of being drawn into the vortex of the Russo-Japanese war, who but America secured for her the privileges of neutrality—thus a second time protecting her national life? And now you turn against us! Is not such conduct condemned by your ancient poet who says:

"'*Ki wo siao yuen, wang wo ta teh*', etc.

(How many acts of kindness done
One small offence wipes out,
As motes obscure the shining sun
And shut his lustre out.')

"If the cause of offence be taken away there is reason to hope that the beneficent action of our country, on those two occasions so big with destiny, will be remembered, and will lead China to look to our flag as an ægis under which she may find protection in time of need. Not till then will our influence, now reduced to the vanishing-point, be integrated to its full value.

PROVOCATIONS TO A BOYCOTT

"The injuries inflicted, though trifling in comparison with the benefits conferred, are such as no self-respecting people should either perpetrate or endure. Take one example, where I could give you twenty. Two young men, both Christians, one rich, the other poor, came to the United States for education. They were detained in a prison-shed for three months, One of them, falling sick, was removed to a hospital; the other obtaining permission to visit him, they made their escape to Canada and thence back to China.

"What wonder no more students come to us and that over 8,000 are now pursuing their studies in Japan![20]

"The present irritation is, we are assured by the agitators, provoked by the outrageous treatment of the *privileged classes* (merchants, travellers, and students) and not by the exclusion of labourers, to which their government has given its assent. Yet in the growing intelligence of the Chinese a time has come when their rulers feel such discrimination as a stigma. It is not merely a just application of existing laws that Viceroy Chang and his mandarins demand. They call for the rescinding of those disgraceful prohibitions and the right to compete on equal terms with immigrants from Europe. If we show a disposition to treat the Chinese fairly, their country and their hearts will be open to us as never before. Our commerce with China will expand to vast proportions; and our flag will stand highest among those that overarch and protect the integrity of that empire."

On November 16, I was received by President Roosevelt. Running his eye over the documents (see below) which I placed in his hands he expressed himself on each point. The grievances arising from the Exclusion Laws he acknowledged to be real. He promised that they should be mitigated or removed by improvements in the mode of administration; but he held out no hope of their repeal. "We have one race problem on our hands and we don't want another," he said with emphasis. The boycott which the Chinese have resorted to as a mode of coercion he condemned as an aggravation of existing difficulties. The interruption of trade and the killing of American missionaries to which it had led made it impossible, he said, to turn over to China the surplus indemnity, as he had intended.

This response is what I expected; but it will by no means satisfy the ruling classes in China, who aim at nothing short of repeal. When I assured him the newspapers were wrong in representing the agitation as confined to labourers and merchants, adding that the highest mandarins, while formally condemning it, really give it countenance, he replied that he believed that to be the case, and reiterated the declaration that nothing is to be gained by such violent measures on the part of China.

---

[20] The conciliatory policy of President Roosevelt is bearing fruit Forty students are about to start to the United States (May, 1906).

From the Executive Mansion, I proceeded to the Chinese Legation, where I talked over the matter with the minister, Sir Chentung Liang. He was not surprised at the attitude of the President. He said the state of feeling towards China in Congress and in the entire country is improving, but that, in his opinion, it will require ten years to bring about the repeal of the Exclusion Laws.

The present hitch in negotiations comes in part from Peking, but he hoped a temporary settlement would soon be arrived at.

The papers referred to above are here appended.

LETTERS REQUESTING GOOD OFFICES
(Translation)

"To the Hon. Dr. Martin.

"Sir:

"During the last three years we have often exchanged views on the subject of education and other topics of the day; and to me it is a joy to reflect that no discordant note has ever marred our intercourse.

"In view of your learning and your long residence of forty years at our capital, besides fifteen years in other parts of China, you are regarded by us with profound respect. When we hear your words we ponder them and treasure them up as things not to be forgotten. It is by your scholarship and by your personal character that you have been able to associate with the officers and scholars of the Central Empire in harmony like this.

"Now, sir, there is a matter which we wish to bring to your attention—a matter that calls for the efforts of wise men like yourself. I refer to the exclusion of Chinese labourers. It affects our mercantile as well as our labouring population very deeply.

"We beg you to bear in mind your fifty-five years' sojourn in China and to speak a good word on our behalf to the President of the United States so as to secure the welfare of both classes.

"If through your persuasion the prohibitory regulations should be withdrawn the gratitude of our Chinese people will know no bounds; your fifty-five years of devotion to the good of China will have a fitting consummation in one day's achievement; and your name will be handed down to coming generations.

"Being old friends, I write as frankly as if we were speaking face to face.

«(Signed) LIANG TING FEN,

"Director of the Normal College for the Two Lake
"Provinces, Intendant of Circuit (Taotai), etc. etc.
"Wuchang, July 8, 1905."

The foregoing translation was made by me, and the original is attached to the copy presented to the President, for the satisfaction of any official interpreter who may desire to see it.

This letter may be regarded as expressing the sentiments of the higher officials of the Chinese Empire. It was written on the eve of my embarkation for home by a man who more than any other has a right to be looked on as spokesman for Viceroy Chang; and the following day the request was repeated by the viceroy himself. These circumstances make it a document of more than ordinary importance.

The outrageous treatment to which the privileged classes (merchants, students, and travellers) have been subjected, under cover of enforcing the Exclusion Laws, has caused a deep-rooted resentment, of which the boycott is only a superficial manifestation. That movement may not be of long duration, but it has already lasted long enough to do us no little damage.

Besides occasioning embarrassment to our trade, it has excited a feeling of hostility which it will require years of conciliatory policy to eradicate.

The letter makes no direct reference to the boycott, neither does it allude to coming negotiations; yet there can be little doubt that, in making this appeal, the writer had both in view. The viceroy and his officials are right in regarding the present as a grave crisis in the intercourse of the two countries.

Their amicable relations have never been interrupted except during a fanatical outbreak known as the "Boxer Troubles," which aimed at the expulsion of all foreigners. The leading part taken by our country in the subsequent settlement, especially in warding off the threatened dismemberment of China, added immensely to our influence. Again, on the outbreak of the Russo-Japanese conflict, which was waged mainly on Chinese territory, it was American diplomacy that secured for China the advantage of neutrality, and once more warded off a danger that menaced her existence.

Yet every spark of gratitude for these transcendent services is liable to be extinguished by the irritation caused by discrimination against her labourers and the consequent ill-treatment of other classes of her people. No argument is required to show how important it is to remove all grounds of complaint in the interest of our growing commerce.

That any sweeping alteration will be made in our existing laws, I have given my mandarin friends no reason to expect. Self-preservation stands on a higher plane than the amenities of intercourse. For many years these laws served as a bulwark without which the sparse population of our Western States would have been swamped by the influx of Asiatics. In early days it was easier for the Chinese to cross the ocean than for the people of our Eastern States to cross the Continent. Now, however, the completion of railroads has reduced the continental transit to five or six days, in lieu of many months; and the population of our Pacific Coast is so considerable that there is no longer any danger of its being overrun by immigrants from the Far East. Is it not therefore a fair question whether the maintenance of these old restrictions is desirable or politic? Swaddling bands, necessary for the protection of an infant, are an impediment to a growing boy. That question can perhaps be best decided by ascertaining the general sentiment of our Pacific States. My impression is that, with the exception of the fruit-growers of California and some others, they are strongly opposed to what they call "letting down the bars."

The Empress of China

The Emperor's Second Wife

Two Portraits of the Empress Dowager

The most feasible way of meeting the difficulty would be, as it appears to me, the enactment of regulations to provide against abuses in the enforcement of our Exclusion Laws. The President has already spoken forcibly in condemnation of such abuses. The "privileged classes" might be construed in a more liberal sense. Provision might be made to mitigate the hardships of detention and repatriation; and a better class of inspectors might be appointed with a general superintendent, whose duty it should be to see that the laws are enforced humanely as well as faithfully.

On December 18, less than three months after the attack on Americans at Lienchow, an attempt was made to destroy the British settlement in Shanghai.

A woman arrested on a charge of kidnapping was sent to the foreign jail to await trial. The Chinese assessor insisted, not without reason, that she ought to be kept in a native jail. No attention being given to his protest, though supported by the *taotai* or local governor, a mob of riff-raff from beyond the limits burst into the settlement, put the foreign police to flight, and began to burn and pillage. Happily a body of marines with gatling guns and fire-engines succeeded in quelling the flames and suppressing the insurrection. A few hours' delay must have seen that rich emporium converted into a heap of ashes. Forty of the rioters were killed and many wounded. Though on ground granted to Great Britain, the settlement is called international and is governed by a municipal council elected by the foreign ratepayers. The Chinese residents, numbering half a million, are allowed no voice in the council; and that also is felt as a grievance. They are, however, protected against the rapacity of their own officials; and it is said they took no part in the riot. In fact had it not been promptly suppressed they must have suffered all the horrors of sack and pillage. After it was over they took occasion to demand recognition in the municipal government; promising to be satisfied if allowed to appoint a permanent committee, with whom the council should consult before deciding on any question affecting their interests.

Modest as this request was, it was rejected by an almost unanimous vote of the foreign ratepayers. They knew that such committee, however elected, was certain to be manipulated by the governor to extend his jurisdiction. Their decision was quietly accepted by the Chinese residents, who appreciate the protection which they enjoy in that strange republic. The question is certain to come up again, and their claim to be heard will be pressed with more insistence as they become more acquainted with the principles of representative government.

The existence of an *imperium in imperio* which comes between them and their people is of course distasteful to the mandarins; and they are bent on curtailing its privileges. If its franchises were surrendered, "Ichabod" might be inscribed on the gates of the model settlement.

The practice of marking out a special quarter for each nationality is an old one in China, adopted for convenience. When, after the first war, the British exacted the opening of ports, they required the grant of a concession in each, within which their consuls should have chief, if not exclusive authority. Other nations made the same demands; and China made the grants, not as to the British from necessity, but apparently from choice—the foreign consul being bound to keep his people in order. Now, however, the influx of natives into the foreign settlements, and the enormous growth of those mixed communities in wealth and population, have led the Chinese Government to look on the ready compliance of its predecessors as a blunder. Accordingly, in opening new ports in the interior it marks out a foreign quarter, but makes no "concession." It does not as before waive the exercise of jurisdiction within those limits.

The above question relates solely to the government of Chinese residing in the foreign "concessions." But there is a larger question now looming on the political sky, viz., how to recover the right of control over foreigners, wherever they may be in the Empire. If it were in their power, the Chinese would cancel not merely the franchises of foreign settlements, but the treaty right of exemption from control by the local government. This is a franchise of vital interest to the foreigner, whose life and property would not be safe were they dependent on the native tribunals as these are at present constituted.

Such exemption is customary in Turkey and other Moslem countries, not to say among the Negroes of Africa. It was recognised by treaty in Japan; and the Japanese, in proportion as they advanced in the path of reform, felt galled by an exception which fixed on them the stigma of barbarism. When they had proved their right to a place in the comity of nations, with good laws administered, foreign powers cheerfully consented to allow them the exercise of all the prerogatives of sovereignty.

How does her period of probation compare with that of her neighbour? Japan resolved on national renovation on Western lines in 1868. China came to no such resolution until the collapse of her attempt to exterminate the foreigner in 1900. With her the age of reform dates from the return of the Court in 1902—as compared with Japan four years to thirty! Then what a contrast in the animus of the two countries! The one characterised by law and order, the other by mob violence, unrestrained, if not instigated, by the authorities!

When the north wind tried to compel a traveller to take off his cloak, the cloak was wrapped the closer and held the tighter. When the sun came out with his warm beams, the traveller stripped it off of his own accord.

The sunrise empire has exemplified the latter method; China prefers the former. Is it not to be feared that the apparent success of the boycott will encourage her to persist in the policy of the traveller in the north wind. She ought to be notified that she is on probation, and that the only way to recover the exercise of her sovereign rights is to show herself worthy of confidence. The Boxer outbreak postponed by many years the withdrawal of the cloak of ex-territoriality, and every fresh exhibition of mob violence defers that event to a more distant date.

To confound "stranger" with "enemy" is the error of Bedouin or Afghan. Does not China do the same when she mistakes hostility to foreigners for patriotism? By this blunder she runs the risk of alienating her best friends, England and America. A farmer attempting to rope up a shaky barrel in which a hen was sitting on a nest full of eggs, the silly fowl mistook him for an enemy and flew in his face. Is not

China in danger of being left to the fate which her friends have sought to avert?

In April a magistrate went by invitation to the French Catholic Mission to settle a long-standing dispute, and he settled it by committing suicide—in China the most dreaded form of revenge. Carried out gasping but speechless, he intimated that he was the victim of a murderous attack by the senior priest. His wounds were photographed; and the pictures were circulated with a view to exciting the mob. Gentry and populace held meetings for the purpose of screwing their courage up to the required pitch—governor and mandarins kept carefully in the background—and on the fifth day the mission buildings were destroyed and the priests killed. An English missionary, his wife and daughter, living not far away, were set upon and slain, not because they were not known to belong to another nation and another creed, but because an infuriated mob does not care to discriminate.

English and French officials proceeded to the scene in gunboats to examine the case and arrange a settlement. The case of the English family was settled without difficulty; but that of the French mission was more complicated. Among the French demands were two items which the Chinese Government found embarrassing. It had accepted the theory of murder and hastily conferred posthumous honours on the deceased magistrate. The French demanded the retraction of those honors, and a public admission of suicide. To pay a money indemnity and cashier a governor was no great hardship, but how could the court submit to the humiliation of dancing to the tune of a French piper? An English surgeon declared, in a sealed report of autopsy, that the wounds must have been self-inflicted, as their position made it impossible for them to have been inflicted by an assailant. But

> "A man convinced against his will
> Is of the same opinion still."

In 1870 France accepted a money payment for the atrocious massacre at Tientsin, because the Second Empire was entering on a life-and-death struggle with Germany. If she makes things easy for China this time, will it not be because the Republic is engaged in mortal combat with the Roman Church?

China's constant friction and frequent collisions with France spring chiefly from two sources; (1) the French protectorate over the Roman missions, and (2) the menacing attitude of France in Indo-China. It was to avenge the judicial murder of a missionary that Louis Napoleon sent troops to China in 1857-60. From this last date the long-persecuted Church assumed an imperious tone. The restitution of confiscated property was a source of endless trouble; and the certainty of being backed up by Church and State emboldened native converts not only to insist on their own rights, but to mix in disputes with which they had no necessary connection—a practice which more than anything else has tended to bring the Holy Faith into disrepute among the Chinese people.

Yet, on the other side, there are more fruitful sources of difficulty in the ignorance of the people and in the unfair treatment of converts by the Chinese Government. While the Government, having no conception of religious freedom, extends to Christians of all creeds a compulsory toleration and views them as traitors to their country, is it not natural for their pagan neighbours to treat them with dislike and suspicion?

In this state of mind they, like the pagans of ancient Rome, charge them with horrible crimes, and seize the slightest occasion for murderous attack. A church spire is said to disturb the good luck of a neighbourhood—the people burn the building. A rumour is started that babies in a foundling hospital have their eyes taken out to make into photographic medicine—the hospital is demolished and the Sisters of Charity killed. A skeleton found in the house of a physician is paraded on the street as proof of diabolical acts—instantly an angry mob wrecks the building and murders every foreigner within its reach. One of these instances was seen in the Tientsin massacre of 1869, the other in the Lienchow massacre of 1905. Nor are these isolated cases. Two American ladies doing hospital work in Canton were set upon by a mob, who accused them of killing a man whose life they were trying to save, and they narrowly escaped murder. But why extend the gruesome list? In view of their mad fury, so fatal to their benefactors, one is tempted to exclaim: *Unglaube du bist nicht so viel ein ungeheuer als aberglaube du!* "Of the twin monsters, unbelief and superstition, the more to be dreaded is the last!"

In China if a man falls in the street, the priest and Levite consult their own safety by keeping at a distance; and if a good Samaritan stoops to pick him up it is at his peril. In treating the sick a medical man requires as much courage and tact as if he were dealing with lunatics! These dark shadows, so harmful to the good name of China, are certain to be dissipated by the numerous agencies now employed to diffuse intelligence. But what of the feeling towards religious missions?

Medical missions are recognised as a potent agency in overcoming prejudice. They reach the heart of the people by ministering to their bodily infirmities; high officials are among their supporters; and the Empress Dowager latterly showed a disposition to give them her patronage. But how about the preaching missionary and the teaching missionary? Are the Chinese hostile to these branches of missionary work?

Unlike Mohammedan or Brahman, the Chinese are not strongly attached to any form of religious faith. They take no umbrage at the offer of a new creed, particularly if it have the advantage of being akin to that of their ancient sages. What they object to is not the creed, but the foreigner who brings it. Their newspapers are in fact beginning to agitate the question of accepting the Christian faith and propagating it in their own way, without aid from the foreigner. That they would be glad to see merchant and missionary leave them in peace, no one can doubt. Yet the influence of missions is steadily on the increase; and their influence for good is acknowledged by the leading minds of the Empire.

Said the High Commissioner Tuan Fang, in an address to the Mission Boards at New York, February 2,1906:

> "We take pleasure this evening in bearing testimony to the part taken by American missionaries in promoting the progress of the Chinese people. They have borne the light of Western civilisation into every nook and corner of the Empire. They have rendered inestimable service to China by the laborious task of trans-

lating into the Chinese language religious and scientific works of the West. They help us to bring happiness and comfort to the poor and the suffering by the establishment of hospitals and schools. The awakening of China which now seems to be at hand may be traced in no small measure to the hand of the missionary. For this service you will find China not ungrateful."

Mission stations, now counted by hundreds, have generally high schools or colleges. Not only is the science taught in them up-to-date, but the conscientious manner in which they are conducted makes them an object-lesson to those officials who are charged with the supervision of government schools. To name only a few:

Here in Peking is a university of the American Methodist Episcopal Church which is not unworthy of the name it bears. At Tungchow, a suburb of the capital, is a noble college of the American Board (Congregationalist) which is in every point a worthy compeer. These coöperate with each other and with a Union Medical College which under the London Mission has won the favour of the Empress Dowager.

The American Presbyterian Mission has a high school and a theological seminary, and coöperates to a certain extent with the three societies above named. A quadrilateral union like this speaks volumes as to the spirit in which the work of Christian education is being carried forward. The Atlantic is bridged and two nations unite; denominational differences are forgotten in view of the mighty enterprise of converting an empire. In the economy of their teaching force they already experience the truth of the maxim "Union is Strength."

In Shantung, at Weihien, there is a fine college in which English Baptists unite with American Presbyterians. The original plant of the latter was a college at Tengchow, which under Dr. Mateer afforded conclusive proof that an education deep and broad may be given through the medium of the Chinese language. In most of these schools the English language is now claiming a prominent place, not as the sole medium for instruction, but as a key to the world's literature, and a preparation for intercourse with foreign nations.

At Shanghai, which takes the lead in education as in commerce, there is an admirable institution called St. John's College which makes English the basis of instruction. Numberless other schools make it a leading branch of study to meet the wants of a centre of foreign trade.

One of the best known institutions of Shanghai is a Roman Catholic College at Siccawei, which preserves the traditions of Matteo Ricci, and his famous convert Paul Sü. In connection with it are an astronomical observatory and a weather bureau, which are much appreciated by foreigners in China, and ought to be better known throughout the Empire.

Passing down a coast on which colleges are more numerous than lighthouses, one comes to Canton, where, near the "Great City" and beautifully conspicuous, rises the Canton Christian College.

These are mentioned by way of example, to show what missionaries are doing for the education of China. It is a narrow view of education that confines it to teaching in schools. Missionaries led the way in Chinese journalism and in the preparation of textbooks in all branches of science. The Society for the Diffusion of Useful Knowledge is spreading broadcast the seeds of secular and religious truth.

Gratitude for the good they have already done, as well as for benefits to come, ought to lead the Chinese Government to accord a generous recognition to all these institutions. At the opening of the Union Medical College, Mr. Rockhill, the American minister, in a remarkable address, proposed the recognition of their degrees by the Government; and as a representative of the Empress Dowager was in the chair on that occasion, there is reason to hope that his suggestion will not be overlooked.

CHAPTER XXXII

THE MANCHUS, THE NORMANS OF CHINA

The Ta-Ts'ing Dynasty—The Empress Dowager—Her Origin—Her First Regency—Her Personality—Other Types—Two Manchu Princes—Two Manchu Ministers—The Nation's Choice—Conclusions

In a wide survey of the history of the world, we discover a law which appears to govern the movements of nations. Those of the north show a tendency to encroach on those of the south. The former are nomads, hunters, or fishers, made bold by a constant struggle with the infelicities of their environment. The latter are occupied with the settled industries of civilised life.

The Goths and Vandals of Rome, and the Tartars under Genghis and Tamerlane all conform to this law and seem to be actuated by a common impulse. In the east and west of the Eastern hemisphere may be noted two examples of this general movement, which afford a curious parallel: I refer to the Normans of Great Britain and the Manchus of China. Both empires are under the sway of dynasties which originated in the north; for the royal house of Britain, though under another title, has always been proud of its Norman blood.

The Normans who conquered Britain had first settled in France and there acquired the arts of civilised life. The Manchus coming from the banks of the Amur settled in Liao-tung, a region somewhat similarly situated with reference to China. There they learned something of the civilisation of China, and watched for an opportunity to obtain possession of the empire. In Britain a kindred branch of the Norman family was on the throne, and William the Conqueror contrived to give his invasion a colour of right, by claiming the throne under an alleged bequest of Edward the Confessor. The Manchus, though not invoking such artificial sanction, aspired to the dominion of China because their ancestors of the Golden Horde had ruled over the northern half of the empire. The Norman conquest, growing out of a family quarrel, was decided by a single battle. The Manchus' conquest of a country more than ten times the extent of Britain was not so easy to effect. Yet they achieved it with unexampled rapidity, because they came by invitation and they brought peace to a people exhausted by long wars. Their task was comparatively easy in the north, where the traditions of the Kin Tartars still survived; but it was prolonged and bloody in the south.

Both houses treated their new subjects as a conquered people. Each imposed the burden of foreign garrisons and a new nobility. Each introduced a foreign language, which they tried to perpetuate as the speech of the court, if not of the people. In each case the language of the people asserted itself. In Britain it absorbed and assimilated the alien tongue; in China, where the absence of common elements made amalgamation impossible, it superseded that of the conquerors, not merely for writing purposes, but as the spoken dialect of the court.

Both conquerors found it necessary to conciliate the subject race by liberal and timely concessions; but here begins a contrast. In Britain no external badge of subjection was ever imposed; in process of time all special privileges of the ruling caste were abolished; and no trace of race antipathy ever displays itself anywhere—if we except Ireland. In China the cue remains as a badge of subjection. Habit has reconciled the people to its use; but it still offers a tempting grip to revolutionary agitators. Every party that raises the standard of revolt abolishes the cue; would it not be wise for the Manchu Government to make the wearing of that appendage a matter of option, especially as it is beginning to disappear from their soldiers' uniform?

The extension of reform in dress from camp to court and from court to people (to them as a matter of option) would remove a danger. It would also remove a barrier in the way of China's admission into the congress of nations. The abolition of the cue implies the abandonment of those long robes which make such an impression of barbaric pomp. Already the Chinese are tacitly permitted to adopt foreign dress; and in every case they have to dispense with the cue. The Japanese never did a wiser thing than to adopt our Western costume. Their example tends to encourage a reform of the same kind in China. A new costume means a new era.

Another point is required to complete the parallel: each victor has given the conquered country a better government than any in its previous history. To Confucius feudalism was a beau-ideal, and he beautifully compares the sovereign to the North Star which sits in state on the pole of the heavens while all the constellations revolve around it, and pay it homage. Yet was the centralised government of the First Hwang-ti an immense improvement on the loose agglomeration of the Chous. The great dynasties have all adopted the principle of centralisation; but not one has applied it with such success, nor is there one which shows so large a proportion of respectable rulers as the house of Ta-ts'ing. Of the first six some account has been given in Part II. As to the next two it is too soon to have the verdict of history. One died after a brief reign of two years and three months, too short to show character. The other now sits at the foot of the throne, while his adoptive mother sways the sceptre. Both have been overshadowed by the Empress Dowager and controlled by her masterful spirit.

China has had female rulers that make figures in history, such as Lu of the Han and Wu of the T'ang dynasties, but she has no law providing for the succession of a female under any conditions. A female reign is abnormal, and the ruler a monstrosity. Her character is always blackened so as to make it difficult to delineate. Yet in every instance those women have possessed rare talent; for without uncommon gifts it must have been impossible to seize a sceptre in the face of such prejudices, and to sway it over a submissive people. Usually they are described much as the Jewish chronicler sketches the character of Jezebel or Athaliah. Cruel, licentious, and implacable, they "destroy the seed royal," they murder the prophets and they make the ears of the nation tingle with stories of shameless immorality.

Among these we shall not seek a parallel for the famous Empress Dowager, so well known to the readers of magazine literature. In tragic vicissitudes, if not in length of reign, she stood without a rival in the history of the world. She also stood alone in the fact that her destinies were interwoven with the tangle of foreign invasion. Twice she fled from the gates of a fallen capital; and twice did the foreign conqueror permit her to return. Without the foreigner and his self-imposed restraint, there could have been no Empress Dowager in China. Did she hate the foreigner for driving her away, or did she thank him for her repeated restoration?

The daughter of Duke Chou (the slave-girl story is a myth), she became a secondary wife of Hienfung in 1853 or 1854; and her sister somewhat later became consort of the Emperor's youngest brother. Having the happiness to present her lord with a son, she was raised to the rank of Empress and began to exert no little influence in the character of mother to an heir-apparent. Had she not been protected by her new rank her childless rival might have driven her from court and appropriated the boy. She had instead to admit a joint motherhood, which in a few years led to a joint regency.

Scarcely had the young Empress become accustomed to her new dignity, when the fall of Taku and Tientsin, in 1860, warned the Emperor of what he might expect. Taking the two imperial ladies and their infant son, he retired to Jeho, on the borders of Tartary, in time to escape capture. There he heard of the burning of his summer palace and the surrender of his capital. Whether he succumbed to disease or whether a proud nature refused to survive his disgrace, is not known. What we do know is, that on his death, in 1861, two princes, Sushun and Tuanhwa, organised a regency and brought the court back to the capital about a year after the treaty of peace had been signed by Prince Kung as the Emperor's representative. Prince Kung was not included in the council of regency; and he knew that he was marked for destruction. Resolving to be beforehand, he found means to consult with the Empresses, who looked to him to rescue them from the tyranny of the Council of Eight. On December 2 the blow was struck: all the members of the council were seized; the leader was put to death in the market-place; some committed suicide; and others were condemned to exile. A new regency was formed, consisting of the two Empresses and Prince Kung, the latter having the title of "joint regent."

What part the Empress Mother had taken in this her first *coup d'état*, is left to conjecture. Penetrating and ambitious she was not content to be a tool in the hands of the Eight. The senior Empress yielded to the ascendency of a superior mind, as she continued to do for twenty years.

There was another actor whom it would be wrong to overlook, namely, Kweiliang, the good secretary, who had signed the treaties at Tientsin. His daughter was Prince Kung's principal wife, and though too old to take a leading part in the Court revolutions, it was he who prompted Prince Kung, who was young and inexperienced, to strike for his life.

The reigning title of the infant Emperor was changed from *Kisiang*, "good luck," to *Tung-chi*, "joint government"; and the Empire acquiesced in the new régime.

One person there was, however, who was not quite satisfied with the arrangement. This was the restless, ambitious young Dowager. The Empire was quiet; and things went on in their new course for years, Prince Kung all the time growing in power and dignity. His growing influence gave her umbrage; and one morning a decree from the two Dowagers stripped him of power, and confined him a prisoner in his palace. His alleged offence was want of respect to their Majesties; he threw himself at their feet and implored forgiveness.

The ladies were not implacable; he was restored to favour and clothed with all his former dignities, except one. The title of *Icheng-wang*, "joint regent," never reappeared.

In 1881 the death of the senior Dowager left the second Dowager alone in her glory. So harmoniously had they coöperated during their joint regency, and so submissive had the former been to the will of the latter, that there was no ground for suspicion of foul play, yet such suspicions are always on the wing, like bats in the twilight of an Oriental court.

On the death of Tung-chi, the adroit selection of a nephew of three summers to succeed to the throne as her adopted son, gave the Dowager the prospect of another long regency. Recalled to power by the reactionaries, in 1898, after a brief retirement, the Empress Dowager dethroned her puppet by a second *coup-d'état*.

During the ruinous recoil that followed she had the doubtful satisfaction of feeling herself sole aristocrat of the Chinese Empire. Was it not the satisfaction of a gladiator who seated himself on the throne of the Cæsars in a burning amphitheatre? Was she not made sensible that she, too, was a creature of circumstances, when her ill-judged policy compelled her a second time to seek safety in flight? A helpless fugitive, how could she conceive that fortune held in reserve for her brighter days than she had ever experienced?

Accepting the situation and returning with the Emperor, the Empire and the world accepted her, and, taught by experience, she engaged in the congenial task of renovating the Chinese people. Advancing years, consciousness of power, and willing conformity to the freer usages of European courts, all conspired to lead her to throw aside the veil and to appear openly as the chief actor on this imperial stage.

Six years ago her seventieth birthday was celebrated with great pomp, although she had forbidden her people to be too lavish in their loyalty. At Wuchang, Tuan Fang, who was acting viceroy, gave a banquet at which he asked me to make a speech in the Dowager's honor. The task was a delicate one for a man who had borne the hardships of a siege in 1900; but I accepted it, and excused the Dowager on the principle of British law, that "The king can do no wrong." Throwing the blame on her ministers, I pronounced a eulogy on her talents and her public services.

The Court in Masquerade

The question arises, did we know her in person and character? Have we not seen her in that splendid portrait executed by Miss Carl, and exhibited at St. Louis? If we suspect the artist of flattery, have we not a gallery of photographs, in which she shows herself in many a majestic pose? Is flattery possible to a sunbeam? We certainly see her as truly as we see ourselves in a mirror!

As to character, it is too soon to express an opinion. *Varium et mutabile semper femina.*

To pencil and sunbeam add word-pictures by men and women from whose critical eyes she did not conceal herself; and we may confidently affirm that we knew her personal appearance as well as we knew that of any lady who occupies or shares a European throne. A trifle under the average height of European ladies, so perfect were her proportions and so graceful her carriage that she seemed to need nothing to add to her majesty. Her features were vivacious and pleasing rather than beautiful; her complexion, not yellow, but subolive, and her face illuminated by orbs of jet, half-hidden by dark lashes, behind which lurked the smiles of favour or the lightning of anger. No one would take her to be over forty. She carried tablets on which, even during conversation, she jotted down memoranda. Her pencil was the support of her sceptre. With it she sent out her autograph commands; and with it, too, she inscribed those pictured characters which were worn as the proudest decorations of her ministers. I have seen them in gilded frames in the hall of a viceroy.

The elegance of her culture excited sincere admiration in a country where women are illiterate; and the breadth of her understanding was such as to take in the details of government. She chose her agents with rare judgment, and shifted them from pillar to post, so that they might not forget their dependence on her will. Without a parallel in her own country, she has been sometimes compared with Catherine II. of Russia. She had the advantage in the decency of her private life; for though she is said to have had favourites they have never dared to boast of her favours, nor was a curious public ever able to identify them.

Her full name, including honorific epithets added by the Academy, was Tse Hi Tuanyin Kangyi Chaoyu Chuangcheng Shoukung Chinhien Chunghi. A few hours before her death, which occurred on the day after the Emperor's, she named his nephew as successor, and the present ruler, Hsuan-Tung, who was born in 1903, began to reign November 14, 1908.

Let the Dowager be taken as a type of the Manchu woman. The late Emperor, though handsome and intelligent, was too small for a representative of a robust race. Tuan Fang, the High Commissioner, is a more favourable specimen. The Manchus are in general taller than the Chinese, and both in physical and intellectual qualities they prove that their branch of the family is far from effete.

Prince Kung, who for fifteen years presided over the imperial cabinet, was tall, handsome and urbane. Despite the disadvantages of an education in a narrow-minded court, he displayed a breadth and capacity of a high order. Prince Ching, who succeeded him in 1875, though less attractive in person, is not deficient in that sort of astuteness that passes for statesmanship. What better evidence than that he has kept himself on top of a rolling log for thirty years? To keep his position through the dethronement of the Emperor and the convulsions of the Boxer War required agility and adaptability of no mean order. Personally I have seen much of both princes. They are abler men than one would expect to find among the offshoots of an Oriental court.

Wensiang, who from the opening of Peking to his death in 1875 bore the leading part in the conduct of foreign affairs, showed great ability in piloting the state through rocks and breakers. His mental power greatly impressed all foreigners, while it secured him an easy ascendency among his countrymen. Such men are sure to be overloaded with official duties in a country like China. Physically he was not strong; and on one occasion when he came into the room wheezing with asthma he said to me: "You see I am like a small donkey, with a tight collar and a heavy load." The success of Prince Kung's administration was largely due to Wensiang. Paochuin, minister of finance, and member of the Inner Council, was distinguished as a literary genius. Prince Kung delighted on festive occasions to call him and Tungsuin to a contest in extempore verse. To enter the lists with a noted scholar and poet like Tung, showed how the Manchus have come to vie with the Chinese in the refinements of literary culture. I remember him as a dignified greybeard, genial and jocose. On the fall of the Kung ministry, he doffed his honours in three stanzas, which contain more truth than poetry:

> "Through life, as in a pleasing dream,
> Unconscious of my years,
> In Fortune's smile to bask I seem;
> Perennial, Spring appears.

> "Alas! Leviathan to take
> Defies the fisher's art;
> From dreams of glory I awake,—
> My youth and power depart.

> "That loss is often gain's disguise
> May us for loss console.
> My fellow-sufferers, take advice
> And keep your reason whole."

In more than one crisis, the heart of the nation has cleaved to the Manchu house as the embodiment of law and order. The people chose to adhere to a tolerably good government rather than take the chance of a better one emerging from the strife of factions.

Three things are required to confirm their loyalty: (1) the abolition of tonsure and pigtail, (2) the abandonment of all privileges in examinations and in the distribution of offices, (3) the removal of all impediments in the way of intermarriage.

This last has been recently authorised by proclamation. It is not so easy for those who are in possession of the loaves and fishes to admit others to an equal share. If to these were added the abolition of a degrading badge, the Manchu dynasty might hope to be perpetual, because the Manchus would cease to exist as a people.

The Presbyterian Mission Press Works, Shanghai

CONCLUSIONS

1. More than once I have demanded the expulsion of the Manchus, and the partition of China. That they deserved it no one who knows the story of 1900

will venture to deny. It was not without reason that *Mene tekel* and *Ichabod* were engraved on the medal commemorating the siege in Peking. If I seem to recant, it is in view of the hopeful change that has come over the spirit of the Manchu Government. Under the leadership of Dowager Empress and Emperor, the people were more likely to make peaceful progress than under a new dynasty or under the Polish policy of division.

2. The prospect of admission to the full privileges of a member of the brotherhood of nations will act as an incentive to improvement. But the subjection of foreigners to Chinese jurisdiction ought not to be conceded without a probation as long and thorough as that through which Japan had to pass. In view of the treachery and barbarism so conspicuous in 1900—head-hunting and edicts to massacre foreigners—a probation of thirty years would not be too long. During that time the reforms in law and justice should be fully tested, and the Central Government should be held responsible for the repression of every tendency to anti-foreign riots.

A government that encourages Boxers and other rioters as patriots does not merit an equal place in the congress of nations. The alternative is the "gunboat policy," according to which foreign powers will administer local punishment. If the mother of the house will not chastise her unruly children, she must allow her neighbours to do it.

3. Prior to legal reform, and at the root of it, the adoption of a constitution ought to be insisted on. In such constitution a leading article ought to be not toleration, but freedom of conscience. As long as China looks on native Christians as people who have abjured their nationality, so long will they be objects of persecution; self-defence and reprisals will keep the populace in a ferment, and peace will be impossible. If China is sincere in her professions of reform, she will follow the example of Japan and make her people equal in the eye of the law without distinction of creed.

4. All kinds of reform are involved in the new education, and to that China is irrevocably committed. Reënforced by railroad, telegraph, and newspaper, the schoolmaster will dispel the stagnation of remote districts, giving to the whole people a horizon wider than their hamlet, and thoughts higher than their hearthstone. Animated by sound science and true religion, it will not be many generations before the Chinese people will take their place among the leading nations of the earth.

The Lockhart Union Medical College, Peking

APPENDIX

I.

THE AGENCY OF MISSIONARIES IN THE DIFFUSION OF SECULAR KNOWLEDGE IN CHINA[21]

While the primary motive of missionaries in going to China is, as in going to other countries, the hope of bringing the people to Christ, the incidental results of their labours in the diffusion of secular knowledge have been such as to confer inestimable benefit on the world at large and on the Chinese people in particular. This is admitted by the recent High Commission.[22]

It was in the character of apostles of science that Roman Catholic missionaries obtained a footing in Peking three centuries ago, and were enabled to plant their faith throughout the provinces. Armed with telescope and sextant they effected the reform of the Chinese calendar, and secured for their religion the respect and adherence of some of the highest minds in the Empire. So firmly was it rooted that churches of their planting were able to survive a century and a half of persecution. Their achievements, recorded in detail by Abbé Huc and others, fill some of the brightest pages in the history of missions. I shall not enlarge on them in this place, as my present task is to draw attention to the work of Protestant missions.

A CENTURY OF PROTESTANT MISSIONS.

It is not too much to claim for these last that for a century past they have been active intermediaries, especially between the English-speaking nations and the Far East. On one hand, they have supplied such information in regard to China as was indispensable for commercial and national intercourse, while on the other they have brought the growing science of the Western world to bear on the mind of China. Not only did Dr. Morrison, who led the way in 1807, give the Chinese the first translation of our Holy Scriptures; he was the very first to compile a Chinese dictionary in the English language.

THE PIONEER OF AMERICAN MISSIONS

It was not until 1838 that America sent her pioneer missionary in the person of Dr. Bridgman. Besides coöperating with others in the revision of Morrison's Bible, or, more properly, in making a new version, Bridgman won immortality by origi-

---

[21] This paper was originally written for Dr. Dennis's well-known work on The Secular Benefits of Christian Missions. As it now appears it is not a mere reprint, it having been much enlarged and brought down to date.

[22] See page 177.

nating and conducting the *Chinese Repository*, a monthly magazine which became a thesaurus of information in regard to the Chinese Empire.

THE PRESS—A MISSIONARY FRANKLIN

The American Board showed their enlightened policy by establishing a printing-press at Canton, and in sending S. Wells Williams to take charge of it, in 1833. John R. Morrison, son of the missionary, had, indeed, made a similar attempt; but from various causes he had felt compelled to relinquish the enterprise. From the arrival of Williams to the present day the printing-press has shown itself a growing power—a lever which, planted on a narrow fulcrum in the suburb of a single port, has succeeded in moving the Eastern world.

The Methodist Episcopal University, Peking

The art of printing was not new to the Chinese. They had discovered it before it was dreamed of in Europe; but with their hereditary tendency to run in ruts, they had continued to engrave their characters on wooden blocks in the form of stereotype plates. With divisible types (mostly on wood) they had indeed made some experiments; but that improved method never obtained currency among the people. It was reserved for Christian missions to confer on them the priceless boon of the power press and metallic types. What Williams began at Canton was perfected at Shanghai by Gamble of the Presbyterian Board, who multiplied the fonts and introduced the process of electrotyping.

Shut up in the purlieus of Canton, it is astonishing how much Dr. Williams was able to effect in the way of making China known to the Western world. His book on "The Middle Kingdom," first published in 1848, continues to be, after the lapse of half a century, the highest of a long list of authorities on the Chinese Empire. Beginning like Benjamin Franklin as a printer, like Franklin he came to perform a brilliant part in the diplomacy of our country, aiding in the negotiation of a new treaty and filling more than once the post of chargé d'affaires.

EXPANSION OF THE WORK

The next period of missionary activity dates from the treaty of Nanking, which put an end to the Opium War, in 1842. The opening of five great seaports to foreign residence was a vast enlargement in comparison with a small suburb of Canton; and the withdrawal of prohibitory interdicts, first obtained by the French minister Lagrené, invited the efforts of missionary societies in all lands. In this connection it is only fair to say that, in 1860, when the Peking expedition removed the remaining barriers, it was again to the French that our missionaries were indebted for access to the interior.

MEDICAL WORK

From the earliest dawn of our mission work it may be affirmed that no sooner did a chapel open its doors than a hospital was opened by its side for the relief of bodily ailments with which the rude quackery of the Chinese was incompetent to deal. Nor is there at this day a mission station in any part of China that does not in this way set forth the practical charity of the Good Samaritan. This glorious crusade against disease and death began, so far as Protestants are concerned, with the Ophthalmic Hospital opened by Dr. Peter Parker at Canton in 1834.

MEDICAL TEACHING

The training of native physicians began at the same date; and those who have gone forth to bless their people by their newly acquired medical skill may now be counted by hundreds. In strong contrast with the occult methods of native practitioners, neither they nor their foreign teachers have hidden their light under a bushel. Witness the Union Medical College, a noble institution recently opened in Peking under the sanction and patronage of the Imperial Government. A formal despatch of the Board of Education (in July, 1906) grants the power of conferring degrees, and guarantees their recognition by the state. For many years to come this great school is likely to be the leading source of a new faculty.

THE SEEDS OF A NEW EDUCATION

Not less imperative, though not so early, was the establishment of Christian schools. Those for girls have the merit of being the first to shed light on the shaded hemisphere of Chinese society. Those for boys were intended to reach all grades of life; but their prime object was to raise up a native ministry, not merely to coöperate with foreign missions, but eventually to take the place of the foreign missionary.

THE EARLIEST UNION COLLEGE

One of the earliest and most successful of these lighthouses was the Tengchow College founded by Dr. C. W. Mateer. It was there that young Chinese were most thoroughly instructed in mathematics, physics, and chemistry. So conspicuous was the success of that institution that when the Government opened a university in Peking, and more recently in Shantung, it was in each case to Tengchow that they had recourse for native teachers of science. From that school they obtained text-books, and from the same place they secured (in Dr. Hayes) a president for the first provincial university organised in China.

METHODIST EPISCOPAL UNIVERSITY IN PEKING

The missions of the Methodist Episcopal Church have of late taken up the cause of education and carried it forward with great vigour. Not to speak of high schools for both sexes in Fukien, they have a flourishing college in Shanghai, and a university in the imperial capital under the presidency of H. H. Lowry. Destroyed by the Boxers in 1900, that institution has now risen phœnix-like from its ashes with every prospect of a more brilliant future than its most sanguine friends ever ventured to anticipate.

AMERICAN BOARD COLLEGE AT TUNGCHOW

A fine college of the American Board at Tungchow, near the capital, met the same fate and rose again with similar expansion. Dr. Sheffield, its president, has made valuable contributions to the list of educational text-books.

These great schools, together with the Medical College of the London Mission, above referred to, and a high school of the United States Presbyterians, have formed a system of cöoperation which greatly augments the efficiency of each. Of this educational union the chief cornerstone is the Medical College.

American Board College at Tungchow, near Peking

A similar coöperative union between the English Baptists and American Presbyterians is doing a great work at Weihien, in Shantung. I speak of these because of that most notable feature—union international and interdenominational. Space would fail to enumerate a tithe of the flourishing schools that are aiding in the educational movement; but St. John's College, at Shanghai (U. S. Episcopal), though already mentioned, claims further notice because, as we now learn, it has been given by the Chinese Government the status of a university.

PREPARATION OF TEXT-BOOKS

Schools require text-books; and the utter absence of anything of the kind, except in the department of classical Chinese, gave rise to early and persistent efforts to supply the want. Manuals in geography and history were among the first produced. Those in mathematics and physics followed; and almanacs were sent forth yearly containing scientific information in a shape adapted to the taste of Chinese readers—alongside of religious truths. Such an annual issued by the late Dr. McCartee, was much sought for. A complete series of text-books in mathematics was translated by Mr. Wylie, of the London Mission; and text-books on other subjects, including geology, were prepared by Messrs. Muirhead, Edkins, and Williamson. At length the task of providing text-books was taken in hand by a special committee, and later on by the Society for the Diffusion of Useful Knowledge, now under the direction of the Rev. Dr. Richard.

So deeply was the want of text-books felt by some of the more progressive mandarins that a corps of translators was early formed in connection with one of the government arsenals—a work in which Dr. John Fryer has gained merited renown. Those translators naturally gave prominence to books on the art of war, and on the politics of Western nations, the one-sided tendency of their publications serving to emphasise the demand for such books as were prepared by missionaries.

Text-books on international law and political economy were made accessible to Chinese literature by Dr. W. A. P. Martin, who, having acted as interpreter to two of the American embassies, was deeply impressed by the ignorance of those vital subjects among Chinese mandarins.

On going to reside in Peking, in 1863, Dr. Martin carried with him a translation of Wheaton, and it was welcomed by the Chinese Foreign Office as a timely guide in their new situation. He followed this up by versions of Woolsey, Bluntschli and Hall. He also gave them a popular work on natural philosophy—not a translation—together with a more extended work on mathematical physics. Not only has the former appeared in many editions from the Chinese press, but it has been often reprinted in Japan; and to this day maintains its place in the favour of both empires. To this he has lately added a text-book on mental philosophy.

A book on the evidences of Christianity, by the same author, has been widely circulated both in China and in Japan. Though distinctly religious in aim, it appeals to the reader's taste for scientific knowledge, seeking to win the heathen from idolatry by exhibiting the unity and beauty of nature, while it attempts to show the reasonableness of our revealed religion.

THREE PRESIDENTS OF GOVERNMENT COLLEGES

It is not without significance that the Chinese have sought presidents for their highest schools among the ranks of Protestant missionaries. Dr. Ferguson of the Methodist Episcopal Mission was called to the presidency of the Nanyang College at Shanghai; Dr. Hayes, to be head of a new university in Shantung; and Dr. Martin, after serving for twenty-five years as head of the Diplomatic College in Peking, was, in 1898, made president of the new Imperial University. His appointment was by decree from the Throne, published in the Government *Gazette*; and mandarin rank next to the highest was conferred on him. On terminating his connection with that institution, after it was broken up by Boxers, he was recalled to China to take charge of a university for the two provinces of Hupeh and Hunan.

CREATORS OF CHINESE JOURNALISM

In the movement of modern society, no force is more conspicuous than journalism. In this our missionaries have from the first taken a leading part, as it was they who introduced it to China. At every central station for the last half-century periodicals have been issued by them in the Chinese language. The man who has done most in this line is Dr. Y. J. Allen, of the Methodist Episcopal Church South. He has devoted a lifetime to it, besides translating numerous books.

Formerly the Chinese had only one newspaper in the empire—the *Peking Gazette*, the oldest journal in the world. They now have, in imitation of foreigners, some scores of dailies, in which they give foreign news, and which they print in foreign type. The highest mandarins wince under their stinging criticisms.

THEY LEAD A VERNACULAR REVOLUTION

It is one of the triumphs of Christianity to have given a written form to the language of modern Europe. It is doing the same for heathen nations in all parts of the earth. Nor does China offer an exception. The culture for which her learned classes are noted is wholly confined to a classic language that is read everywhere, and spoken nowhere, somewhat as Latin was in the West in the Middle Ages, save that Latin was really a tongue capable of being employed in speech, whereas the classical language of China is not addressed to the ear but to the eye, being, as Dr. Medhurst said, "an occulage, not a language."

The mandarin or spoken language of the north was, indeed, reduced to writing by the Chinese themselves; and a similar beginning was made with some of the southern dialects. In all these efforts the Chinese ideographs have been employed; but so numerous and disjointed are they that the labour of years is required to get a command of them even for reading in a vernacular dialect. In all parts of China our missionaries have rendered the Scriptures into the local dialects. so that they may be understood when read aloud, and that every man "may hear in his own tongue the wonderful works of God." In some places they have printed them in the vernacular by the use of Chinese characters. Yet those characters are clumsy instruments for the expression of sounds; and in several provinces our missionaries have tried to write Chinese with Roman letters.

The experiment has proved successful beyond a doubt. Old women and young children have in this way come to read the Scriptures and other books in a few days. This revolution must go forward with the spread of Christianity; nor is it too much to expect that in the lapse of ages, the hieroglyphs of the learned language will for popular use be superseded by the use of the Roman alphabet, or by a new alphabet recently invented and propagated by officials in Peking.

In conclusion: Our missionaries have made our merchants acquainted with China; and they have made foreign nations known to the Chinese. They have aided our envoys in their negotiations; and they have conferred on the Chinese the priceless boon of scientific text-books. Also along with schools for modern education, they have introduced hospitals for the relief of bodily suffering.

W. A. P. M.

PEKING,
Aug. 4. 1906.

II.

UNMENTIONED REFORMS[23]

The return of the Mission of Inquiry has quickened our curiosity as to its results in proposition and in enactment. All well-wishers of China are delighted to learn that the creation of a parliament and the substitution of constitutional for autocratic government are to have the first place in the making of a New China. The reports of the High Commissioners are not yet before the public, but it is understood that they made good use of their time in studying the institutions of the West, and that they have shown a wise discrimination in the selection of those which they recommend for adoption. There are, however, three reforms of vital importance, which have scarcely been mentioned at all, which China requires for full admission to the comity of nations.

1. A CHANGE OF COSTUME

During their tour no one suggested that the Chinese costume should be changed nor would it have been polite or politic to do so. But I do not admire either the taste or the wisdom of those orators who, in welcoming the distinguished visitors; applauded them for their graceful dress and stately carriage. If that indiscreet flattery had any effect it merely tended to postpone a change which is now in progress. All the soldiers of the Empire will ere long wear a Western uniform, and all the school children are rapidly adopting a similar uniform. To me few spectacles that I have witnessed are so full of hope for China as the display on an imperial birthday, when the military exhibit their skilful evolutions and their Occidental uniform, and when thousands of school children appear in a new costume, which is both becoming and convenient. But the Court and the mandarins cling to their antiquated attire. If the peacock wishes to soar with the eagle, he must first get rid of his cumbersome tail.

This subject, though it savours of the tailor shop, is not unworthy the attention of the grand council of China's statesmen. Has not Carlyle shown in his "Sartor Resartus" how the Philosophy of Clothes is fundamental to the history of civilisation? The Japanese with wonderful foresight settled that question at the very time when they adopted their new form of government.

When Mr. Low was U. S. Minister in Peking some thirty years ago, he said to the writer "Just look at this tomfoolery!" holding up the fashion plates representing the new dress for the diplomatic service of Japan. Time has proved that he was

---

[23] Written by the author for the *North-China Daily News*.

wrong, and that the Japanese were right in adopting a new uniform, when they wished to fall in line with nations of the West. With their old shuffling habiliments and the cringing manners inseparable from them, they never could have been admitted to intercourse on easy terms with Western society.

The mandarin costume of China, though more imposing, is not less barbaric than that of Japan; and the etiquette that accompanies it is wholly irreconcilable with the usages of the Western world. Imagine a mandarin doffing his gaudy cap, gay with tassels, feathers, and ruby button, on meeting a friend, or pushing back his long sleeves to shake hands! Such frippery we have learned to leave to the ladies; and etiquette does not require them to lay aside their hats.

Quakers, like the mandarins, keep their hats on in public meetings; and the oddity of their manners has kept them out of society and made their following very exiguous. Do our Chinese friends wish to be looked on as Quakers, or do they desire to fraternise freely with the people of the great West?

Their cap of ceremony hides a shaven pate and dangling cue, and here lies the chief obstacle in the way of the proposed reform in style and manners. Those badges of subjection will have to be dispensed with either formally or tacitly before the cap that conceals them can give way to the dress hat of European society. Neither graceful nor convenient, that dress hat is not to be recommended on its own merits, but as part of a costume common to all nations which conform to the usages of our modern civilisation.

It must have struck the High Commissioners that, wherever they went, they encountered in good society only one general type of costume. Nor would it be possible for them to advise the adoption of the costume of this or that nationality—a general conformity is all that seems feasible or desirable. Will the Chinese cling to their cap and robes with a death grip like that of the Korean who jumped from a railway train to save his high hat and lost his life? As they are taking passage on the great railway of the world's progress, will they not take pains to adapt themselves in every way to the requirements of a new era?

2. POLYGAMY

We have as yet no intimation what the Reform Government intends to do with this superannuated institution. Will they persist in burning incense before it to disguise its ill-odour, or will they bury it out of sight at once and for ever?

The Travelling Commissioners, whose breadth and acumen are equally conspicuous, surely did not fail to inquire for it in the countries which they visited. Of course, they did not find it there; but, as with the question of costume, the good breeding of their hosts would restrain them from offering any suggestion touching the domestic life of the Chinese.

The Commissioners had the honour of presentation to the Queen-Empress Alexandra. Fancy them asking how many subordinate wives she has to aid her in sustaining the dignity of the King-Emperor! They would learn with surprise that no European sovereign, however lax in morals, has ever had a palace full of concubines as a regular appendage to his regal menage; that for prince and people the ideal is monogamy; and that, although the conduct of the rich and great is often such as to make us blush for our Christian civilisation, it is true this day that the crowned heads of Europe are in general setting a worthy example of domestic morals. "Admirable!" respond the Commissioners; "our ancient sovereigns were like that, and our sages taught that there should be *'Ne Wu Yuen Nu, Wai wu Kwang-tu'* (in the harem no pining beauty, outside no man without a mate). It is the luxury of later ages that keeps a multitude of women in seclusion for the pleasure of a few men, and leaves the common man without a wife. We heartily approve the practice of Europe, but what of Africa?"

"There the royal courts consider a multitude of wives essential to their grandeur, and the nobles reckon their wealth by the number of their wives and cows. The glory of a prince is that of a cock in a barn-yard or of a bull at the head of a herd. Such is their ideal from the King of Dahomey with his bodyguard of Amazons to the Sultan of Morocco and the Khedive of Egypt. Not only do the Mahommedans of Asia continue the practice—they have tried to transplant their ideal paradise into Europe. Turkey, decayed and rotten, with its black eunuchs and its Circassian slave girls, stands as an object-lesson to the whole world."

"We beg your pardon, we know enough about Asia; but what of America—does polygamy flourish there?"

"It did exist among the Peruvians and Aztecs before the Spanish conquest, but it is now under ban in every country from pole to pole. Witness the Mormons of Utah! They were refused admission into the American Union as long as they adhered to the Oriental type of plural marriage."

"Ah! We perceive you are pointing to the Mormons as a warning to us. You mean that we shall not be admitted into the society of the more civilised nations as long as we hold to polygamy. Well! Our own sages have condemned it. It has a long and shameful record; but its days are numbered. It will do doubt be suppressed by our new code of laws."

This imaginary conversation is so nearly a transcript of what must have taken place, that I feel tempted to throw the following paragraphs into the form of a dialogue. The dialogue, however, is unavoidably prolix, and I hasten to wind up the discussion.

With reference to the Mormons I may add that at the conference on International Arbitration held at Lake Mohonk last July, there were present Jews, Quakers, Protestants and Roman Catholics, but no Mormons and no Turks. Creeds were not required as credentials, but Turk and Mormon did not think it worth while to knock at the door. Both are objects of contempt, and no nation whose family life is formed on the same model can hope to be admitted to full fraternity with Western peoples.

The abominations associated with such a type of society are inconsistent with any but a low grade of civilisation—they are eunuchs, slavery, unnatural vice, and, more than all, a general debasement of the female sex. In Chinese society, woman occupies a shaded hemisphere—not inaptly represented by the dark portion in their national symbol the *Yinyang-tse* or Diagram of the Dual principles. So completely has she hitherto been excluded from the benefits of education that a young man in a native high school recently began an essay with the exclamation—"I am glad I am not a Chinese woman. Scarcely one in a thousand is able to read!"

If "Knowledge is power," as Bacon said, and Confucius before him, what a source of weakness has this neglect of woman been to China. Happily she is not excluded from the new system of national education, and there is reason to believe that with the reign of ignorance polygamy will also disappear as a state of things repugnant to the right feeling of an intelligent woman. But would it not hasten the enfranchisement of the sex, and rouse the fair daughters of the East to a nobler conception of human life if the rulers would issue a decree placing concubinage under the ban of law? Nothing would do more to secure for China the respect of the Western world.

3. DOMESTIC SLAVERY

Since writing the first part of this paper, I have learned that some of the Commissioners have expressed themselves in favour of a change of costume. I have also learned that the regulation of slavery is to have a place in the revised statutes, though not referred to by the Commissioners. Had this information reached me earlier, it might have led me to omit the word "unmentioned" from my general title, but it would not have altered a syllable in my treatment of the subject.

Cheering it is to the well-wishers of China to see that she has a government strong enough and bold enough to deal with social questions of this class. How urgent is the slave question may be seen from the daily items in your own columns. What, for example, was the lady from Szechuen doing but carrying on a customary form of the slave traffic? What was the case of those singing girls under the age of fifteen, of whom you spoke last week, but a form of slavery? Again, by way of climax, what will the Western world think of a country that permits a mistress to beat a slave girl to death for eating a piece of watermelon—as reported by your correspondent from Hankow? The triviality of the provocation reminds us of the divorce of a wife for offering her mother-in-law a dish of half-cooked pears. The latter, which is a classic instance, is excused on the ground of filial duty, but I have too much respect for the author of the "Hiaoking," to accept a tradition which does a grievous wrong to one of the best men of ancient times. The tradition, however unfounded, may serve as a guide to public opinion. It suggests another subject, which we might (but will not) reserve for another section, viz., the regulation of divorce and the limitation of marital power. It is indeed intimately connected with my present topic, for what is wife or concubine but a slave, as long as a husband has power to divorce or sell her at will—with or without provocation?

Last week an atrocious instance, not of divorce, but of wife-murder, occurred within bow-shot of my house. A man engaged in a coal-shop had left his wife with an aunt in the country. The aunt complained of her as being too stupid and clumsy to earn a living. Her brutal husband thereon took the poor girl to a lonely spot, where he killed her, and left her unburied. Returning to the coal-shop, he sent word to his aunt that he was ready to answer for what he had done, if called to account. "Has he been called to account?" I enquired this morning of one of his neighbours. "Oh no! was the reply; it's all settled; the woman is buried, and no inquiry is called for." Is not woman a slave, though called a wife, in a society where such things are allowed to go with impunity? Will not the new laws, from which so much is expected, limit the marriage relation to one woman, and make the man, to whom she is bound, a husband, not a master?

Confucius, we are told, resigned office in his native state when the prince accepted a bevy of singing girls sent from a neighbouring principality. The girls were slaves bought and trained for their shameful profession, and the traffic in girls for the same service constitutes the leading form of domestic slavery at this day—so little has been the progress in morals, so little advance toward a legislation that protects the life and virtue of the helpless!

But the slave traffic is not confined to women; any man may sell his son; and classes of both sexes are found in all the houses of the rich. Prædial servitude was practised in ancient times, as it was in Europe in the Middle Ages, and in Russia till a recent day. We read of lands and labourers being conferred on court favourites. How the system came to disappear we need not pause to inquire. It is certain, however, that no grand act of emancipation ever took place in China like that which cost Lincoln his life, or that for which the good Czar Alexander II. had to pay the same forfeit. Russia is to-day eating the bitter fruits of ages of serfdom; and the greatest peril ever encountered by the United States was a war brought on by negro slavery.

The form of slavery prevailing in China is not one that threatens war or revolutions; but in its social aspects it is worse than negro slavery. It depraves morals and corrupts the family, and as long as it exists, it carries the brand of barbarism. China has great men, who for the honour of their country would not be afraid to take the matter in hand. They would, if necessary, imitate Lincoln and the Czar Alexander to effect the removal of such a blot.

It is proposed, we are told, to limit slavery to minors—freedom ensuing on the attainment of majority. This would greatly ameliorate the evil, but the evil is so crying that it demands not amelioration, but extinction. Let the legislators of China take for their model the provisions of British law, which make it possible to boast that "as soon as a slave touches British soil his fetters fall." Let them also follow that lofty legislation which defines the rights and provides for the well-being of the humblest subject. Let the old system be uprooted before a new one is inaugurated, otherwise there is danger that the limiting of slavery to minors will leave those helpless creatures exposed to most of the wrongs that accompany a lifelong servitude.

The number and extent of the reforms decreed or effected are such as to make the present reign the most illustrious in the history of the Empire. May we not hope that in dealing with polygamy and domestic slavery, the action of China will be such as to lift her out of the class of Turkey and Morocco into full companionship with the most enlightened nations of Europe and America.

III.

A NEW OPIUM WAR

The fiat has gone forth—war is declared against an insidious enemy that has long been exhausting the resources of China and sapping the strength of her people. She has resolved to rid herself at once and forever of the curse of opium. The home production of the drug, and all the ramifications of the vice stand condemned by a decree from the throne, followed by a code of regulations designed not to limit, but to extirpate the monster evil.

In this bold stroke for social reform there can be no doubt that the Government is supported by the best sentiment of the whole country. Most Chinese look upon opium as the beginning of their national sorrows. In 1839 it involved them in their first war with the West; and that opened the way for a series of wars which issued in their capital being twice occupied by foreign forces.

Their first effort to shake off the incubus was accompanied by such displays of pride, ignorance and unlawful violence that Great Britain was forced to make war—not to protect an illegal traffic, but to redress an outrage and to humble a haughty empire. In this renewed onslaught the Chinese have exhibited so much good sense and moderation as to show that they have learned much from foreign intercourse during the sixty-seven years that have intervened.

Without making any appeal to the foreigner, they courageously resolved to deal with the evil in its domestic aspects. Most of the mandarins are infected by it; and the licensed culture of the poppy has made the drug so cheap that even the poor are tempted to indulge.

The prohibitory edict asserts that of the adult population 30 or 40 per cent. are under the influence of the seductive poison. This, by the way, gives an enormous total, far beyond any of the estimates of foreign writers.

Appalled by the signs of social decadence the more patriotic of China's statesmen were not slow to perceive that all attempts at reform in education, army, and laws must prove abortive if opium were allowed to sap the vigour of the nation. "You can't carve a piece of rotten wood," says Confucius. Every scheme for national renovation must have for its basis a sound and energetic people. It was this depraved taste that first made a market for the drug; if that taste can be eradicated the trade and the vice must disappear together, with or without the concurrence of Great Britain.

Great Britain was not, however, to be ignored. Besides her overshadowing influence and her commercial interests vast and varied, is she not mistress of India, whose poppy-fields formerly supplied China and are still sending to the Chinese market fifty thousand chests per annum? No longer an illegal traffic, this importation is regulated by treaty. Concerted action might prevent complications and tend to insure success. The new British Government was approached on the subject. Fortunately, the Liberals being in power, it was not bound by old traditions.

A general resolution passed the House of Commons without a dissentient voice, expressing sympathy with China and a willingness to adopt similar measures in India. "When asked in the House what steps had been taken to carry out the resolution for the abolition of the opium traffic between India and China, Mr. Morley replied, that he understood that China was contemplating the issue of regulations restricting the importation, cultivation, and consumption of opium. He had received no communication from China; but as soon as proposals were submitted he was prepared to consider them in a sympathetic spirit. H. B. M.'s minister in Peking had been instructed to communicate with the Chinese Government to that effect."

The telegram containing these words is dated London, October 30. The imperial edict, which initiated what many call "the new crusade," was issued barely forty days before that date (viz., on September 20). Let it also be noted that near the end of August a memorial of the Anti-Opium League, suggesting action on the part of the Government, was sent up through the Nanking viceroy. It was signed by 1,200 missionaries of different nations and churches. Is it not probable that their representations, backed by the viceroy, moved the hand that sways the sceptre?

The decree runs as follows:

> "Since the first prohibition of opium, almost the whole of China has been flooded with the poison. Smokers of opium have wasted their time, neglected their employment, ruined their constitutions, and impoverished their households. Thus for several decades China has presented a spectacle of increasing poverty and weakness. It rouses our indignation to speak of the matter. The Court is now determined to make China powerful; and it is our duty to urge our people to reformation in this respect.

> "We decree, therefore, that within a limit of ten years this harmful muck be fully and entirely wiped away. We further command the Council of State to consider means for the strict prohibition both of opium-smoking and of poppy-growing."

Among the regulations drawn up by the Council of State are these:

That all smokers of opium be required to report themselves and to take out licenses.

Smokers holding office are divided into two classes. Those of the junior class are to cleanse themselves in six months. For the seniors no limit of time is fixed. Both classes while under medical treatment are to pay for approved deputies, by whom their duties shall be discharged.

All opium dens are to be closed after six months. These are places where smokers dream away the night in company with the idle and the vicious.

No opium lamps or pipes are to be made or sold after six months. Shops for the sale of the drug are not to be closed until the tenth year.

The Government provides medicines for the cure of the habit.

The formation of anti-opium societies is encouraged; but the members are cautioned not to discuss political questions.

The question no doubt arises in the mind of the reader, Will China succeed in freeing herself from bondage to this hateful vice? It is easy for an autocrat to issue a decree, but not easy to secure obedience. It is encouraging to know that this decisive action is favoured by all the viceroys—Yuan, the youngest and most powerful, has already taken steps to put the new law in force in the metropolitan province. A flutter of excitement has also shown itself in the ranks of Indian traders—Parsees, Jews, and Mohammedans—who have presented a claim for damages to their respectable traffic.

On the whole we are inclined to believe in the good faith of the Chinese Government in adopting this measure, and to augur well for its success. Next after the change of basis in education, this brave effort to suppress a national vice ranks as the most brilliant in a long series of reformatory movements.

W. A. P. M.

PEKING, January, 1907.

ENDNOTES

[A] Such as *Om mani padmi hum* ("O the jewel in the lotus")

[B] Mt. Meru, the Indian Olympus.

[C] She is often so represented, as the symbol of present Providence.

[D] *Lunhui*, the wheel of destiny, within which birth and death succeed without end or interval.

[E] She escapes the wheel, but remains on the border of Nirvana, where, as her name signifies, she "hears the prayers of men."

INDEX

Lector House believes that a society develops through a two-fold approach of continuous learning and adaptation, which is derived from the study of classic literary works spread across the historic timeline of literature records. Therefore, we aim at reviving, repairing and redeveloping all those inaccessible or damaged but historically as well as culturally important literature across subjects so that the future generations may have an opportunity to study and learn from past works to embark upon a journey of creating a better future.

This book is a result of an effort made by Lector House towards making a contribution to the preservation and repair of original ancient works which might hold historical significance to the approach of continuous learning across subjects.

HAPPY READING & LEARNING!

LECTOR HOUSE LLP
E-MAIL: lectorpublishing@gmail.com